Replanning the blitzed city centre

THEMES IN THE TWENTIETH CENTURY

Series Editor: Pat Thane, Reader in History,
                Goldsmiths' College, University of London

Replanning the blitzed city centre

A comparative study of Bristol, Coventry and Southampton 1941–1950

Junichi Hasegawa

Open University Press
Buckingham • Philadelphia

Open University Press
Celtic Court
22 Ballmoor
Buckingham
MK18 1XW

and
1900 Frost Road, Suite 101
Bristol, PA 19007, USA

First Published 1992

British Library Cataloguing in Publication Data

Hasegawa, Junichi
    Replanning the blitzed city centre: A comparative
    study of Bristol, Coventry and Southampton,
    1941–1950. – (Themes in the twentieth century)
    I. Title II. Series
    307.10942

    ISBN 0-335-15634-7
    ISBN 0-335-15633-9 pbk

Library of Congress Cataloging-in-Publication Data

Hasegawa, Junichi, 1961–
    Replanning the blitzed city centre: a comparative study of
    Bristol, Coventry, and Southampton, 1941–1950 / Junichi Hasegawa.
        p.   cm. – (Themes in the twentieth century)
    Includes bibliographical references and index.
    ISBN 0-335-15634-7. – ISBN 0-335-15633-9 (pbk.)
    1. Urban renewal – England – Bristol – History. 2. Urban renewal –
    England – Coventry – History. 3. Urban renewal – England –
    Southampton – History. 4. Central business districts – England –
    Bristol – Planning – History. 5. Central business districts –
    England – Coventry – Planning – History. 6. Central business
    districts – England – Southampton – Planning – History. 7. Bristol
    (England) – History – Bombardment, 1940 – 1941. 8. Coventry (England) –
    History – Bombardment, 1940–1941. 9. Southampton (England) –
    History – Bombardment, 1940–1944. I. Title. II. Series.
    HT178.G72B754   1992
    307.1′216′0942 – dc20   91–44092
                                                                    CIP

Typeset by Graphicraft Typesetters Limited, Hong Kong
Printed in Great Britain by Biddles Ltd, Guildford and King's Lynn

Contents

Series editor's introduction

A great deal both of everyday conversation, and of everyday academic analysis of contemporary society, embodies assumptions about the past, including the quite recent past, for which actual evidence is slight. Indeed, the history of Britain in the first half of the twentieth century seems sometimes to have taken on an almost mythic character. This is largely because until very recently social historians have been reluctant to explore history beyond the First World War. Because British empirical sociology did not take off on a large scale until the 1950s, there has been an important gap in our knowledge of the twentieth century, which has distorted interpretation of the whole time-span and limited our understanding of post-war Britain by deracinating it.

Recent work has begun to dispel some widely held convictions about this period, though most of it has yet to be absorbed either into everyday consciousness or academic social science. It is now clear, to take just a few examples, that there was not a significant movement of women into 'male' occupations during the First World War;[1] that such a shift is not the main explanation for the partial concession of votes to women in 1918;[2] that feminism did not die away after women obtained the vote but was especially vibrant in the 1920s;[3] that the 1930s was not a time of overwhelming 'slump', but of contrasting prosperity and recession in different regions;[4] that women were not peremptorily ejected from the paid labour market after the Second World War, but rather exhorted to stay on.[5]

The aim of this series is to take the demythologizing further by subjecting previously unexplored areas of recent British history to empirical scrutiny in order to deepen our understanding of major themes in the twentieth-century experience. An exceptional number of myths cluster around the Second World War: that the war peculiarly promoted cohesion and consensus across classes;[6] that it exceptionally accelerated progressive social change;[7] that a conscious aim of politicians, civil servants and other influential figures, from early in the war and with popular support, was the planning of a post-war 'New Jerusalem'.[8] The latter illusion has recently been firmly lodged in the chatter of the chattering classes by Corelli Barnett, for whom this supposed consensual devotion to social reconstruction provides the explanation for Britain's post-war economic decline.[9]

Hasegawa's study of three major blitzed cities challenges all of these assumptions while also making a scholarly, and vivid, contribution to the rather under-researched history of British town planning. His account of the social politics of the (partially) planned reconstruction of Coventry, Bristol and Southampton shows clearly how social, economic and political divisions persisted throughout the war, through demonstrating how conflicts based on property ownership overrode any potential consensus about local planning. These interests opposed imaginative planned reconstruction, as did politicians and civil servants, after a brief period of enthusiasm early in the war and there were few signs of popular enthusiasm. Both at the central and local levels, the vogue for New Jerusalems was very limited and very short-lived. And, contrary to the belief that the war strongly promoted the influence of 'experts' in all fields, Hasegawa stresses how slight was the audience for the newly developing expertise in town planning.

The post-war Labour government also started out apparently committed to 'bold' city planning, but also speedily retreated into compromise and muddle. Part of the reason was continued pressure from property and trading interest groups, but more important was the growing awareness of the overriding need to focus resources upon the exporting industries and on the secondary priority of building up welfare services. Similarly, during the war the priority given to particular perceptions of how to reconstruct local economies shaped or constrained plans for city reconstruction.

Hasegawa's work suggests that Barnett is mistaken to set welfare investment and industrial investment in opposition as competitors for scarce resources – they were, and were seen to be, complementary. The reconstruction of the local economies of the blitzed cities required 'welfare' investment on housing reconstruction to ensure adequate supplies of labour. When, both during and after the war choices seemed unavoidable between industrial and social investment, the former took priority. Whether the industrial investment was wisely directed is an important but quite separate question. Tiratsoo has taken the argument further, pointing out that in post-war Coventry it was 'growing official concern with exports and rearmament that damaged the achievement of welfare goals and not vice versa'.[10]

Coventry, indeed, experienced fewest constraints upon its planned reconstruction. This was partly because, unlike Bristol and Southampton, it was under the continuous control of one political party from before the war and throughout the 1940s; and Coventry's Labour council was developing, even before the war and the blitz, very necessary plans to reconstruct a city whose inter-war economic expansion was bursting the bounds of its ancient infrastructure. In Coventry, there was a momentum for change independent of the experience of war.[11] In consequence, there were fewer local conflicts over Coventry's plans and it was somewhat protected from central government constraints by its unique symbolic role in blitz mythology. The degree of reconstruction it managed to achieve took on a further symbolic role in post-war culture, and has been mistakenly read as typifying post-blitz planning. Rather, it was a quite untypical near-success story within a larger narrative of muddle and conflict. Hasegawa's account presents in vivid microcosm a persuasive account of wartime and post-war policy making in its social context which emphasizes detail, complexity and local variety without falling into random empiricism or losing sight of the major themes and questions in twentieth-century society.

Pat Thane

Acknowledgements

I would like to thank the Centre for the Study of Social History, University of Warwick, for providing me with the opportunity to compile a PhD thesis on which this work is based. I am particularly indebted to Drs James Hinton and Tony Mason for their assistance and kindness during the course of this research. I also received considerable help from a number of archivists, particularly the staff at the City Record Offices in Bristol, Coventry and Southampton, at the Local Studies Section of Coventry City Library, as well as at the Newspaper Library and the Public Record Office in London.

I have indeed been fortunate in all those who have helped me with various aspects of this research, especially Dr Mark Clapson, Dr Richard Coopey, Dr John Davis, Dr Steve Fielding, Dr James Kilmartin, Mrs Ros Lukas, Mr Michael Rowland and Mr Tatsuya Tsubaki. However, of all the many academic colleagues who have been most helpful, I must mention Dr Nick Tiratsoo, himself an expert on reconstruction in Britain after the Second World War, for providing me with invaluable advice and inspiration throughout the research. I owe a more general debt to Dr Pat Thane and to the staff of Open University Press who gave encouragement and good counsel during the preparation of the manuscript of this volume. I also acknowledge with gratitude the remarkable accuracy and forbearance of Mrs Dee Hewitt in typing the manuscript.

Finally, I would like to thank Professor Takao Matsumura, and my parents, Haruo and Ryoko Margaret Hasegawa, for the encouragement they gave me over the five years I spent in England, and dedicate this work to them.

Junichi Hasegawa

Notes on sources and abbreviations

This study is based on the following main archive sources:

1   Material in the Bristol City Record Office (BRO), particularly the minutes of the City Council's Planning and Public Works Committee (PPWC) and the Planning and Reconstruction Committee (PRO); and the annual reports, minutes and various papers of the Bristol Incorporated Chamber of Commerce and Shipping (BRO 38605).
2   Material in the Coventry City Record Office (CRO), particularly the minutes of the City Council's City Re-development Committee, subsequently the Planning and Reconstruction Committee (CRC); and the Town Clerk's files (CRO Sec./CF/1).
3   Material in the Local Studies Section of Coventry City Library, particularly the local newspapers – *The Midland Daily Telegraph* (*MDT*), the *Coventry Evening Telegraph* (*CET*) and *The Coventry Standard* (*Standard*).
4   Material in the Southampton City Record Office (SRO), particularly the Borough Council's Town Planning and Development Committee (TPDC), City Architect's Department Records (SRO SC/BA), City Engineer's Department Records (SRO SC/EN), Town Clerk's Records (SRO TC Box), City Treasurer's Department Records (SRO SC/T), the minutes and various papers of the Central Area Association (SRO D/Z), and various collections of papers disposed by Alderman James Matthews (SRO D/Mat).
5   The local Bristol and Southampton newspapers in the Newspaper Library, London; for Bristol – the *Bristol Evening Post* (*BEP*), the *Bristol*

Evening World (*BEW*), the *Bristol Observer* (*Observer*) and the *Western Daily Press and Bristol Mirror*; and for Southampton – the *Southern Daily Echo* (*SDE*).

6   Various files in the Public Records Office, London (mainly those in BT, CAB and HLG).

one

Introduction

The main theme of this volume is devoted to a description of how the replanning of the blitzed city centres proceeded in the 1940s. The work is arranged around the three case studies of Bristol, Coventry and Southampton, the first provincial cities in Britain to suffer the German blitz in 1940. This is, therefore, very much a local study of three urban cities in the twentieth century. At the same time, justification for such an exercise should also be found by placing it in such wider contexts as the history of British town planning, post-war reconstruction, and Labour politics both at the central and local level.

As the existing literature shows, British town planning up to the Second World War had been characterized by a number of personalities and organizations each armed with a variety of ideas. Their aims were to overcome the impoverished and insanitary conditions of the industrial cities and towns – the outcome of uncontrolled development since the Industrial Revolution – and to create more humane living standards. It is acknowledged, however, that the most influential figure in the history of British town planning is Ebenezer Howard, whose book *Tomorrow* first appeared in 1898. His idea was the 'Garden City' principle – self-contained towns of limited size where people could work near their homes, exist in helpful neighbourliness, and enjoy all the advantages of city and country life. The 'Garden City' principle was vigorously advocated by the Garden Cities Association, which, with its energetic secretary, F. J. Osborn, became one of the strongest propaganda organizations in town planning circles.[1]

What turned out to be particularly important for those associated with town planning was to call for more positive and comprehensive state intervention, i.e. national planning. The government had offered only partial and *ad hoc* solutions to particular problems of industrialized society. In the nineteenth century, the main task of government had been to provide preventative measures against insanitary conditions in the older central areas of the industrial cities. In the twentieth century, it was to facilitate the provision of houses for the working classes on new estates, which sprang up in the suburbs of large cities. As it was observed, however, there was a serious lack of machinery for comprehensive planning: first, there was no central planning authority and, secondly, planning legislation was inadequate both for the built-up central areas and for the suburbs where new development was taking place. These shortcomings had led to overcrowding and traffic congestion in the large cities and towns, and an indiscriminate sprawl of housing in the countryside.[2] The state of city centres was especially appalling, embedded in such problems as overcrowded and out-of-date housing, the inadequacy and maldistribution of open space, the jumble of housing, shops and industry compressed along narrow roads, and traffic congestion that was both dangerous and a waste of travellers' time.[3]

The call for national planning was intensified in the 1930s by those politicians, businessmen and academics, of both Left and Right, associated with so-called 'middle opinion', whose voices were echoed in such organizations as the New Fabian Research Bureau, the Next Five Years Group and Political and Economic Planning. It was argued that the wide range of economic and social problems the country was facing should be tackled through collectivist means. At the same time, emphasis was placed upon the technocratic approach to problems by making the best use of the experience, knowledge and opinions of experts.[4] Gradually, governments had taken action. Particular attention had been paid to what the experts thought to be the worst evil of contemporary society, i.e. the unbalanced distribution of industry and the industrial population. The south – especially London – had become overgrown, whereas those areas based on the old staple industries were in serious decline. In 1937, a Royal Commission was set up to investigate the question. Its conclusions, published in January 1940 as the Barlow Report, declared that the situation was disadvantageous to national life, and that positive government action, based on national planning, would be necessary to improve the imbalance.[5]

Thus it was now keenly realized that town planning should be part and parcel of national planning and not a local matter as it had been. The demand for a new central authority in one form or another was already great among town planners,[6] and some new ideas and techniques were being aired.[7] Town planning needed to cease being a partial and *ad hoc* solution to specific problems, and the first essential seemed to be determined government action.

The Second World War prompted the government to take such action, with the realization that there would be a need for reconstruction. Town planning had been expected to play a vital part in the pursuit of national planning, and this was reflected in the appointment of Lord Reith in October 1940 as minister responsible for the study of appropriate methods and machinery for dealing with post-war town and country planning. One of his first moves was to set up a panel of experts to examine the various problems involved in town planning. The area that attracted most attention was the redevelopment of built-up areas, especially city centres.

The German blitz on London and other provincial cities in late 1940 had created the opportunity for comprehensive replanning by local authorities. Bristol, Coventry and Southampton were chosen by the government as 'test cases' in an attempt to identify the kind of legislation that would be needed for the redevelopment of built-up areas. Moreover, Reith encouraged the local authorities in question to plan boldly. The replanning of city centres had become symbolic of post-war reconstruction as a whole and, as Esher and Ravetz observe, the mood of the time was that the experts, with confidence and enthusiasm, would create a totally new and better Britain.[8] Cullingworth's extensive research into the public records also demonstrates that the government made considerable efforts, leading to the setting up of the Ministry of Town and Country Planning in 1943 and two Town and Country Planning Acts, 1944 and 1947. Because of the nature of his work – an official history of the Ministry – Cullingworth emphasizes the importance of the part played by civil servants in establishing the legislative framework of post-war town planning.[9]

However, in studies dealing with the task of reconstruction under the wartime coalition government and Labour between 1945 and 1951, city centre replanning has not been given the attention that might have been expected.[10] Among the general studies of town planning and works of local history, fairly frequent reference has been made to the case of Coventry, because, as they often emphasize, the city's uniquely imaginative plan not only received a great deal of contemporary publicity, but it is regarded from a technical viewpoint as a model of post-war city centre replanning.[11] What seems to be lacking here is a detailed analysis of the essence of city centre replanning, i.e. the process by which consensus was sought in support of the plans of the three local authorities – Coventry, Bristol and Southampton.[12] A close examination of this process shows how diversified opinions were as to the future of the city centre. This was true of all three plans. It also shows how the plans were affected by a variety of differing opinions. Both local interests and the government departments concerned applied various pressures on the local authorities so that their views would be represented in the final outcome. However, each of the three local authorities, all of which were Labour councils during the second half of the 1940s, responded to such pressures in quite different ways, depending on a number of factors: the perception of the industrial future, the council's financial position, political conflicts between councillors or corporation officials regarding the plans, and the attitude of the public.

By examining the replanning process in these three case studies, and placing it in a wider perspective, this volume brings into relief the fate of that optimistic, early period when the idea of reconstruction stood for a peaceful and fairer post-war world. For ease of exposition, what follows is divided into three parts, the first of which serves as an introduction to the main theme. Chapter 2 analyses a variety of views about post-war reconstruction, placing an emphasis on the government's attitude towards the opinions of experts. Chapter 3 describes the pre-war character of the three cities – Bristol, Coventry and Southampton – from an economic, political and social point of view; the chapter also comments on the destruction caused by the bombing of 1940–41. The second part of the book examines the replanning process during the war with regard to Coventry (Chapter 4), Southampton (Chapter 5) and Bristol (Chapter 6) respectively. The main point of discussion in the final part is how much recognition these plans had received – especially by the ministry responsible – by the time the construction of permanent buildings commenced at the end of the 1940s (Chapters 7 and 8). Finally, Chapter 9 attempts a concise comparison of the three case studies, and presents some brief conclusions.

two

Development of reconstruction policy during the war

The case for national planning put forward in the Barlow Report was rather suddenly in the limelight as a result of an air raid on London in September 1940, followed by a series of heavy blitzes throughout the country. As Ian McCallum, author of *The Architects' Journal*'s weekly feature 'Notes and Topics' wrote in retrospect in 1945:

> From the moment of this first big attack on London the interest of the British people in planning was awakened; it began in fervent hope and determination to use the damage done by bombs to good purpose.[1]

The interest was so keen that

> the mere contemplation of plans for the future was a stimulus to the almost back-breaking efforts of the present. Hopes loomed vaguely but largely behind the dust and smoke of war damage and the uncertainty of the struggle itself.[2]

In early 1941, the minister responsible called for expert assistance in planning the future Britain, and also told those local authorities which had been blitzed to plan boldly and comprehensively. But hopes gradually turned to disappointment as the government adopted *ad hoc* solutions to the immediate problems. In particular, those experts in whom so many had placed their faith for building a future Britain, did not achieve very much at the national level because of the government's fear of drastic change and its preference for the conventional approach. As McCallum observed in 1945:

Four years have passed since this bold planning began; and now the
scene has changed in a most significant way. The bold conceptions are
being analyzed down into detail, and every detail is a cause of controversy. The well-known slogan *First Things First*, that gained such
currency in the planning period of the mid-war years, has quietly
changed its meaning. It no longer suggests that the most important
post-war aims should be firmly placed in the forefront, but that the
most immediate ones are all we have time to consider.[3]

*   *   *

The realization in the 1930s of the need for national planning gained
even further currency as the war progressed. Because of the devastation
caused by enemy action, town planning provided a focal point for discussion
about Britain's post-war future. In particular, public interest centred
around the replanning of the heavily damaged city centres. During the
winter of 1941–42, the BBC broadcast a series of weekly talks, entitled
'Making Plans'. In the first programme – 'Bombed Out' – a London manu-
facturer said:

> The bombs are levelling our old cities. In my view there's got to be a
> lot more levelling, not only of old slums and buildings, but of outworn
> institutions too; and a better opportunity and more security for the
> majority than there has ever been before. That can only be achieved
> if private and sectional plans are fitted into national schemes, and
> judged in the light of the national balance sheet...
>   The key to it all lies in a true democracy where all of us can play
> our part, both in making plans, and in carrying them out. That's what
> most of us are fighting for.[4]

Despite the talk of 'democracy', however, the most remarkable feature of
those days was 'an almost boundless professional self-confidence among
architects and others involved with town planning'.[5] The Town and
Country Planning Association (thus renamed in 1941, incorporating the
Garden City Association and the Town Planning Association) remained the
most active propaganda body. Its annual conferences became the hub of
discussion about planning.[6] No less important were its publications such
as *The Rebuilding Britain Series*[7] (started in 1941) and *The Planning and
Reconstruction Year Book*[8] (started in 1942), both including comprehensive
material on a wide range of issues related to town planning. Another
important body was The Royal Institute of British Architects (RIBA), the
views of which were most comprehensively advanced in *Rebuilding Britain*,
published for their exhibition held in February 1943.[9] Although there were
differing views among various bodies and individuals as to what was needed
(notably in regard to the question of density), there was agreement that
drastic change would be inevitable in replanning the country, especially
those areas which had been badly damaged by air raids.

The initial response of the government to the blitz was swift and promising. In October 1940, Lord Reith was appointed Minister of Works and Buildings, and was personally charged with responsibility for reporting to Cabinet on the methods and machinery required for post-war town and country planning. In January 1941, Reith announced that the government had accepted one of the recommendations of the Barlow Commission to set up an Expert Committee on Compensation and Betterment, and Mr Justice Uthwatt's Committee was accordingly appointed. On 26 February, Reith told the House of Lords that the government accepted in principle the idea of national planning and of a central planning authority. He also announced the establishment of a Consultative Panel on Physical Reconstruction, to which he said he attached great importance, and the beginning of an examination of planning problems through consultation with experts outside the government. Meanwhile, Reith encouraged the London County Council to draw up a plan with the help of Professor Abercrombie, a leading town planning figure at the time. Reith also chose Coventry, Birmingham, Bristol and Southampton as test cases in a survey of the existing planning system and of its future requirements. Most importantly he told the local authorities of these and other severely damaged cities to plan boldly and comprehensively.

The Uthwatt Committee published its interim report in June 1941 (Cmd. 6291), just six months after its appointment. Its recommendations were: the adoption of the value of land at 31 March 1939 as the 'ceiling' price for public acquisition; the setting up of a central planning authority; and the definition of 'reconstruction areas' (i.e. those areas of substantial devastation caused by enemy action that were likely to be involved in consequent redevelopment schemes) within which no building should be permitted, except under central licence, until reconstruction schemes had been prepared. On 17 July, Lord Reith announced that the government accepted the Uthwatt Committee's recommendations in principle. It was also suggested that, pending the creation of the central planning authority in its final form, a Council of Ministers – consisting of Reith as chairman, the Secretary of State for Scotland and the Minister of Health – would work together. In October, Lord Justice Scott's Committee on Land Utilization in Rural Areas was appointed to consider the rural repercussions of the Barlow Report policy of decongestion and dispersal.[10]

Behind the scenes consideration was also being given by civil servants to the question of replanning those areas devastated by enemy action. By the end of February 1941, the results of four test surveys of blitzed cities were brought to the Interdepartmental Committee of Officials on Reconstruction. The chief inspector of the surveys pointed out the most urgent requirements: tighter and more positive interim control needed to be given to the planning authorities in question; these authorities needed to prepare outline plans for the guidance of such control as soon as possible; and powers of purchase needed to be simplified and made more expeditious – this applied not only to sites of destroyed buildings but also to areas of convenient shape and size suitable for redevelopment.[11] Consequently, strenuous efforts were made to draft a Bill that would provide the machinery for the reconstruction of devastated areas, and strengthen the planning system so as to prevent prejudice to reconstruction during the war and immediate post-war period. Of particular importance was the contribution of this interdepartmental committee's sub-committee (under the chairmanship of T.D. Harrison of the Ministry of Health) whose various reports 'formed the basis of much of the legislation which was eventually enacted in the early post-war years'.[12] By November 1941, the Harrison Committee had completed two important reports: the first recommended the amendment of legislation so extending interim development control over the country to the local authorities; the second dealt with the provisions related to 'Reconstruction Areas'.[13]

Thus, by November, Reith was in a position to submit a draft Town and Country (Reconstruction) Bill to the Cabinet Committee on Reconstruction Problems. At the meeting of the committee, however, the main discussion centred around the nature of the proposed central planning authority, which was a first indication of a lack of coherence in the government's decision making. On 11 February 1942, Reith announced the government's decision to establish a central planning authority by transferring the planning functions of the Ministry of Health to a renamed Ministry of Works and Planning. A fortnight later, however, Reith – 'distrusted by Churchill' – was suddenly replaced by Lord Portal, and 'had to content himself with token honours for the rest of his life'.[14] From then on, the government became more and more indecisive about important matters, and frustration soon grew among experts at large.

With Lord Reith went his Consultative Panel on Physical Reconstruction. Its members had been recruited in early 1941 from various fields concerned with planning,[15] and divided into groups to consider and advise the minister[16] on such questions as: the recruitment and training of planners; the strengthening of planning control over the design and external appearance of buildings, with a view to providing a system of guidance on the technique of development;[17] the preparation of a series of maps, to similar scale and size, with a view to reserving land for agriculture and for recreational purposes or as national parks; and the study of industries suitable for location in country areas.[18] Meanwhile, the publication of the Uthwatt Committee's interim report and the preparation of a Town Planning (Reconstruction) Bill necessitated the setting up of a sub-group to consider special problems arising out of the redevelopment of reconstruction areas – the exercise of compulsory purchase powers by local authorities and the method of redevelopment, redevelopment finance, and the procedures and priorities of work in such areas.[19]

Interestingly, at its second meeting on 10 October 1941, the unofficial members of this group expressed views as to the undesirability of local authorities' large-scale purchase and redevelopment of land. They argued that the ultimate use of purchase powers would be unduly restrictive of private enterprise;[20] the probable cost of purchasing central areas would be so great as to be quite beyond the local authority's resources;[21] and if the local authority were allowed to acquire and develop considerable areas of land, a local land monopoly might be created and the local authority would have a powerful vested interest in the use of the land.[22] Ministry officials were not impressed with such views. One thought that 'we are fighting for democracy and I see no reason why we should not give local authorities the chance to rise to their responsibilities'.[23] In the end, it was agreed to have a further meeting to consider this subject along with others. No further meetings, however, seem to have been held. The curtailment of the Reconstruction Bill obviously poured cold water on the initiative. As a ministry official pointed out to one outside member, it would not include any provisions for reconstruction areas; and, he continued, 'On this footing the fundamental questions which the Group discussed will not arise on this Bill.'[24]

The consultative panel itself soon ceased to function. Once Lord Reith was dismissed, ministry officials became more and more cautious about any consultative machinery on such a large scale. Moreover, while the setting up of the new Ministry of Works and Planning would require the reorganization of the structure and work of existing staff, these same officials also felt that it would take a long time to create a proper central planning authority. As one official put it, they should 'not get the complete picture' until they had created the new planning system.[25] When the Ministry of Town and Country Planning was eventually set up in 1943, one of the original members of the consultative panel sent a letter to the new minister, which illustrates the frustration of the members. As he put it:

> A number of us were appointed as members of a Panel by Lord Reith. Has this Panel lapsed on the creation of the new Ministry? And if so will a new one be appointed? I was asked to serve on a committee to deal with the practical problem of redevelopment of city centres, and this made a start and promised to be useful. Is there any intention to call it, or a similar committee, together again?[26]

*   *   *

The publication of the Scott Committee's Report (Cmd. 6378) in August and of the Uthwatt Committee's Final Report (Cmd. 6386) in September 1942 intensified those voices demanding immediate positive action by government. Within the Ministry of Works and Planning, anxiety about the effect on public opinion of any government prevarication regarding the two reports caused concern even before their publication. Arguing for the appointment of a 'top-notch' public relations officer, one official deplored the lack of positive publicity:

> The prime justification for the existence of a Ministry of Planning during the war is one of morale. Its success or failure must be largely

measured by whether it is making people more hopeful of the future and thereby more willing to endure the present. The best way of achieving this is by producing visible results, i.e. legislation. When this is impossible, the next best way is to explain why the results are not immediately forthcoming and to give assurance that everything possible is being done to produce them and that they will, in fact, be produced by the time they are really needed.[27]

Thus, for the moment, it was imperative for such a public relations officer to 'attempt to persuade the public that only a short Bill on immediate emergency measures is possible this year [1942] and that implementation of Scott and Uthwatt [reports] must wait over until later'.[28]

The publication of Uthwatt's final report was believed to remove, as *The Times* put it, 'the last excuse for further postponement of official action in the field of national planning',[29] and its contents were discussed in the most heated way. Its main recommendations were:

1 The State acquisition of development rights of all land outside built-up areas, with fair compensation on a 'global' basis in ratio to market values at 31st March, 1939, such land to be compulsorily acquired at the residual agricultural value if and when needed for development, and to be granted to the developer on leasehold only.

2 Powers to be given to planning authorities to purchase war-damaged and obsolete or unsatisfactory built-up areas needing redevelopment as a whole. All land so acquired to be leased, not sold outright.

3 A periodic levy of 75 per cent of the increase of annual site values of all developed land, whatever the reason for such increase of values, the values to be assessed quinquennially for rating purposes.

4 An expedited procedure for compulsory acquisition of land.

Not surprisingly, there were strong objections to the Uthwatt proposals from the landowners' organizations. The National Federation of Property Owners, for instance, regarded the Uthwatt proposals as 'a fatal deterrent to individual initiative, thrift, and enterprise'. Claiming that the increase in the value of land was created more often by the enterprise of individual owners than by the state or local authorities, they argued:

The majority of the proposals are aimed at avoiding the rights and freedoms of individuals, and would mean the creation of officials at whose mercy the property owner would be. Some of the methods suggested would cause a grave injustice to owners of property – dictatorship methods, in fact.[30]

At the other extreme, the Labour Party argued that 'The Uthwatt Report does not appear to indicate a clear comprehension of the difficulties confronting Planning or Housing Authorities in urban areas.' The high cost of urban land, especially in the central areas of larger towns, had so far prevented local authorities from providing open spaces or working-class housing in such areas because of the fear of heavy rate burdens on their ratepayers. The only satisfactory solution was, they argued, 'nationalization of urban land':

> Once the land was nationalized, the State would either lease or sell to the Planning Authorities the land comprised in their area. These authorities would then be in a position to plan their areas as a whole, and develop them to the best advantage regardless of what any particular piece of land had originally cost... In this way open spaces, housing, public buildings, commercial buildings, and industry could each be sited in the most suitable and convenient position.[31]

Nevertheless, the Labour Party eventually conceded:

> ... if fairly and carefully administered ... the periodic levy of 75 per cent of the increases in annual site values, with all its defects, might be accepted as a step in the right direction. It is a valuable though partial recognition of the principle that increases in site values, in a special sense, are created by efforts and activities of the community, and properly belong to the community. Whatever are the defects of the proposed levy, it cannot be impugned on the ground that it is injustice to owners of land.[32]

In 1943, criticism was focused on the government's failure to announce its findings. In February 1943, the Town and Country Planning Act was passed, establishing a new ministry to take over the planning functions of the Ministry of Works and to concentrate solely on planning. Then, in July 1943, the Town and Country Planning (Interim Development) Act was passed to bring under planning control from an 'operative date' (22 October 1943) land which was not yet subject to a scheme or resolution under the Town and Country Planning Act 1932. These measures, however, could not really pacify the widespread impatience. As a *Times* leader stated in October 1943, it had been suggested that:

> the difficulties [for the government] are centred upon the Uthwatt proposals for a national requisitioning of the development rights in land lying outside built-up areas and for an expedited and enlarged power of purchase by local authorities of land within those areas. If so it will be wiser policy to publish the nature of these difficulties than to maintain an evasive official silence. By such a course opinion would at least be instructed, and the chances of a practicable solution advanced. Without some such disclosure the suspicion will grow that the reports have been successfully resisted by interests affected by them, and their effective consideration indefinitely postponed. Yet if the Uthwatt recommendations or some other proposals of equivalent effect were not essential as a preliminary to a reconstruction

programme, the Government would have had no occasion to appoint the Committee at all.[33]

Just 2 days after this article, W.R.S. Morrison, the Minister of Town and Country Planning, announced that the government's findings on the Uthwatt Report were almost 'ready for presentation'. They were, however, the mere acceptance of the two pledges already given, i.e. the principle of the public acquisition of all land in reconstruction areas, and the principle of compensation for the public acquisition or control of land not exceeding the value at 31 March 1939. At the same time, he underlined the fact that the government had been determined not to be hustled into premature conclusions:

> There are some who speak as though the Uthwatt report was a panacea of all planning difficulties, as though all that the Government had to do was to say 'Aye' and all the problems of the planning would then automatically sort themselves out like a complete jigsaw puzzle ... The report does not pretend ... to provide a blueprint of all the administrative machinery which their solution would demand.
>
> The Government pledges on the Uthwatt report mean that the local authorities can go ahead with the making of plans, secure in the knowledge that they will have possession of the land in those areas. The planning authority of every district should now review its resources and its needs in the stark light of 1943 and make a plan to balance them.[34]

*   *   *

Meanwhile, the Uthwatt proposals had been considered by a sub-committee of officials of various departments, again chaired by T.D. Harrison.[35] At the end of 1942, an official of the Ministry of Works and Planning on the committee, reporting to L. Neal (Deputy Secretary of the Ministry) on the progress of its work, said:

> In this connection, I should like to raise once again the urgency of the contemplated investigation into Coventry and other 'blitzed' areas. At their meeting yesterday ... the committee were informed, forcefully, by the representative of the Valuation Department that the cost of land acquisition in reconstruction areas will reach astronomical figures. If this is so it is of the highest importance that before we introduce the Reconstruction Areas Bill in May we should have the broad measure of the problem and know the lines on which it is proposed to deal with the matter.[36]

Within the Ministry of Works and Planning, the setting up of a Blitzed Cities Committee had been contemplated and, by September 1942, the scope and nature of its task was already drafted by Neal, but had been postponed pending the establishment of the Ministry of Town and Country Planning (hereafter MOTCP). Now in February 1943, Neal urged Whiskard, secretary to the ministry, to take up the matter immediately. The problems which local authorities had to face in the reconstruction of the central areas of blitzed cities would 'transcend local interest, and constitute one of the earliest – and most formidable – tasks of national planning':

> This is a matter in which not only the population of the cities concerned, but the public generally, may be expected to take a keen interest. They would probably not be content to leave to a Government Department the task of formulating the principles to be followed. It is therefore suggested that a small committee, so constituted as to command public confidence, should be appointed, and should be asked to advise, within a short period, on the problems and the programme of the reconstruction of central urban areas.[37]

Whiskard was somewhat concerned about the inevitable publicity, given a formal committee. Accordingly, the minister held a meeting with the parliamentary secretary, Whiskard, Neal and Pepler, and it was agreed that the minister would invite a small team of unofficial advisers to assist his officers in making a study of the matter.[38]

The Advisory Panel on Redevelopment of City Centres was appointed in May 1943.[39] Its terms of reference were:

> To examine the main planning issues involved in the redevelopment of city centres which have been devastated by bombing, to redefine and measure the problems of finance and organisation connected therewith and to set out the relevant considerations on which central and local Government policy in regard to such redevelopment should be based.[40]

It was pointed out that the panel's problem could be solved 'only by visits to some of the cities concerned and by discussions with the responsible people on the spot'.[41] Accordingly, seven cities – Southampton, Portsmouth, Coventry, Swansea, Bristol, Hull and Plymouth – were chosen and visited by the panel by the end of 1943. In selecting cities, they excluded 'on the one hand, the "conurbations" such as London and Liverpool', for they had their own quite special problems. On the other hand, 'the medium sized or small towns such as Exeter and Canterbury' were also excluded on the understanding that:

> ... the general run of our findings can be applied broadly to other cities and towns whose centres have been heavily damaged. It should be remarked, however, that the cities chosen by us illustrate devastation in its severest form.[42]

Just before the panel submitted its report to the Minister of Town and Country Planning in August 1944, the government's answer to the Uthwatt proposals finally appeared in June as the White Paper on the Control of Land Use (Cmd. 6537) and the Town and Country Planning Bill. The former, mainly concerned with Uthwatt's Development Rights Scheme, did not contain the settled policy of the government, but presented some modified thoughts on their own suggestions for public discussion to discover what measure of support they might command. It was the latter that provided the measures for the acquisition of land for the purpose of redeveloping the bombed and derelict central parts of towns, that could and had to be settled urgently. There were difficulties in reaching agreement with all concerned. After lengthy debates at all levels and consequent amendments, the Bill eventually received the Royal Assent in November 1944.[43] Dissatisfaction was, however, rife, especially among the local authorities concerned. A 1939 'standard' instead of 'ceiling' basis of compensation, for instance, would prevent local authorities from buying much land at less than 1939 prices. On the other hand, the pressure from many Conservative politicians who did not like the idea that landowners could get no more than 1939 prices for compensation had led to a supplementary payment to all owner-occupiers of up to 30 per cent of the 1939 value of the payments. Government assistance under the Act was a grant equal to the loan charges for two years on the cost of purchase and clearing of land in war-damaged areas, such grants possibly being extended to ten years, after which time it was assumed that the reconstruction scheme would be self-supporting (i.e. the local authority's receipts from the scheme would be sufficient to meet outgoings). Many local authorities regarded this as too optimistic a view, as their schemes were usually designed to provide ample open spaces and other amenities that did not produce rates revenue.

The Minister of Town and Country Planning claimed that the new Act showed 'the welcome green light to those who wanted to get on with the rebuilding of our bombed towns and cities'.[44] But, as *The Times* pointed out, the general feeling was that the only legitimate excuse for the enactment of such imperfect measures was that 'to delay further the legislative remedy for the war-damaged areas is a choice which cannot seriously be made'.[45] The criticism from socialists was much more acute. As G.D.H. Cole and R. Postgate put it, for instance, the Uthwatt proposals had been:

> ... hotly opposed by landowners and anti-socialists, and after long delays were finally rejected by the Government without any alternative plans covering most of the ground being put forward in their place. As the war advanced it became increasingly plain that any measures of post-war reconstruction which in any way limited private property rights or proposed an extension of public ownership would be strenuously resisted by vested interests both in and outside Parliament and by the main body of Conservative and capitalist opinion.[46]

The provisions of the Town and Country Planning Act 1944 were in fact no less disappointing to members of the ministry's Advisory Panel on Redevelopment of City Centres. Originally it was hoped that the panel would help the officials of various government departments to draw up the

Town and Country Planning Bill. The panel emphasized, from their observations of the heavily damaged towns, that any financial arrangement between the government and the local authorities should make it possible for the local authorities to choose such plans and programmes as would secure the long-term interests of the community at large, rather than those that might, at the expense of proper planning, most quickly restore local rateable values.[47] Consequently, their recommendations with regard to government financial assistance for the redevelopment of city centres was fairly generous. Under their scheme, central government would make good the local authority's net deficit on its reconstruction revenue for 12 years. If a local authority's reconstruction accounts for any year should show a net deficit, central government would provide an advance of that amount. At the end of 12 years, should there be advances still outstanding, central government would, as a justifiable national charge, cancel them.[48] Moreover, while it was practically certain that there would be a short-term net deficit during the first 12 years, it was also possible that there might in certain instances be a longer-term net deficit too, because the reconstruction plan would often justifiably necessitate a destruction or shift of old site values; the time taken over rebuilding together with high building costs would make it difficult to re-establish new values; and there might be other unfavourable factors outside the control of local authorities (e.g. the reconstruction scheme of itself might not prove fully successful in attracting new development, or the town itself might at some future time decline in prosperity).[49] For this reason, it would be necessary to consider methods of continued government financial assistance in the long term,[50] and of establishing organizations to secure maximum speed of reconstruction, both of which were virtually ignored by the 1944 Act.[51]

The advisory panel's elaborate consideration, however, did not exert any particular influence on the provisions of the Town and Country Planning Bill. In early 1945, an 'abridged' version of the panel's report was sent to about 60 local authorities, including the seven cities which it visited, as a private circulation. There was no mention of the unofficial members, the seven cities chosen preserved anonymity, and any part related to their own recommendations about the 12-year financial assistance had to be omitted as superseded by the 1944 Act. In reply to the chairman of the panel, who proudly claimed that the report had been well received,[52] one outside expert member stated:

> I am so glad that the Report has been considered useful but it makes me regret that it could not have been sent out in its original form with the backing of legislation – it would then, I think, have been of real service.[53]

Thus towards the end of the war it was quite clearly felt that bold and comprehensive planning with the aid of experts, as promised by the government in the early days of the war, was not going to materialize. One obvious reason for this was the government's retreat from a bold and more interventionist stance to a concern with economizing and protecting private interests. On the other hand, the government did not really grant any particular importance to experts, as the cases of Lord Reith's consultative panel and the Advisory Panel of the Ministry of Town and Country Planning clearly indicate. At the same time, these experts were, apart from their hostility to the present state of affairs, radically divided about what was needed, and could not offer the public consensus about the ideal society of the future. There was certainly conflict between modernism and traditionalism among planners,[54] which may have inhibited their capacity to mobilize public opinion on these issues.[55] Some experts on the consultative panel, who were themselves officers of local authorities, expressed their own doubts about the competence of local authorities to undertake the redevelopment. Although these experts became fairly confident about the abilities of local authorities by the time they sat on the Advisory Panel on Redevelopment of City Centres, the essence of their proposals did not see the light of day due to the government's – if not the ministry's – neglect of them. Because of the highly technical nature of town planning, the failure of experts to consolidate their divergent views more often resulted in the fading away of interest on the part of the public, rather than their positive participation in the decision-making process. Not surprisingly, the experts were now worried that enthusiasm among the public, once looming so large, was about to disappear. As one authority put it, town planning was 'for the mass of the people ... still something shapeless and remote from their daily lives ... There is no reason why discussion of planning issues should not become at least as widespread and as intelligent as the recent discussions on Beveridge.'[56]

The local authorities had to replan their blitzed city centres under such difficult and indeed rather unpromising circumstances. There were also other factors to be reckoned with, such as quick restoration of the loss of the rateable value destroyed by enemy action, the industrial and demographic future of the cities and the local authority's ownership of land as against the concerns of certain private interests. As these factors were closely related to a town's economic, social and political characteristics and the effect of devastation caused by air raids, it is time to make a close examination of these aspects with regard to the three cities of Bristol, Southampton and Coventry.

three

Bristol, Coventry and Southampton before the war and the impact of the bombing

Bristol[1]

Situated on the River Avon about five miles from the Severn estuary, Bristol had grown to be a world port, the main city of the west of England, and a centre of commercial activity and of university life. At the beginning of the twentieth century, its population was already greater than 300 000, and by 1939 it had grown beyond 400 000 (see Table 3.1).

The port of Bristol was one of the chief centres of maritime trade in the country, and served a very large area, including the western and

Table 3.1 Population growth in Bristol, Coventry and Southampton

Year	Bristol		Southampton		Coventry	
	Total	%[a]	Total	%[a]	Total	%[a]
1901	328 945[b]	83	104 824[b]	60	69 978[b]	42
1911	357 048[b]	90	119 012[b]	68	106 349[b]	64
1921	376 975[b]	95	160 994[b]	91	128 157[b]	77
1931	396 918[b]	100	176 025[b]	100	167 046[b]	100
1938	415 500[c]	105	180 100[c]	102	229 900[d]	138
1939	419 200[c]	106	181 400[c]	103	224 267[d]	134

[a] 1931 = 100.
Sources: [b] Census, [c] Treasurers' Reports, [d] Annual Reports of the Medical Officer of Health.

south-western counties, Birmingham and the Midlands. Yet Bristol was not dependent exclusively on its port. The industries of Bristol were remarkable for their variety, there being about 300 different types in all. Those industries employing large numbers of workers included building and contracting, general engineering, vehicle and aircraft building, transport and communication, paper and printing, distributive trades, and food, drink and tobacco. Government service (national and local), the professions and entertainment were other important sources of employment. Bristol was therefore to some extent immune from those consequences of depression experienced in other centres which were dependent on one or two staple industries only.

Politically, the local Labour Party obtained for the first time a majority on the city council in 1937. In the following year, however, the Citizen Party (a coalition of Conservatives and Liberals) wiped it out.[2] Consequently, the two parties – with 56 representatives each – were to share power for the duration of the war.

As the city grew, there was considerable building activity, especially in the inter-war period: a total of 36 000 houses were built, 14 000 of them by the corporation. The city council was also well advanced in planning outer areas – whether inside or beyond its formal boundaries.

In March 1923, the city council set up a town planning committee and appointed B.F. Brueton executive planning officer to act under the supervision of the city engineer. The new committee soon invited the neighbouring local authorities to form the Bristol and Bath and District Joint Regional Planning Committee. This committee, although disbanded by the time war broke out, published a Regional Survey and Plan in 1930 prepared by Professor Abercrombie and Brueton. When war did break out, the corporation had five statutory schemes comprising 95 765 acres, of which more than 78 862 acres were outside the city.[3]

The planning machinery of the council had also been strengthened during the 1930s. In June 1932, Marston Webb was appointed city engineer and became responsible for the preparation and supervision of town planning schemes. In May 1938, J. Nelson Meredith was appointed city architect, with a brief to undertake all of the architectural requirements of the corporation. He was also asked to collaborate with the city engineer in preparing and administering those town planning schemes in which it was necessary to take into account the design of buildings.[4]

When it came to the replanning of the central area, however, there was no comprehensive planning scheme. The city centre served as a regional centre of commercial and cultural activities with long traditions. However, its hilly topography had created a problem: because the factories and commercial premises had concentrated on the limited number of flat areas, the centre had become very congested, and there were no wide open spaces, only small patches here and there.

The main shopping centre ran east–west, following Wine Street and Castle Street. The area was closely confined by two rivers, the Avon to the

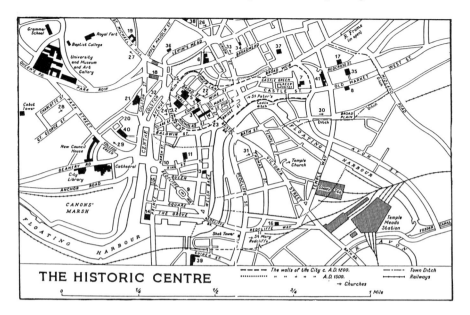

The central area of Bristol before the 1940 Blitz
Source: B. Little, *The City and County of Bristol* (1954), pp. 68–9.

south and the Frome to the north, which were only 150 yards apart. Consequently, all development had been constrained within very narrow and
tortuous streets.

Traffic congestion, too, was acute. Bristol was the principal focus of all
traffic within its region, and was the meeting place of ten first-class radial
roads. These roads amalgamated within the city and concentrated most of
their traffic in the city centre. Among the various schemes aimed at relieving the problem, was the construction of a southern inner ring road known
as Redcliffe Way and Temple Way.

In 1935, a scheme to create an 11-acre civic centre in the College Green
area was ratified.[5] When war broke out the construction of a dignified
neo-Georgian Council House (one of the last products of the great town
hall and civic building boom of the inter-war period) had been well
advanced. Generally speaking, however, there was not much enthusiasm
for the comprehensive replanning of the central part of Bristol, as existed
in Coventry and, to some extent, in Southampton. As we shall see later, it
was the experience and the opportunity provided by the German blitz that
inspired serious consideration of the matter.

* * *

Southampton[6]

In 1939, Southampton had a population of 180000. It ranked first among British ports for passenger traffic and fourth for freight trade, and was often called the 'Gateway to England', being located within easy and convenient reach of London, the Midlands and the West. Not surprisingly, its main industries were shipping, shipbuilding and repairing, and other ancillary industries.

Politically, the Ratepayers' Party (a coalition of Conservatives and Liberals) had been the majority party on the borough council. As a result of the 1938 local elections, it had 12 aldermen and 28 councillors, whereas the Labour Party had two aldermen and 23 councillors, although Labour polled 296 votes more than the Ratepayers' Party in that election (19857 to 19561).[7]

Southampton's rapid growth took place alongside the development of the docks. The Old Docks were begun in 1838, the railway from London arrived in 1844, and so prompted a rapid increase in the transatlantic shipping trade. In 1934, the New Docks were opened, forming part of the Extension Scheme for the reclamation of 407 acres of tidal mudland in the bay of the River Test, where many firms became established. Between 1918 and 1938, more than 18700 houses were built, of which the council were responsible for 4450.

Yet towards the end of the 1930s, there was growing concern about the industrial future of Southampton. Councillor Matthews, deputy Labour leader and acknowledged expert on town planning, argued in 1938, for example, that the fact that over one-third of Southampton's workers were directly engaged in shipping and allied services made it too dependent on shipping, which in turn was vulnerable to the uncertainties of domestic and world trade. He also pointed out that the number of workers engaged in shipping had fallen from 17000 in 1930 to 11000 in 1938, not only because of the worldwide depression but also because of rationalization in the industry, which was expected to continue in the years ahead. In conclusion, he urged that it was 'in every way desirable that a variety of industrial development should be encouraged in Southampton'.[8]

Southampton's importance as a port had made its central area a commercial magnet of some consequence. The principal shopping street ran from the civic centre down to the Town Quay, and consisted of two sections, separated by the Bargate, known as Above Bar and High Street. The central area had developed along a north–south axis, in the form of an 'internal ribbon development', measuring a mile long by a quarter of a mile wide.[9]

Within the central area the outstanding features were the new civic centre, the open spaces and what remained of the ancient walled town. The town was exceptionally lucky to have extensive town parks stretching for half a mile through the heart of the central area, while within walking distance of it lay the Commons of 375 acres, still thickly wooded. The origins of the new civic centre dated back to proposals in the late nineteenth century for a town hall to replace the old guildhall over the Bargate and the old municipal offices. After years of prevarication, in 1928 the council eventually approved a design by the London architect E. Berry Webber, and between 1932 and 1939 a complex of four blocks of buildings was erected: municipal offices and council chambers; law courts and police offices; the guildhall; and a general public library, art gallery and the School of Arts and Crafts. It was regarded as 'one of the best examples of inter-communicating civic buildings' in the country.[10]

Southampton's lengthy history had left its mark on the town in a varied collection of antiquities and historical remains. One fine example was the Bargate, which had formed the principal entrance to the city from the north and was now preserved in the middle of the main street. However, its presence exacerbated one of the main problems of the town centre, i.e. traffic congestion in Above Bar/High Street. With only a single narrow arch, the Bargate allowed only for one line of traffic to pass through at a time.

Although this specific problem was partially relieved in 1938 by the city council's scheme for the construction of two roadways around the outside of the Bargate, traffic congestion in Above Bar/High Street continued to deteriorate. The crux of the matter was that this was the most direct route to and from the docks, and at the same time the primary business and shopping street. Dock workers and passengers/visitors to and from the liners passed through it, and many shoppers and businessmen parked their cars along the kerbs leaving only the central portion of the roadway open to through traffic.

This problem was especially serious to the north end of Above Bar, at the junctions with Commercial Road and civic centre–New Road, where the congestion was exacerbated by the stream of cross-traffic between the east and the west, and through traffic from the north. As the volume of traffic increased with the opening of New Docks and the reclamation of land, the congestion continued to deteriorate.[11]

The question of traffic congestion was much considered in the 1930s in connection with the replanning of the lower part of the town (i.e. below the Bargate). As the retail zone had extended northwards since the late nineteenth century, so that Above Bar had become outstandingly successful, High Street had declined in importance, and warehouses were interspersed with retail shops.[12] In 1934, the local civic society and the chamber of commerce presented reports on the question to the city council. With the rejuvenation of business life in the area below Bargate as the primary object, they argued not only for the completion of the Bargate Scheme, but also the provision of markets and car parking, the building of flats for the dock workers, and a new north–south road from the Old Docks parallel to Above Bar/High Street.[13]

Planning problems in the central area had been brought to light in this way, and they had been to some extent considered by the borough council before the war. For instance, a preliminary plan for an alternative north–south road to Above Bar had been under consideration in the late 1930s.[14] There were, however, serious defects in the planning machinery of the local authority. At the municipal level, there wasn't even a full town planning committee on the borough council, nor was there an independent town planning department. And the town planner to the corporation, who was only an assistant to the borough engineer, had not been given full authority or responsibility in the matter. As we shall see later, it was not until the German blitz destroyed the town's central area that these administrative defects were seriously considered by the borough council.

*   *   *

Coventry[15]

In the late 1930s, Coventry was both a mediaeval town, with many historic buildings and streets, and a rapidly expanding modern industrial city, producing a wide variety of goods – from motor vehicles and aero engines to artificial silk. It had a long and varied history of craftsmanship and industry. From the fourteenth to the sixteenth centuries, it was the chief centre for woollen manufacture in the Midlands. Then it turned to silk ribbon weaving until the 1860s and watchmaking until the 1880s, both of which declined because of foreign competition. Its very rapid industrial expansion, however, began around the turn of the century with the coming of motor vehicle production, following the rise of the cycle industry in the 1890s, which soon became the principal trade of the city. Added to this were the aircraft industry, machine tools, rayon, radio and telephone equipment manufacture. The population grew at a very fast rate as its thriving industry and relatively high wages attracted immigrants from various parts of the country.

Within a decade up to 1938, nearly 26 000 houses were built, of which about 22 500 were erected by private enterprise.[16] There was a remarkably high rate of owner-occupation, which was reflected in the rapid growth of building societies, e.g. the Coventry Permanent Economic Building Society had increased its assets from a little more than £1.75 million in 1932 to around £4 million in 1937.[17] The city council was responsible for the planning of 25 914 acres in 1939, of which 8598 acres were outside the city boundaries. One scheme was already operative in 1938, and four others were being prepared.

The city's central area, however, had never been covered by a planning resolution. It remained substantially mediaeval in character and became extremely inadequate for the ever-increasing tasks of a modern city. The narrow and winding streets in the city centre became increasingly congested by traffic,[18] but early attempts to construct new streets to remedy the situation were shelved because of opposition from local citizens concerned to protect old streets and properties. Between 1910 and 1940, in fact, only two new conduits were completed – Corporation Street and Trinity Street[19] – and these were described quite rightly by a local newspaper as 'patchwork expedients, two isolated, incomplete and separate links'.[20] The city engineer and the chief constable expressed alarm in 1938, the streets in the central area being:

> ... no longer wide enough to permit an uninterrupted flow of the present volume of traffic in both directions and at the same time to have uncontrolled waiting for such purposes as loading and unloading of goods vehicles, making business calls, picking up and setting down people using large passenger carrying vehicles, collection of refuse, etc. All these matters create serious congestion and traffic delays.[21]

Another pressing problem was the inadequacy of municipal buildings such as the Council House,[22] central police station and courts of justice,[23] and the lack of such cultural amenities as an art gallery and a museum.[24] Because of this, some began to urge the development of a civic centre, and E. Ford, newly appointed city engineer, set to this task on his arrival in 1924. In the mid-1930s, the matter proceeded rapidly. In 1934, the city council set up a Civic Centre Sub-committee, and within 1 year it was decided to promote a Parliamentary Bill for schemes for various public buildings based on the city engineer's plan.[25] The corporation's scheme put the question of the replanning of the central area in the limelight. Some local architects,[26] the Coventry City Guild[27] and a local councillor[28] put forward their own ideas for a civic centre, and the question was much discussed in the local press. As these suggestions often saw a new civic centre as part of the replanning of a much wider area, the discussion soon focused on a new city centre as a whole.[29]

The corporation, however, confined their scheme to a small area in Earl Street and Little Park Street where the possibility of further extension was limited, and they could not settle the question of sites for an art gallery and a museum. The opening-up of Broadgate to the Cathedral to gain the vista contemplated in the city engineer's plan was dropped altogether. What constrained the council from considering any comprehensive replanning was the fact that the Town and Country Planning Act 1932, which supposedly allowed for the planning of built-up areas for the first time, in fact provided little opportunity. As Coventry's Town Clerk put it:

> ... it will be out of the question to attempt the town-planning of the built-up areas of Coventry as a whole. The best policy seems to be to prepare, as occasion arises, town-planning schemes for selected built-up areas ... where experience has shown the need to be greatest.[30]

The crux of the matter was liability for compensation, which prevented, among other things, the city engineer's proposal for the opening up of Broadgate, where the cost of acquiring the shop properties was thought to be prohibitive. Gradual acquisition of land thus became the best possible way forward, for by that process the council would 'save money by avoiding a certain amount of trade claim'[31] – claims for compensation for loss of trade.

The problem of compensation was directly related to the problem of increasing rates. In 1937, the Labour Party took over the control of the city council from the Progressive Party, the coalition of Conservatives and Liberals, whose major concern was to keep the rates as low as possible. The Labour Party thought that there was much need for municipal intervention. They set up a Policy Advisory Committee to supervise the work of other committees and departments, so that the work of the corporation should be centralized. Its first Five Year Programme of Capital Expenditure, covering £1.57 million for various projects, promised among other things new streets and more open spaces. In order to carry out these developments in a co-ordinated way, it was also decided to set up a City Architect's Department so that in future all of the corporation's architectural work would be handled by a single department.

However, no mention was made in this five-year capital programme of a civic centre. It was estimated that a 6d increase in the rate from 13s to 13s 6d in the pound was necessary to carry through the projects proposed in the programme. As G. Hodgkinson, one of the Labour leaders, said: 'If the five-year programme was enlarged to cover more ambitious projects obviously a 13s 6d rate would not be sufficient.'[32] Around this time the need for the replanning of the central area was most intensively urged in the local press. But Hodgkinson had to say:

> The view of the Labour Party is that we feel that the more pressing problems at the moment are those provided by the new areas on the outskirts of the city, and these have to take first place as against any claims for the development of a civic centre ...
>
> We know that the ratepayers are not too happy about the recent rate imposition, and if they say that they are not prepared to pay any more they cannot have improved schemes in the centre of the city.[33]

The problems of expansion were aggravated when Coventry was chosen as a centre for the government's armament programme. It has been estimated that there was an influx of at least 30 000 munition workers and their families, which took the city's population over 250 000 in 1939.[34] Altogether eight shadow factories were operating in the Coventry area during the war.[35] Naturally, any hopes of city centre replanning quickly disappeared. Some even argued – as the Mayor for 1936–37 said rather jokingly – that it would be better to wait for the bombing, because 'then the land would be cleared free of all charges'.[36] Elsewhere, somewhat different reasoning led to the same conclusion. For example, Alderman Halliwell, another leader of the Labour Party, argued that any city centre scheme under the present form of government would mean very little for ordinary citizens, because 'an improved centre would simply create additional vested interests in property', unless there was 'conscription of wealth'.[37]

Thus it seemed that any effort towards future city centre development was totally futile. Yet there were some ideas which proved to be important for the future. Donald Gibson, a Liverpool University graduate in his early 30s, was appointed the first city architect in 1938. He was able to recruit with ease enthusiastic young architects for his staff, for they felt that the creation of a City Architect's Department was 'a noteworthy step ... [towards showing] that a Municipal Authority could do work comparable to the best in private practice'.[38] Although town planning was not at first considered part of their tasks, they set about the job by planning a new city centre, for:

> We believed that a beautiful city could result only when each building in the programme was designed to respect its neighbouring buildings, in height, shape and colour and, too, in the arrangements of the roads and gardens around them.
>
> Here was the genesis of precinctual treatment of buildings and their surroundings. The desired result could, we felt, be obtained only when an overall picture could be produced before building began; and in our view the architect-planner ... was the person best fitted for this task.[39]

Gibson assigned four members of his staff the work of designing a co-ordinated scheme for all the civic buildings considered necessary, and of preparing a large model for display purposes, 'hoping that by this means we should be given the chance to prove our case'.[40] The team was headed by the city's first principal planning officer, Percy Johnson-Marshall, another young Liverpool graduate.

In fact, as Gibson recalled, the preparation work was 'a voluntary task – undertaken at home in the evenings – shared by wives and sweethearts of members of the Department and some enthusiasts who were not in local government service'.[41] Within months they produced a model of the scheme for grouped public buildings, taking an area of 40 acres and forming a precinct around the cathedral with a new central park. As Johnson-Marshall admitted, while the main theoretical source and inspiration came from Le Corbusier's *The city of tomorrow*, all of the buildings in their plan 'were kept comparably low in order to emphasise the verticality of the Cathedral and St. Michael's Church, and were to be faced with brick and stone to harmonise with the local red sandstone of the latter buildings'.[42]

The next step was to make the public 'planning and design conscious'.[43] So the Coventry branch of the Association of Architects, Surveyors and Technical Assistants, which was almost entirely composed of members of the City Architect's Department, decided to hold a planning exhibition in the summer of 1940. The 'Coventry of Tomorrow' exhibition, attended by several thousand people, featured not only the above-mentioned model, but also evening lectures on town planning delivered by famous town planners and architects, and presided over by a number of city councillors. 'So', as Gibson recalls, 'the seeds of a later harvest were being sown.'[44] When the blitz wiped out the central area of the town about six months later, those councillors:

> ... remembered the model which we had produced at the St. Mary's Hall exhibition, and invited me to join forces with the City Engineer and to prepare a new plan for the city centre ...
> At last we as architects had been given the opportunity to present to the City Council our views on town planning and civic design. Because of our pre-war studies the new plan did not take long to prepare.[45]

*   *   *

Destruction[46]

The pattern and effects of the major air raids on the three cities were quite similar. The bombing was concentrated in the winter and early spring of 1940–41 as shown in Table 3.2. And yet the damage caused was, as Table 3.3 illustrates, still serious at the end of the war. When it came to the destruction of houses, however, Coventry and Southampton sustained much more severe damage than Bristol, as shown in Table 3.4. But the extensive destruction, as shown in Table 3.5, tended to be localized in the central areas, which led the government to make special surveys in early 1941.

These 'test case' surveys in the three cities revealed damage to the main

Table 3.2 Major blitzes on the three cities

	Date	*High explosive (tons)*
Coventry	14 November 1940, 8 April 1941	818
Southampton	17 and 23 November, 30 November–1 December 1940, 19 January 1941	647
Bristol (and Avonmouth)	24 November, 2 and 6 December 1940, 3–4 January, 16–17 March, 11–12 April 1941	919

Sources: T. Harrisson, *Living through the blitz* (Harmondsworth, 1978), p. 356; R. Winstone, *Bristol in the 1940s* (Bristol, 1961), pp. 23–5.

Table 3.3 The number of properties and floor space destroyed, damaged and not repaired by May 1945

	Shops	*Commercial buildings*	*Factories and warehouses*
Coventry			
no. of properties	826	149	108
floor space (ft²)	290 000	351 000	3 394 000
Southampton			
no. of properties	730	311	141
floor space (ft²)	1 124 000	1 642 000	1 415 000
Bristol			
no. of properties	996	190	403
floor space (ft²)	3 388 000	901 000	4 778 000

Source: HLG 71/595, 'Ministry of Town and Country Planning: An estimate of war damage to shops, commercial buildings, factories and warehouses in a few selected "Blitzed" towns', 19 March 1945.

business and commercial areas, especially to the principal shopping streets, which were almost wiped out. In Coventry, Smithford Street was 'practically burnt out';[47] in Southampton, about 75 per cent of all properties destroyed had their frontage on Above Bar/High Street; in the Castle Street area of Bristol, of 185 shops, 139 were completely destroyed and 36 were damaged.

The severe damage sustained by these main shopping areas led to the local authorities' finances being badly hit, because shop property was the most profitable to the corporation in terms of rates revenue. The test case survey report revealed that the rates income of Coventry was reduced by about 17 per cent, while Southampton had lost one-third of its rates revenue by early 1941. The restoration of the rateable value was thus of great importance for the local authorities concerned.

As Table 3.6 shows, however, Coventry and Bristol recovered better financially than Southampton. As the ministry pointed out in 1943, Coventry – although badly damaged in terms of business premises – had in fact gained

Table 3.4 Housing destroyed and seriously damaged due to enemy action

	No.	*% of total houses*
Coventry	23 577	30.3
Southampton	13 610	29.9
Bristol	5 197	4.9

Source: HLG 71/593, 'Revised appreciation of war damage based on injury to houses', Ministry of Town and Country Planning, April 1944.

Table 3.5 Approximate extent of major devastated area (in acres)

Coventry	Southampton	Bristol
53	60	40

Source: HLG88/9, 'Report of Advisory Panel on Redevelopment of City Centres', Ministry of Town and Country Planning, 1944.

industries rather than lost them, for a number of shadow factories had been built in the vicinity. Consequently, its economic activity recovered considerably, while the need for accommodation for munitions workers seemed to contribute a lot to the enhancement of rateable value.[48] As for Bristol, although the damage to the Castle Street area was quite considerable, the city had a number of subsidiary shopping areas still standing,[49] while the war brought about a spectacular rise in the scale of, among other things, government services. In Southampton, however, the damage to the shopping centre, particularly to Above Bar, and its effect on the local authority's finance, was formidable.

As Tables 3.6 and 3.7 show, loss of rateable value in Above Bar alone accounted for more than 25 per cent of the total loss. Moreover, Southampton was unfortunate that its industry was dependent on shipping and allied activities. Unlike Bristol, which enjoyed a fairly diversified structure, Southampton suffered severely once its port activities came to a standstill.

At the same time, it was recognized by all sides that the bombing, by clearing the previously congested central areas, provided a great opportunity for the comprehensive replanning of such areas. The local authorities were very keen to grasp their chance, especially in Coventry, where two plans for the central area – drawn up by the city engineer and the city architect – already existed. The author of the test case survey also admitted that the carrying out of either scheme had been 'greatly facilitated by the bombardment'.[50]

In fact, Coventry received by far the greatest publicity and attention, with interest focusing on both the destruction which it had suffered and on the redevelopment plan which was now proposed. The city was often cited as the first victim of the blitz, with the spire of the ruined cathedral standing defiantly in a vacuum. Then the bold plan for a new city centre, so

Table 3.6 The rateable value of the three cities

Year	Coventry	Southampton	Bristol
1939–40	£1 634 883	£1 632 255	£3 433 087
1945–46	£1 577 987	£1 428 679	£3 326 926

Sources: Abstracts of Accounts of the three cities.

Table 3.7 The rateable value (RV) of Southampton shopping centre

Street	1 October 1939		1 April 1946	
	No. of properties	RV (£)	No. of properties	RV (£)
London Road	109	10 701	51	4 223
Above Bar	256	78 703	90	23 802
East Bargate	25	3 418	23	4 698
West Bargate	3	197	3	224
High Street	222	37 022	84	16 942
Hanover Bldgs	46	3 559	24	1 694
East Street	104	25 067	54	8 045
Total	765	158 667	329	59 628

Source: SRO SC/T9/100, 'Rateable value of shopping centre', Borough Treasurer, 17 April 1946.

quickly adopted and so confidently supported by the city council, became the symbol for post-war reconstruction. It is appropriate, therefore, to turn to a more lengthy discussion of the Coventry case.

four

Replanning the city centre: Coventry 1940–45

Being one of the first provincial towns to suffer from the blitz, Coventry attracted nationwide attention because of the destruction of its central core and the redevelopment plan that was subsequently prepared. At the very beginning of the replanning of the future city centre, the minister concerned, Lord Reith, encouraged the city council to plan boldly. Two plans were prepared: the city engineer's plan, in the ministry's words, 'suffered from some lack of imagination', while the city architect's plan 'suffered from rather too much imagination'.[1] Although the government inspector appointed to assess these documents reported rather optimistically that 'a compromise plan based on the good features in both schemes would be acceptable',[2] it soon proved very difficult to arrive at any compromise.

The city council adopted the city architect's plan and waited for the ministry's reaction to it, while refusing any consultations with the local interests affected by it. The ministry, and particularly its Regional Planning Officer (hereafter RPO), were very concerned about this lack of consultation at the local level. Some features of the Coventry plan, notably the arcaded shopping precinct and civic centre, also caused the ministry anxiety because of their boldness.

Following the visit to Coventry of the advisory panel in the summer of 1943, the ministry worked very hard to persuade the city council to meet local interests and to consider a possible new plan on a more modest scale. The task was not an easy one. The council stood firm in sticking to its plan. The provisions of the Town and Country Planning Bill 1944, obviously disappointing to the local authorities concerned, added to the ministry's anxieties. As one official put it, there was 'a very serious risk of Coventry becoming the centre of the hostile elements opposed to the Government proposals', especially in view of 'the strong sentiment which surrounded Coventry in the public eye as the first small city to endure the weight of the German air assault'.[3] Also worrying was 'the grandiose nature' of the plan, which 'would lend itself particularly well to an outcry that the Government for reasons of financial stringency, as opposed to planning, were attempting to force the blitzed cities to cut their proposals to the bone'.[4]

Although the ministry could avoid the worst potential scenario taking place, they thought that there was still much left to be done. All they could claim in late 1945 was, as the able RPO put it:

> For the past three years we have been gradually working the City Council off the idea that a long term plan can be prepared in less than three months at the height of a blitz without consulting any outside interest. That is very broadly what happened at Coventry.[5]

*　　*　　*

Within a month of the November blitz, the city council set up the City Reconstruction Committee (hereafter CRC) to consider the redevelopment of the city, especially that of the heavily damaged central area. The city engineer and city architect were asked to collaborate in preparing a plan for that area.[6] In early January 1941, the council sent a deputation on the initiative of Alderman Hodgkinson to Lord Reith, Minister of Works and Buildings. While the bombing gave Coventry an excellent opportunity to replan its central area, the council was apprehensive about making the most of it in view of the lengthy procedures and enormous amount of money involved under the existing legislation. As Hodgkinson told the minister:

> It may be that none of us around this table today will see in our life-time the city that ought to emerge from the ruins of Coventry, but what we are concerned with is taking the right steps and building in such a way that future generations will not curse someone or other for making false steps now, and we believe that your Department may be able to help us very considerably in reaching the ideal we wish to achieve.[7]

The minister, suggesting that Coventry would be made a test case (for future legislation), told the deputation:

> The City of course cannot do more than it can do, and possibly you are entitled from that to form an optimistic conclusion about future help.

I would hope that you would be able to proceed with your wider plan, and not just the conservative one. I would hope you would find encouragement later on to proceed on a pretty broad basis.[8]

The conference with the minister undoubtedly gave tremendous heart to the city council. As the *Coventry Standard* (hereafter *Standard*) reported Hodgkinson telling the council:

... [he] had not the least doubt, having regard to the smooth way in which they were received in London, that they would get a great deal of help, and probably much more help than they thought before they went into that conference. 'That delegation was the most fruitful I have been to of any Government department', he commented. 'In so far as this job can be speeded up, we shall get every assistance from London.'[9]

By early February, two plans for the city centre were submitted to the CRC by Ford and Gibson respectively. Although they were asked to collaborate, they could not see eye to eye.[10] Ford placed primary emphasis on the need for the quick restoration of business premises and of rateable value, by disturbing as little as possible the traditional pattern. Consequently, his plan consisted in the main of street improvements along existing lines, which would in most cases avoid trouble over ownership.[11] Gibson emphasized, however, the far-reaching potential of the council's position. As he put it in his report to the CRC:

The city is being made a test case, and its solutions will form a guide to the other cities which have been similarly devastated. The decisions of the Council will therefore, have a national and not merely a local effect ...

We have an opportunity in front of us that has never occurred before, born it is true, out of a catastrophe of colossal magnitude, but an opportunity to be grasped with both hands. Let it not be said by future generations that the people of Coventry failed them, when the ideal was within their reach.[12]

On 25 February, the city council adopted Gibson's plan by an overwhelming 43 votes to six. They were struck by the new Coventry, bordered by an inner ring road and divided into a number of zones based on function. Among the spectacular features included were a civic centre consisting of a library, police offices and law courts, civic hall, museum, municipal offices, adult educational institution, school of art and art gallery, with generous provision of open spaces; and a traffic-free shopping precinct, possibly arcaded, of six- or seven-storey buildings connected to a new retail market, replacing the old shopping area of Smithford Street and Hertford Street.[13]

Outside the council, the boldness of Gibson's plan attracted favourable comments, including those of various national newspapers.[14] Of particular importance was the King's visit to Coventry in early 1942, as the monarch

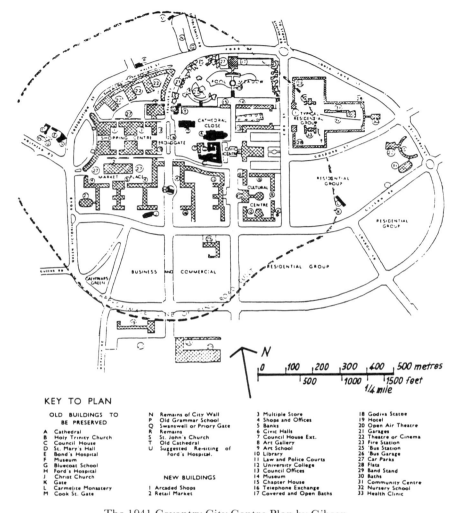

The 1941 Coventry City Centre Plan by Gibson

Source: T. Gregory, 'Coventry', in J. Holliday (ed.) *City Centre Redevelopment* (1973), p. 100. The map plan originally appeared in the *Midland Daily Telegraph*, 13 March 1941.

KEY TO PLAN

OLD BUILDINGS TO BE PRESERVED		
A	Cathedral	
B	Holy Trinity Church	
C	Council House	
D	St. Mary's Hall	
E	Bond's Hospital	
F	Museum	
G	Bluecoat School	
H	Ford's Hospital	
J	Christ Church	
K	Gate	
L	Carmelite Monastery	
M	Cook St. Gate	

N	Remains of City Wall
P	Old Grammar School
Q	Swanswell or Priory Gate
R	Remains
S	St. John's Church
T	Old Cathedral
U	Suggested Re-siting of Ford's Hospital.

NEW BUILDINGS

1	Arcaded Shops
2	Retail Market

3	Multiple Store
4	Shops and Offices
5	Banks
6	Civic Halls
7	Council House Ext.
8	Art Gallery
9	Art School
10	Library
11	Law and Police Courts
12	University College
13	Council Offices
14	Museum
15	Chapter House
16	Telephone Exchange
17	Covered and Open Baths

18	Godiva Statue
19	Hotel
20	Open Air Theatre
21	Garages
22	Theatre or Cinema
23	Fire Station
24	'Bus Station
25	'Bus Garage
26	Car Parks
27	Flats
28	Band Stand
30	Baths
31	Community Centre
32	Nursery School
33	Health Clinic

pronounced himself 'particularly satisfied' with an idea for arranging a shopping precinct on the arcading principle. He expressed the opinion that in all replanning schemes of blitzed towns, the future amenities for citizens were 'of supreme importance', and hoped that 'his visit ... would help to make such plans materialise'.[15] But how would the government react to such a plan? There was some concern about the financial implications of this bold plan, the cost of which had not yet been estimated. While the

An artist's impression of the proposed shopping precinct of Coventry

Source: City of Coventry, *The Future Coventry* (Coventry, 1945), p. 15.

majority of the council were confident of the government's generosity, there was strong doubt, as the *Standard* expressed, about 'the gift of the realisation of an otherwise impossible dream'.[16]

Within the Labour Party, Alderman Halliwell thought it was absolutely necessary to call on the government to introduce 'conscription of wealth' (or socialization of land), without which any rebuilding scheme would be impossible to operate. While his Labour colleagues agreed that socialization of land would be the best measure, they did not think it could be realized very quickly.[17] They thought, therefore, that it would be enough in the first instance to secure access to the land required for redevelopment by 'sterilization' (so that no buildings other than those of a temporary nature should be permitted on the cleared site, pending a proper redevelopment plan),[18] a method that could be pursued under existing legislation. Subsequently, it was hoped, the government might move well beyond this position. At the same February council meeting, Halliwell could not find a seconder for his amendment, and the council's adoption of Gibson's plan led to his resignation from the CRC and from the Coventry Labour Party.[19]

The Labour Party stood very firm indeed on the question of temporary buildings. As early as December 1940, the CRC had recommended that any building be subject to the submission of a proper plan for the approval of the Town Planning and Buildings Committee and the duration of the approval be for only 1 year.[20] It faced an amendment (from members of the Progressive Party) at the council meeting, that its duration be three years or until six months after the termination of the war. It was pointed out that property owners could not afford to build temporary premises to let on such a short-term basis, nor could shop owners hope to establish themselves and recoup their capital costs within that time. Labour contended that, in order to safeguard future redevelopment from prejudicial building, it was absolutely necessary to have as firm control as possible over land, and defeated the amendment by 20 votes to 15.[21]

Members of the local chamber of commerce were not at all content with the council's decision. They maintained that the duration should be much longer than 12 months, so that goodwill could be re-established. They also criticized Gibson's approach to the redevelopment of Coventry, and asked the CRC to receive a deputation to discuss whether the latter should contain co-opted members from outside the council.[22] The CRC simply said that it did 'not think a deputation would serve any useful purpose',[23] and proceeded to delegate to Gibson primary responsibility for the re-planning.[24] It was not until late 1943 that the CRC invited the chamber of commerce to discuss Gibson's plan. If anything, the city council were intently awaiting the government's reaction during the first half of the war, while the boldness of Gibson's plan and Lord Reith's encouragement were beginning to loom large in the minds of government officials.

*   *   *

The reaction from the Ministry of Works and Buildings to Gibson's plan was not as promising as the council had expected. In February 1942, the ministry wrote to Coventry, asking about the progress of work in connection with it. In reply, the CRC expressed 'surprise', for the plan had been investigated in detail by the ministry's inspector a year previously and, 'to make the position quite explicit', they resolved to make an application for the minister's formal approval of the plan.[25] This fitted in with the committee's wider decision that it would not make any further move unless and until the ministry demonstrated its own position.[26] Thus, in late 1942, E.H. Doubleday, newly appointed Regional Planning Officer of the Birmingham region of the ministry, found that little progress had been made regarding Coventry's replanning scheme. He asked the ministry in London to send a letter to Coventry about new development. Accordingly, the letter was sent in December 1942, stating that no formal approval could be given, because no planning resolution was operative regarding the centre of Coventry. Instead, the letter suggested reviewing the plan in relation to a wider area of the city, to make a detailed survey of changes in the conditions of the area caused by war damage, and to discuss the matter with the RPO.[27] The CRC had a conference with Doubleday and decided to carry out the suggested detailed survey of a wider area.[28]

Nevertheless, Doubleday had to write again to the ministry in London in April 1943. As he put it:

> The crux of the whole matter is finance. An air of uncertainty exists locally as to the intentions of the Government regarding assistance to 'blitzed areas', and this has created, in this region at any rate, a position of stalemate.[29]

Doubleday had been trying to discuss amending the 1941 plan with the corporation officers through informal monthly meetings, and, at the same time, to promote discussions about Coventry's 1941 plan between the council and business and industrial interests of the city by speaking to different council members on various occasions. His efforts, however – especially those to promote discussions with local interests – had been unsuccessful, as the council was most reluctant to make any further move under the existing legislation. Concluding that letter, he urged the ministry in London that:

> ... evidence on all sides points to the fact that the next phase in redevelopment lies with the Government. In this respect there is also much evidence that they (Coventry and Birmingham) are expecting a great deal from our new Ministry [of Town and Country Planning] now that we are solely responsible, and the opportunity is ripe for development.[30]

As already seen in Chapter 2, however, the government was suffering from great difficulties regarding decision making, especially with regard to the Uthwatt proposals.

The ministry's advisory panel provided important opportunities to discuss the matter with several of the most heavily blitzed cities. Before its visit to Coventry on 13 July 1943, it was already concerned about the grouping together of all of the civic buildings, and the replacement of an ordinary shopping street by arcaded shops of uniform design, which had not yet been discussed with commercial interests.[31]

At the meeting between the panel and the corporation, the latter were anxious to discover what the likelihood of formal approval of its 1941 plan was and the scope of any government financial assistance. In reply, the panel pointed out that 'the Government could not be expected to sign a blank cheque', and urged the need for some financial estimates regarding the scheme.[32] During discussion of the council's proposal to replace Smithford Street by an arcaded shopping precinct, the panel found:

> The Council are unaware of any objection, on the part of traders, to go into a 'precinct' instead of an ordinary shopping street ... Although the Council have had no official consultation with the traders and have not worked out the cost of the expected revenue from the shops they are apparently confident that the arcade scheme will be a success.[33]

Immediately after this visit, the panel decided that Doubleday should 'insinuate into the minds of the Council' the need for consultation with business and industrial interests.[34] Accordingly, he met the town clerk and reported to the ministry in London:

> The visit of the Panel to Coventry has had a most salutary effect, and I am glad to say that the Town Clerk now appreciates the need to consult business and industrial interests in the Town. This is a big step forward, and on my next visit to Coventry I will discuss with him ways and means of making a start on this long overdue matter.[35]

The local atmosphere was, however, getting worse. In October, Alderman Moseley, chairman of the CRC since its inauguration, commented on the recent announcement of the Minister of Town and Country Planning stating that the government's findings on the Uthwatt Report were ready for presentation:

> I am surprised at the wide attention that has been directed to the statement made this week by the Minister ... In fact, if there is anything new in the Minister's statement it seems to suggest that little in the way of financial assistance will be forthcoming from the Government, and, if I am interpreting the statement correctly, this is serious.[36]

Around this time, Hodgkinson also stated:

> It was feared that the bombed towns were going to be treated like old soldiers in days gone by – forgotten and left to their own resources

when the war was ended. Bombed towns would be like wounded, limbless soldiers unless the Government did its duty by them. So far there had been little evidence of Government enthusiasm in this connection.[37]

Meanwhile, the survey of a wider area suggested by the ministry was well advanced. In October, the CRC formally recommended the acceptance of a reconstruction area covering 383 acres. The committee stressed the importance of this decision, as it would 'form a basis for discussion with the Government as to the extent and character of State assistance'.[38] By this time, the Town and Country Planning (Interim Development) Act was passed, which gave power to local authorities to grant an interim development permission for a limited period only. The CRC recommended in September that the initial period of permission should be one year.[39] The last possible challenge from the chamber of commerce through Councillor Corbett (president of the chamber) at the October council meeting was defeated by 32 votes to 24.[40]

Under such circumstances, the CRC decided for the first time to invite the chamber of commerce to discuss the new shopping provisions of the 1941 plan.[41] Things thus eventually began to move. The ministry came to realize the gravity of Coventry's case more acutely, especially through the efforts of the RPO and through the visit of the advisory panel. The corporation became highly frustrated at the indecisiveness of the ministry and, in particular, at the uncertainty of financial assistance. At the same time, the corporation also decided to face up to local traders' criticisms of an arcaded shopping precinct.

In 1944, some features of the corporation's plan, notably an arcaded shopping precinct of multi-storey buildings, came under vigorous attack from the local chamber of commerce and the ministry. At the same time, the ministry faced a period of uncertainty in its dealings with Coventry, due in part to the lack of unity of opinion among officials, but most importantly because of their failure to introduce long-awaited general legislation.

*   *   *

The meeting between the CRC and the chamber of commerce was held in February 1944. The chamber conveyed their objections to the shopping provisions in the corporation's scheme, particularly to the idea of an arcaded traffic-free shopping precinct. They argued that the precinct principle 'would, due to its restriction in size, tend to create monopolies, and would prevent any further addition or expansion'; arcade shopping was not favoured either, because it would be 'unpopular with the general public'; they further maintained that the existing main shopping streets should not be eliminated altogether, because the inclusion of vehicle traffic was essential to the success of the shopping area. In this connection, it was stated that, under their auspices, an alternative layout for a shopping area was being prepared.[42] In reply, the CRC stated that they were willing to consider the points made by the chamber, and also to examine the suggested alternative layout on its merits.[43] The president of the chamber thought of this meeting as 'a good-natured, long, and friendly talk', and went on to say, as reported in the local press:

> The real objection was the layout of the City Architect, and it was strongly felt that the old idea of street shopping was much better than what was called 'cloistered precincts'.[44]

The proposed alternative plan prepared by Messrs Woolworth's architect[45] was considered by the CRC on 19 June 1944. The plan envisaged a self-contained shopping area in the shape of a semi-circle, surrounded by a 60-ft wide road, with a kind of 'underground city' beneath, in that goods and service access roads would be provided by excavation below the present ground level. The CRC observed, however, that the sandstone of the area was so charged with water that the maintenance of the suggested underground roads would be impracticable.[46] They concluded that they were not in favour of the alternative scheme, adding though that they would 'be pleased to consider any further observations which the Chamber [might] wish to make'.[47]

While there were obvious signs of some mutual understanding between the corporation and the chamber of commerce, the much tougher battle was going on behind the scenes between Coventry and the Ministry of Town and Country Planning. At ministry headquarters, L. Neal, Deputy Secretary of the Ministry, became rather impatient at the slow progress of Coventry's replanning. Admitting the importance of informal monthly meetings organized by the RPO, Neal repeatedly requested more direct action by the ministry in the form of an official letter of criticism of the 1941 plan. At first, Doubleday resisted such an idea, for he felt that in Coventry 'one has to steer a steady if not a fast course'. As he continued:

> Coventry can, and probably will say that the Government's difficulty in coming to a decision on reconstruction legislation has severely embarrassed them in the preparation of their scheme with public support. In this they will be strongly backed by other 'blitzed' cities ... [And] the feeling 'agin' the Government appears to be getting deep-rooted and somewhat bitter.[48]

Doubleday made the most of these monthly meetings with the help of other ministry officials and of F. Smith, Town Clerk of Coventry, who strongly opposed Gibson's proposals, especially the elimination of Smithford Street. They exposed Gibson to considerable criticism. At the February 1944 meeting, for instance, the precinct principle of six- or seven-storey high buildings was severely attacked by the town clerk and the city treasurer. Gibson replied that at any rate the city council was fully prepared to back his plan. Smith argued, however, as recorded in the ministry's file:

Confidentially, he interpreted the Council's attitude in this way. Excessive publicity had been given to the damage sustained by Coventry and, in consequence, the Council had developed an idea that they had suffered more than any other town and, therefore, had a greater claim than any other town to have all their reconstruction done for them at the expense of the nation. On the wave of this attitude, they had adopted without a period of inquiry and with undue haste the plan proposed to them as a final plan and were, in consequence, committed to a great deal [which], in his view, would certainly have to be revised.[49]

The pressure on Gibson was so strong that, towards the end of the meeting, he himself agreed that if a plan of a different character was asked for, he would prepare one.[50] At the meeting in May, Gibson was again under fierce attack. He tried to defend the precinct concept, citing Plymouth which had also envisaged a precinct shopping centre. Those representing the ministry pointed out that while Plymouth was a pre-eminent shopping centre within its region, without any rivals of importance, Coventry was never an established shopping centre and it was too near to Birmingham to have prospects of becoming one. Gibson held on, maintaining that if the council acted as a developer, his shopping centre would be a great success. At this point, the town clerk hurriedly interrupted to state that Gibson's view was not backed at all by local business and commercial interests. Hearing this, the ministry side stated categorically that 'it was improbable that the local authority would be able to obtain the capital from the Government for a scheme which was objected to by the commercial interests on the grounds that it was a risky business'.[51] Reporting it to headquarters, one ministry official observed:

> None of the officials of the Corporation with whom we have been having conversations, except Gibson (and his views have been slightly modified) believe in the Plan as it now stands.[52]

At the same time, ministry officials – but most especially Doubleday – began to feel that a new stimulus other than the monthly meetings was necessary because of 'the stubbornness on the part of the Council to agree to amend their present proposals' and of his informal knowledge about 'associations between certain members of the Council and political factions which do not approve of the present attitude of the Government in regard to planning and reconstruction'.[53] By this time Neal became so impatient that he directed Doubleday to prepare to instruct Coventry to draw up a fresh plan within three months.[54]

The forthcoming Reconstruction Bill made such a direct and official approach all the more imperative. As one official put it, the financial proposals of the Bill:

> ... have been whittled down in such a way as to leave the question of redevelopment for blighted areas in abeyance for the moment and

generally to give the whole proposal a somewhat smaller scale, which to Coventry, always insistent on Lord Reith's 'Plan boldly', is likely to appear thoroughly mean.

The question is not whether Coventry are right in this view of theirs. The difficulty is that the present bill offers them a fresh opportunity to make political capital out of the Government's attitude to their plan. Now that this has been pointed out I must admit that any controversy which may arise from direct criticism of the Coventry plan before the bill is published is likely to be less than the difficulties caused by making the same criticism after the bill has been published, when Coventry are likely to say that we have made up our criticisms in order to cut down their plan and make it fit into what they will call the Government's inadequate financial proposals.[55]

Those representing the ministry agreed to write a letter of criticism as soon as practicable, and Doubleday sounded out the town clerk as to the possible reception of such a letter. The main ground of criticism was that the plan lacked the support of local traders. On this point, the town clerk expressed his concern:

> ... that if this lack of public support were used as the main ground of criticism, he rather thought that the Council might then embark on a campaign to win public support to the plan, and he would not be surprised if the Council obtained a majority of public support in numbers as opposed to values in the City, mentioning, as a guess, a two-thirds majority in favour.[56]

Smith repeatedly made the point that any criticism which gave rise to political arguments had to be avoided, for he thought that 'some of the Labour members of the Council would not be averse to such publicity "agin" the Government'.[57]

Accordingly, Doubleday produced a detailed critical report of the Coventry plan based on purely technical grounds. The most striking criticism regarded the extraordinarily large amount of land devoted to civic use, which would not be able to produce any ground rents for a considerable time to come. In criticizing this, however, Doubleday noted:

> ... one should not minimise the strong socialist tendencies of the Council, who may reply that they intend to see that these civic buildings are provided, a point which may have a strong local appeal. Care should be taken, I suggest, to keep one's criticism to the doubtful merits of such a large concentration with its effects on the shopping centre, a line which seems to me to be non-political.[58]

Back at the ministry in London, however, Neal thought a shorter, less critical letter to be less likely to upset Coventry. Accordingly, on 19 May 1944 a letter was sent to Coventry asking for a general statement as to the recent work carried out on the redevelopment scheme, and for their proposals regarding zoning, the re-establishment of displaced under-takings, and the programming of the reconstruction works.[59] The letter was considered by the CRC on 19 June, just one day before the introduc-tion of the Bill. Around this time, discussions between Coventry and the Ministry of War Transport were being held as to the route of the inner ring road. A plan showing the route had been submitted by the planning officers to the CRC for approval. As the committee maintained that the demar-cation of the areas of use would depend to a far greater extent upon the alignment of the inner ring road than the other way around, the ministry's letter of 19 May made them hurry over the question of alignment. Thus they resolved to approve the proposed route in principle and to submit the plan to the ministries concerned, so that they could consider the questions in the ministry's letter in the near future.[60]

As for the Bill now in Parliament, Alderman Moseley, chairman of the CRC, told the local press:

> On the whole my own feeling is one of disappointment. At the same time, it has to be realised that the bombed towns are fairly numer-ous, so, in total, making the problem a big one from the national point of view, and if the Bill is the Government's last word, we shall have to make the best of it and cut our coat according to our cloth.[61]

Thus headquarters observed:

> ... that it looks as though our letter of the 19th May may have succeeded in its attempt to prevent the Coventry Plan from becoming a battle cry of the opposition to the Bill. The discussion is now on technical grounds, while at the same time we have given the necess-ary stimulus from the Ministry.[62]

The question was, therefore, whether the ministry should present Coventry City Council with their detailed criticisms of the Coventry plan. Doubleday did not think the time was yet ripe. First, he agreed with the council that in the meantime they should concentrate on the question of the inner ring road.[63] Moreover, there were some positive signs in favour of the ministry. For instance, the planning officers had prepared certain modifications to the 1940 plan, allowing for the line of Smithford Street to be retained as a service-way. Alderman Moseley, who had been rather a problem for the ministry as chairman of the CRC, was to retire. His successor, Councillor Grindley, had mentioned to Doubleday on several occasions his impression that the 1940 plan was 'based on aspirations without foundation work'.[64]

By October, however, the ministry in London was determined to make a further move. As one official put it:

> My impression on reading the earlier minutes and correspondence is that it was a pity that the possibility of political repercussions was considered serious enough to make us take a much weaker line with Coventry than was at first intended. This fear seems to have

influenced our action throughout. There is no doubt that Mr. Doubleday has done good work in very difficult circumstances, but I still feel that an earlier tactful but firm prod from Headquarters would have produced better results and more rapid progress.[65]

The ministry was now in favour of putting forward its detailed criticisms of the Coventry plan in the form of a further official letter.

With the passing of the Bill into law, the city council was also expected to get on with the ground work in connection with the city's plan. The first move was supposed to follow the report of the town clerk on the Town and Country Planning Act 1944,[66] which was to be submitted to the meeting of the CRC on 29 November. As Doubleday observed, 'This is the kick-off for which we have all been waiting, and I think the game will be fast and furious thereafter.'[67]

*   *   *

At the meeting of 29 November, the CRC resolved to initiate a series of conferences with the trading and other interests affected by the redevelopment scheme, and to invite, in the first instance, the chamber of commerce on 14 December.[68] At this first conference, the chamber's concern was focused on the desirability or otherwise of the precinct idea. To their surprise, they were told by the corporation that the precinct proposals had been limited to approximately one-fifth of the total shopping frontage because it was not practicable to extend the idea further in the present scheme. What is more, Gibson promised in reply to a request from the representative of multiple shops, that provision would be made so that it would be possible to convert the shopping precinct into a normal street if experience showed that it was unsuccessful from the commercial point of view.[69]

The chamber's attention was now narrowed down to the question of the Smithford Street precinct. As maintained in a *Memorandum on Coventry Redevelopment: Shopping Facilities* forwarded to the corporation, they still preferred a through road to the shopping precinct.[70] The CRC left consideration of the matter to further discussions between the planning officers and the chamber of commerce, which implied the committee's inclination towards an amended design.[71] As the president of the chamber of commerce told the local press in May 1945, there had been 'a great change in the atmosphere, and he did not think anyone could grumble now at the consideration given to the Chamber by the Corporation'.[72] In the same month, Professor Holford (Technical Adviser to the Ministry) suggested to the corporation's officers that they should make some kind of compromise with the trading interests, although it did not have to be the abandonment of the precinct principle.[73]

At last, the planning officers made the final decision. While the revised plan retained the principle of a shopping precinct in the Smithford Street area, some concessions were made to the views of the chamber of commerce. Among other things was a new north–south road intersecting the precinct area,[74] with a flyover bridge to carry road traffic over the precinct. While the actual shopping area would be free from traffic, highway access to it would be provided.[75]

The chamber of commerce was not in favour of a traffic bridge, partly because they considered it would block a possible future road through the precinct, and instead suggested two footways. They also continued to maintain that a shopping precinct was less desirable than a through road. However, the planning officers pointed out that the suggested through road would very likely be used as a through way and thus nullify the effect of the ring road.[76] The CRC made the final decision, deciding not to proceed with the idea of a traffic bridge and approving in principle the proposed subways. At the same time, they held the view that the shopping precinct was preferable to the suggested through road and, accordingly, decided to adhere to the precinct.[77]

Thus at the local level a compromise was made between the corporation and the local traders as to the shopping provisions of the city centre plan as a result of a number of consultations. At first the consultations pleased the ministry. They soon became irritated, however, by the lack of progress, due mainly to the over-cautious attitude of the town clerk. No further conferences with local interests were arranged to follow those with the chamber of commerce. As Doubleday thought, 'the pressure to which he is subjected by the political elements in the Council is proving to be an overburdening factor of his approach to the Reconstruction Scheme'.[78]

The ministry was still very concerned about plans for a civic centre in the Coventry plan, and, consequently, they kept applying pressure for the council to reconsider. Several conferences were held but all the ministry could find was that the local authority was 'much up against the Ministry, on the ground that they had been told to plan boldly and were now finding themselves hedged about by departmental restrictions'.[79] Eventually, the ministry sent an official letter to the city council in June 1945, throwing strong doubt on allocating a large area to include all the public buildings with ample open spaces surrounding them.[80] In response, the CRC recorded in a strong manner that the points raised in the letter were:

> ... essentially matters to be decided by the judgment of the local authority; and that, the Committee see no reason to make any material change in the land-allocations in the 'civic' area, or in the proposals for the inclusion in that area of specific buildings.[81]

They also decided to prepare a balance sheet for the redevelopment scheme as a whole, including the net site costs likely to result after the government's grants ceased, and the cost of the buildings involved.[82]

The ministry thought, somewhat optimistically, that this letter 'stimulated the Council to test the finances of the proposals from the long-period aspect'.[83] At the same time, whereas the ministry wanted

Coventry to make rapid progress, by submitting a formal application for compulsory purchase under the Town and Country Planning Act 1944, the council could rightly refuse to submit an application until the proposed financial tests had been completed. And this financial examination in turn was expected to take quite some time. Moreover, the local elections were fast approaching and it was recognized that no particular change would occur until they were over. Once completed, however, the fierce battle was expected to resume. As one ministry official put it, 'it must be admitted that if they [the Council] submit the scheme as it stands at present we may have to insist on its being considerably modified'.[84]

Just before the local elections took place, the ministry's insistence on modification was expressed in public by Lewis Silkin, the newly appointed Minister of Town and Country Planning. In October 1945, commemorating the city's 600th anniversary of the granting of its Charter of Incorporation, the 'Coventry of the Future' exhibition was held, featuring a model for a new city centre as its main attraction. It received 57 500 visitors over two weeks, equivalent to one in four of the city's entire population. As the *Midland Daily Telegraph* reported, the exhibition:

> ... has proved in unmistakable manner that, contrary to what has been said so often, the ordinary ratepayer is intensely interested in the affairs of his city, and that he is quite prepared to receive the enlightenment which is so necessary in municipal administration and has been so lacking in the past.
>
> No more effective method could have been devised for creating the determination that will be necessary to convert the 'dream city' into reality.[85]

On the opening day, however, Mayor Hodgkinson and Silkin expressed two conflicting views. At a civic luncheon, Hodgkinson spoke quite strongly of the ministry's 'tremendous delay' in giving formal approval to Coventry's plan. As he put it:

> There has been all sorts of manoeuvring in order to edge Coventry away from the splendid designs it had.
>
> I hope we have now come to a stage where we can halt, where no more modifications will be required, and no more vetting of our plan. I hope the Minister will give approval to what we want to do without further modification.[86]

Declaring the exhibition open, Silkin responded:

> In every reconstruction scheme the local planning authority has to reconcile the call for boldness and imaginative conception with the need for ensuring that reconstruction should so proceed as not to outstrip at any stage the resources of men, materials, and finance available to it, and particularly with the need for ensuring that the community shall be able to proceed actively with its business while

> step by step the process of reconstruction advances ... All my indications are that Coventry is well on the way to securing that reconciliation.[87]

From Coventry's viewpoint, reconciliation had already been secured by making concessions to the chamber of commerce about the shopping provisions in the plan. In this sense, Coventry was the victim of the government's retreat from bold planning to economy and conventionalism. The long-delayed Town and Country Planning Act 1944 was quite restrictive in its provisions, especially those of financial assistance. As the central commercial area, which suffered most heavily from the blitz, was the area that contributed considerably to the city's finances, the council had to ensure that the plan was acceptable to local traders. And in this respect pressure from the ministry played an important role.

Nevertheless, the council did adhere to the principle of a shopping precinct despite strong opposition to it from the chamber of commerce, and, when it came to the ministry's further objection to a civic centre, they showed no sign of compromise. Labour, as the majority on the council, thought that the new city centre formed as important a part of the future Coventry as the improved housing, education and public health.[88] The municipal elections in October 1945 brought three gains to Labour[89] and, with this strengthened majority, they were reasonably confident to 'go forward with all schemes for the city's development'.[90]

There were two things which sustained the council's belief in Gibson's plan. First, there was immense interest in and support for the plan, reflected for example in extensive nationwide publicity and the King's comment, from which it was firmly established that Coventry's bold plan was a symbol for the rebuilding of Britain. Secondly, the local Labour Party was confident that the majority of the people of Coventry were with them in pursuit of the dream plan. This confidence squashed completely the ministry's argument that Coventry's plan lacked public support. Consequently, the ministry, which did not like the imaginative nature of some of the proposals – notably that of a civic centre – had to be extremely cautious in being critical for fear of political repercussions. The position of the ministry was further marred by delays in introducing the promised legislation, and the inadequate provisions of the 1944 Planning Bill almost panicked ministry officials. When the ministry at last ventured to put forward their strong doubt (and yet articulate criticism) of the civic centre proposal to the council, the latter easily bluffed it out, saying that it was a matter to be judged by themselves. Coventry's case thus demonstrates that the belief on the part of the council and the enlightened public that bold replanning of the blitzed city centre would be of ultimate benefit and credit to the local community and to the country after the war, overcame the attempts of vested interests and of the ministry during the war to overturn it. Attention will now turn to the case of Southampton.

five

Replanning the city centre: Southampton 1940–45

An early start was made to the replanning of Southampton's blitzed central area, and it was favourably comparable even to Coventry. In the first place, the planning machinery of the borough council was strengthened through the efforts of Councillor Matthews, deputy leader of Labour and an acknowledged expert on planning. He was appointed southern regional researcher of the Nuffield College Social Reconstruction Survey in the early war years, which gave him new ideas about the city's industrial future. It was not an easy task persuading the Conservative majority on the council of the need for the drastic changes that town planning required, but his influence certainly had some effect. Among other things, Professor S. Adshead, one of the most experienced planners in the country, was appointed planning consultant by the council.

The report and plan were prepared by Adshead and H.T. Cook, town planning and development officer of the council, by early 1942. As regards the central area, their plan envisaged a fairly bold road system and a new shopping centre in the form of a promenade, called the 'Circus'. After discussions with traders and the ministries concerned, the idea of a shopping promenade was abandoned completely, and attention turned exclusively to enhance the values of the main pre-war shopping street of Above Bar/High Street.

The Ministry of Town and Country Planning was quite satisfied with the progress made in Southampton during the war. The borough council were, unlike in Coventry, very receptive to suggestions from the interests concerned, and amended their plan accordingly. Not surprisingly, ministers were rather taken aback as they came to realize that the replanning of Southampton's central area had become the major political issue of the municipal elections in November 1945, and that as a result of this contest, the existing plan was to be replaced by a totally new scheme.

*   *   *

In Southampton, the borough council held their first discussions on replanning in January 1941, just a month after the major bombing. The council were considering a motion moved by Alderman Woolley (leader of the Ratepayers' Party) asking the town planning sub-committee to consider the procedure necessary for the reconstruction of the central portion of the town, and to consult the Ministry of Works and Buildings with a view to the presentation of a preliminary report.

Woolley argued that while any long-term reconstruction was out of the question at that time, there was a great deal that could be done towards restoring the normal life of the city. Of particular importance was to allow the traders the opportunity to return to their businesses on their original sites as soon as possible. Alderman Mouland, Ratepayers' member and chairman of the works committee and its town planning sub-committee since the latter's inauguration in 1928, noted that a scheme for the redevelopment of Southampton city centre was being prepared in line with Woolley's argument.

Matthews was somewhat alarmed at the Ratepayers' Party's approach to the replanning of the city – rush action for the sake of quick restoration of business. Planning required the consideration of much wider issues, such as the population and industry of the town as a whole, which would be influenced considerably by government policy. It had to be considered as a long-term policy in an appropriate manner. As he maintained in a private memorandum, before commencing the replanning of the city, there were several essential steps that needed to be taken: the appointment of a town planning consultant from outside the council to prepare an advisory report on the replanning of the city; measures to safeguard the proposals from prejudicial actions in the future; government intervention at an early stage to secure replanning on the right lines from the outset; and the strengthening of the council's town planning machinery. He deplored the fact that in the town planning sub-committee 'no more than two members have any deep interest in and knowledge of planning'. As regards officials, they had H.T. Cook, town planning assistant, attached to the borough engineer. Although Matthews regarded Cook as 'a first class man', he was:

> ... handicapped by his subordination to the Borough Engineer and by the prevailing attitude of Council members to any drastic planning proposals. That is why the appointment of an eminent Town Planning consultant is essential. But in addition to this the Town Planning work of the Council should be constituted either as a separate

Department, or Mr. Cook, as Town Planning Officer, be given special status.[1]

At the January council meeting, Matthews, while seconding Woolley's motion, also stated:

> We are asking for bold, big and [effective] planning, but we do not want consideration of the miscellaneous problems presented to this Council in a month's time and be asked to call that planning. That is nothing of the kind. I want to plan reasonably and well, and to have first-class brains and first-class thought on the job.[2]

The council meeting ended with Alderman Woolley's withdrawal of his motion on an assurance that the town planning sub-committee be called together as soon as possible to consider the whole matter in the light of the discussion which had taken place at the council meeting.[3]

However, Matthews' most important proposals for the preparation of a long-term plan – including the appointment of a consultant and a borough architect, and the creation of a planning department and committee – were not discussed at all by the planning sub-committee.[4] This seemed to indicate the prevailing negative attitude of other sub-committee members to any drastic change in the matter of planning. Keeping silent himself, Matthews was looking for an opportunity to press his case. Such opportunity was soon to be created by the visit of Lord Reith, Minister of Works and Buildings.

*   *   *

In March, Lord Reith came to Southampton with G.L. Pepler and met the sub-committee. They asked the minister whether they were to plan boldly and comprehensively:

> Lord Reith said, most emphatically, 'Yes.' That advice was definitely valuable to the committee, because it will dissipate any doubt about the official attitude to long-term redevelopment policy. It connoted, moreover, that ... the local authorities, who must be responsible for the plans but can hardly be expected to bear the expense, will have the support of the Government.[5]

Soon after the minister's visit, the planning sub-committee started to consider the setting up of a planning department, with only Mouland, the chairman, opposing it. But even then, the proposal to appoint a planning consultant, now seconded by Councillor Lane (Ratepayers' Party), was defeated,[6] and the sub-committee eventually decided to defer consideration of the appointment for six months.[7] The *Southern Daily Echo* predicted that the matter would certainly be raised in the council before long. The point was whether such an appointment might be premature in view of the necessary preliminary research progressing.[8] Matthews thought that the importance of such research made such an appointment all the more necessary. For, by this course:

> ... he will be able to be in at the birth of the scheme and give his advice in the preparation of the data upon which he will build his proposals. His experience and knowledge would probably save unnecessary labour. Further, he himself would benefit materially by being able to study the scheme from the outset.[9]

At last, at the June council meeting, Alderman Woolley proposed to ask the advice of the Minister of Works and Buildings,[10] a request which resulted in Reith recommending an immediate appointment.[11] In August, the planning sub-committee resolved unanimously to recommend the appointment of Professor S.D. Adshead as town planning consultant. The scope of his work was to prepare an outline redevelopment plan and report for Southampton, with particular reference to the bombed-out city centre. The work was to be carried out within a period of six months from the date of appointment.[12]

With 40 years' experience, Stanley Adshead was one of the most eminent figures in town planning. When the country's first Department of Civic Design was created at Liverpool University in 1909, he was invited to be its first Professor. Five years later, he was offered the Chair of Town Planning at London University, which he retained for 21 years until his retirement.[13] Regarded as one of the best architectural draughtsmen of his day, he was also aware of the importance of social and administrative questions concerning town planning, leading him to write *Town planning and town development* in 1923. In this book he introduced the concept of a 'promenade', a feature often seen on the continent.[14] His appointment was a timely one, for as well as his profound knowledge and wide experience of town planning, he was determined to create a better England after the war, something he expounded in *A new England*, published in 1941.[15] Adshead's partner in the preparation of a redevelopment plan was H.T. Cook, who had just recently been promoted to head the newly created town planning and development department in July 1941.[16]

The preparation of a plan for the new Southampton proceeded rapidly, and in February 1942 Adshead and Cook's joint report was submitted to the city council.[17] This report was relatively comprehensive in that it dealt with such subjects as post-war housing requirements, the future population of the city and proposals for industrial zoning with the object of encouraging new industries. As regards the city centre, several interesting proposals were made. For example, blocks of new and larger tenement buildings of four or six storeys were proposed to the south of Houndwell for those working at the Old Docks.[18] In order to improve the lower part of the city, new meat and fruit markets were to be built in High Street; on recently reclaimed land, a youth centre, a swimming pool and a new park were

An artist's impression of the proposed town centre of Southampton

Source: *Southern Daily Echo*, 29 April 1942.

envisaged. The two most attractive features in the report, however, were the new road system and the creation of a new city centre.

The new road system was designed to relieve the traffic congestion afflicting the city's main shopping street of Above Bar/High Street. The inner ring was to circumscribe the central area and serve to provide connections between important points on existing radial roads. Much of it would be composed of dignified new roads. With regard to the east–west route through the centre, the report proposed a new road leading straight to the front of the guildhall. Its width was to be 100 feet, increasing to 150 feet for the section between the new north–south road and Above Bar. For the new north–south route, a 120-foot wide dual carriageway (the New Dock Road) was proposed. It was to run parallel in the east with the main shopping street, and cater principally for through traffic. Relieved of through traffic, the main shopping street needed only to be widened to 80 feet.[19]

As the report pointed out, Southampton had no central square or plaza comparable to those of many other mediaeval towns. In replanning the city centre, that section upon which all the main roads would converge was designed to form such a centre. The guildhall entrance to the civic centre would be the dominant feature at the western end. It would be an open space approximately 400 feet wide, while the buildings on the east side of Above Bar were to be set back to complete the effect of a large open fore-court in front of the guildhall. The eastern end was composed of a large circular plaza (the 'Circus'), 500 feet in diameter, at the intersection of the new north–south road and that from the east. In view of the great volume of traffic converging upon the Circus, the report proposed to construct bridges for pedestrians at first-floor level over the main roads. Around the Circus and along both sides of the city centre between Above Bar and the new north–south road, the report suggested erecting shops of a uniform elevation.[20]

The design of the circus allowed for the construction of a promenade, or shopping way, $12\frac{1}{2}$ feet wide around the blocks of shops at first-floor level behind a row of columns. The promenade was to be reached by steps and, possibly, lifts. As the report claimed:

> It would be a unique arrangement in this country, where never before has there been a good opportunity for putting it into practice. If the bridges were constructed as already suggested, shoppers could walk all round the circus at first floor level under cover; the nearest design of a comparative nature in this country being 'The Rows' at Chester, though there are many examples of such arcade walks in foreign countries.[21]

The Adshead/Cook report was referred to the new Town Planning and Development Committee, finally created though still without Alderman Mouland's support. Although he was one of the committee's members, he soon resigned from it.[22] The new committee's first chairman during the war was Councillor Lane, and the first vice-chairman was Matthews. While

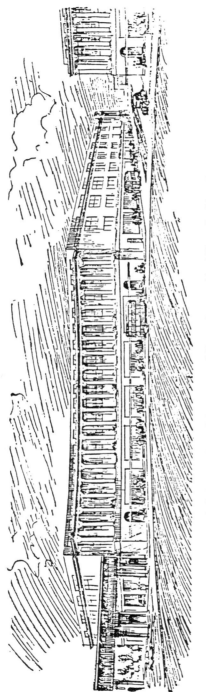

An artist's impression of the proposed Town Centre (the 'Circus') of Southampton

Source: *Southern Daily Echo*, 29 April 1942.

Lane was a Ratepayers' councillor and also a director of the chamber of commerce (by profession he was a surveyor), he remained in agreement with Matthews for most of this period.

The city centre plan put forward by Adshead and Cook was, as Cook wrote to an official of the Ministry of Town and Country Planning, generally favoured by the planning committee. He thought that it would receive the approval of the council in a few months' time.[23] However, the plan – especially the idea of a shopping promenade – met strong opposition from local traders and from the ministries concerned, the Ministry of War Transport in particular.

The local traders stated that they had little confidence in the success of such a proposal, since the shops would not form a natural extension of the existing main shopping street and, consequently, shoppers would have the choice of shopping either in Above Bar or in the new promenade. At a meeting of the chamber of commerce, W. Dixon (former president of the chamber and president of the High Street Association) said that he could see 'no real grounds for planning such an extension of shopping facilities', and wondered 'if in the planning of the town the planners had not been mesmerised by this new shopping centre, which would impinge a new centre on one which already existed'.[24] The Ministry of War Transport was strongly opposed to the proposal on the grounds that it would create conditions dangerous to pedestrians.[25]

A revision of the plan seemed necessary, but the task was assigned to Cook only. The planning committee turned down an offer from Professor Adshead to continue as consultant in January 1943 (without mentioning any particular reason).[26] In March 1943, the revised plan was submitted to the city council. The most significant change from the original 1942 plan was the omission of shops around the Circus. This was a real disappointment to Adshead who had been very keen on the idea of a shopping promenade. As he wrote to Cook:

> I don't understand the Ministry of Transport's point of view. ([Is] it safety, then they can have a railing, as shown on my drawing. I thought it was bridges they wanted, and we gave them bridges.) I [don't] know that a circus is the last word, but it fits the site and is a [splendid] feature if everyone can be persuaded to adopt it ...
>
> It is only natural that owners and the majority of [shop] keepers should hesitate at such innovations, but there will be a lot of innovations to be got used to, after the war, if this is to be a go ahead country.[27]

In the revised plan, it was also suggested that endeavour should be made to attract retail trade into Above Bar and High Street, particularly the latter, which for some years had been in decline from a shopping point of view. For this purpose, several proposals were put forward. Existing buildings adjoining the town quay, except those of historical or archaeological interest, should be demolished. Those of historical interest were to be left standing in suitably laid out open spaces. Bargate Circus (the bottleneck between Above Bar and High Street) was to be entirely reconstructed so as to create greater continuity between the two streets. The wholesale distribution of fruit and vegetables, which had previously taken up a considerable part of High Street, was to be re-established on a site other than the lower part of High Street, as originally suggested.[28]

The focus of discussion at the March council meeting, however, shifted from these new proposals to the rights of property owners. The planning committee asked the council to approve the revised plan in principle, pending clarification of government policy, especially the level of financial assistance likely to be available. If generous financial assistance could eventually be guaranteed from the government, then rebuilding should start as soon as possible. The intention of this resolution was, as Councillor Lane told the council, the 'sterilization' of properties within the area under the plan, which would mean that no buildings other than those of short-lived materials should be permitted on the cleared site pending a final re-development plan. It was a clear warning to individual property owners that the future of the area was within the council's discretion and that they were no longer allowed to rebuild as they liked. Alderman Woolley proposed that the plan be adopted in principle only, as a mere expression of the council's intention to replan along the suggested lines, but should not be a ban on the right of property owners to remain or rebuild on their original sites. In reply, Councillor Lane expressed the opinion that it would be better to have a council debate on the question of sterilization and arrive at a settled policy. At this time, the committee had to have some backing from the council. As Lane observed:

> We have got to face the fact that at some period, if we hope to re-plan and re-build Southampton on better lines, we must be prepared to accept the sterilisation of certain sections. I think it would be more convenient to sterilise now, when other factors are already sterilising, than it would be to do so at some date after the cessation of hostilities when everybody will want to get on with plans for re-building.
>
> There is bound to be some sterilisation, and the committee are very mindful of the necessity to minimise it to the greatest possible degree, but that doesn't mean that we can completely eliminate it.[29]

Nevertheless, he was no longer able to defy the leader of his party. Rather mysteriously, the Labour Party, especially Matthews, put up a rather weak challenge, and it was eventually agreed to embody Woolley's suggestion in the resolution.[30] Knowing the council's decision, Adshead lamented in a letter to Cook:

> It is what must be expected, 'small profits and quick returns'. We were told to plan boldly, and we took a long distance view. It would

have taken nearly two generations to complete our scheme, and Southampton would have been the finest town in England.

The line that seems to be taken is to rebuild as quickly and as like the past as possible. Everyone will be rejoicing and in ten years lamenting.[31]

Adshead was now preparing a plan for York, which 'in a town of Museums and archaeological and ecclesiastical remains, and there is little more wanted than restoration, very different from Southampton'.[32] In reply, Cook emphasized that the council's approval had only been tentative. Thus, referring to the shops around the Circus, he observed: 'Since this [the Circus] remains as open space, it does not preclude the erection of shops in this position later if the necessity for them arises.'[33] Encouraged by this letter, Adshead wrote to the *Southern Daily Echo* and to Councillor Lane. As he admitted on reflection, 'my views were not presented to the Committee and to [the] Council as they would have been, had I been there'. There was, nevertheless, still time 'to prevent Southampton from being allowed to drift on easy but commonplace lines, instead of making it a great city'.[34] Although his letter, pressing the case of the shopping promenade, appeared in the *Southern Daily Echo* in June,[35] it did not seem to change the councillor's mind. As Cook told Adshead in July:

> With regard to the shopping circus, while no finality has yet been reached as to the precise treatment of this junction, the Council are naturally influenced by the aversions of the traders to the scheme and the strong opposition which the proposal has aroused with the Ministry of Transport.[36]

*   *   *

Meanwhile, the Ministry of Town and Country Planning had formed a favourable opinion about Southampton's city centre plan. The ministry appreciated the fact that fairly close contact had been kept between Cook and certain ministry officials,[37] and that the original plan of 1942 had gone through several revisions as a result of the local authority's consultation with local traders[38] and with the ministries concerned.[39]

As shown in Chapter 2, the Ministry of Town and Country Planning set up the Advisory Panel on Redevelopment of City Centres in May 1943, and chose seven badly bombed towns for detailed study. Southampton was the first town to be visited by the panel in June 1943. At the meeting between the panel and Southampton Council, the latter emphasized that they should be enabled to restore their shopping district within a couple of years after the war, so as to revive their rateable values, reduced drastically as a result of air raids.[40] After some consultation with local traders, the council was confident that its plan was likely to be acceptable to them. After the visit, one member of the panel expressed the opinion that too much emphasis had been placed on the restoration of rateable values and too little on finding the ideal plan, and that the plan hardly seemed to be bold enough.[41] It was pointed out, however, that their primary concern should be with the successful re-creation of the main shopping area, which had suffered the most extensive devastation. Both because it was the social magnet of a large and widespread community, and because it was so large a contributor to the city's revenue, its speedy rehabilitation was thought to be essential to the city's future.[42]

At the same time, in view of its proximity to Portsmouth and Bournemouth, any strong conflict of interest had to be avoided. Accordingly, it would be necessary to guard against too ambitious redevelopment.[43] However, the panel thought that the council would be well aware of this, for they had in their ranks Councillor Matthews, who had undertaken the Nuffield Social Reconstruction Survey that covered Southampton, Portsmouth, Bournemouth and Poole, and the planning officer, H.T. Cook, who was also planning officer to the local joint planning committee and a member of a regional advisory planning body for the county.[44] The plan for the borough itself was comprehensive, unlike Coventry, which limited its plan strictly to the city centre.[45] After its visit to Coventry, the panel formed the opinion that Southampton's plan was sufficiently advanced to form a basis for their findings, but Coventry's was far behind. They even thought, rightly, that Southampton was unique in this respect and that none of the other remaining cities would be very far advanced with their plans.[46] As for the general layout of Southampton's redevelopment plan for the city centre, the panel arrived at the provisional conclusion that it 'appears to us to be sound'.[47]

Whether Southampton knew of the panel's provisional conclusion or not, it did not seem to help the local authority very much. What Southampton needed among other things, were, as they told the panel:

1 Early legislation along the lines of the Uthwatt proposals granting them powers to purchase those areas covered by the plan with a view to the principle of public retention of freeholds.
2 Financial assistance from the government in the form of a loan, which should be free from interest and redemption payments during the early post-war years.[48]

As mentioned in Chapter 2, however, the government was facing great difficulty in reaching a conclusion regarding the Uthwatt proposals. Thus in early 1944, H.T. Cook reported that:

> ... little progress has so far been possible with preparations for active rebuilding of the central shopping and business area. This is due to uncertainty as to the future disposal of land and the financial terms upon which such decision will be made. Both of these are dependent upon Government policy.[49]

As government policy was about to be made public as the Town and

Country Planning Bill 1944, consideration of the final details of the scheme for Southampton city centre was carried a stage further. A planning scheme sub-committee consisting of Councillors Burrow, Lane and Matthews was set up in May 1944.[50] Five months later the further revised plan was submitted to the council.[51] Matthews told the council that they had included a magnificent square in front of the guildhall. An open space approximately 235 feet wide would be left in front of the guildhall, and shops on the east side of Above Bar would also be recessed to a similar width. The width of the main shopping street would be 100 feet. Then, at the bottom of it, a fine park would be created by extending public open space at Queen's Park to the Royal Pier and by closing the bottom end of High Street. Nevertheless, as Matthews himself admitted, the revised plan was rather:

> ... an orthodox plan, much more limited than those of many other blitzed towns. If we take away the two main features – the Guildhall Square and a large open space at the bottom of the town facing the docks – we shall destroy the plan altogether.[52]

Alderman Woolley still had something to say. He proposed an amendment to reduce the width of the main shopping street to 80 feet, and to reconsider the layout of Guildhall Square and the site between the town quay and the proposed southern end of High Street. He was particular about the 100-foot width of the shopping thoroughfare. As ample provision had been made for heavy through traffic, there was no need to provide extra road width to accommodate heavy traffic in the main shopping thoroughfare:

> It is doing the job twice over. It is incurring needless expense. It is docking off considerable depth of building line unnecessarily. It is, in my opinion, absolutely spoiling the thoroughfare for the purpose for which it is intended, namely, shopping.[53]

Matthews argued that the amendment was against the weight of technical opinion. The traders wanted pedestrians as well as cars to stop outside their premises. If vehicles were allowed in, then the road had to be sufficiently wide. At the same time, the council would have no power to exclude heavy traffic from this road, although they would do their best to persuade traffic not to use it. In the end, the amendment was carried by 23 votes to 18, although the mover agreed to leave the consideration of the layout of Guildhall Square and of the end of High Street to the planning committee.[54]

The committee soon asked Cook and H. Bennett – the first borough architect, appointed in October 1943 – to submit a revised layout of the areas in question.[55] Bennett expressed his particular concern about the financial consequences of the layout of the Guildhall Square: the deep setback on the east side of Above Bar was likely to diminish the value of the property fronting the east side of the square; the isolation of the small buildings on the north side of the square, caused by the island at the junction of Commercial Road and Above Bar, made it impossible to use them for retail distribution purposes.[56] His solutions were first that the size of the square should be reduced in order to maintain continuity of shopping along the east side of Above Bar; and, secondly, that the approach to the square from the New Dock Road should be one road on the axis of the square, rather than two horn roads, thus eliminating the traffic island in question.[57]

By early 1945, Cook submitted the further revised layout to the committee. The setback of the building block on the east side of Above Bar was greatly reduced. The approach to the square was also altered, by which, as Cook put it, 'the opportunity of erecting a building block, sufficiently large to retain its value as a retail trading site, can be secured'.[58]

Meanwhile, the passing of the Town and Country Planning Bill into law in 1944 made the question of the acquisition of land a very urgent matter. The planning committee asked Cook to indicate the maximum extent of the city centre over which powers of compulsory purchase might be exercised. Although Cook reported to the committee that 463 acres could so be purchased, [59] he expressed his concern that the 1944 Act was by no means clear on many points.[60] Accordingly, it was proposed that a deputation should be sent to W.S. Morrison, Minister of Town and Country Planning,[61] and the meeting took place in February 1945.

Just before this meeting, Matthews hinted in public his disappointment at the government's attitude towards planning. Although Lord Reith told Southampton to plan boldly, a very great gap between what they wanted and their capacity to carry it through had prevented them from replanning boldly. For example, Matthews believed that the government had dithered completely on the question of land utilization.[62] The chamber of commerce also expressed their concern about the reconstruction of the city centre after the war and maintained that a definite declaration by the local authority as to their policy for acquisition of land was essential.[63] The ministry were in fact of the opinion that Southampton should go ahead. As L. Neal, Deputy Secretary of the Ministry, recorded in early 1945, Southampton:

> ... is probably further advanced than any other blitzed city with its reconstruction proposals. These have been adopted by the Local Authority and a considerable measure of agreement has been reached with the Government Departments concerned. Moreover, preliminary negotiations with mmany individual traders have gone some way.[64]

The meeting with the minister gave considerable encouragement to the deputation, or at least to Matthews. The minister told the deputation to make a speedy decision regarding their acquisition proposals through an application for the designation of an area under the 1944 Act. That designation should be as extensive as possible and any specific exclusion should be minimized. He also told them that the local authority should not be too worried about grant, and encouraged them to remain ground landlords of the land acquired under the Act so as to maintain effective control of the property through the leasehold system.[65]

*   *   *

A reconstruction committee was set up to deal with all future matters related to the acquisition and disposal of land.[66] The next essential step, therefore, was to decide the area that should be included for compulsory acquisition under the 1944 Act. Unfortunately, progress thereafter was very slow. As Councillor Lane, chairman of the Town Planning and Development Committee pointed out, one reason was that 'We have one member who is very persistent, over-persistent, in exercising his right to object.' This was Alderman Sir Sidney Kimber, former leader of the Ratepayers' Party but by this time a maverick, sitting on the council as an 'Independent'. He had strong views against any infringement of the rights of property owners. Consequently, he continued to object on that ground to almost any proposals related to the replanning of the city centre, often being the only dissident in the council. The work of the council had inevitably been held up by these 'frivolous objections', which were attacked from both sides of the council.[67] What was more, there emerged the possibility of drafting an entirely new plan for the city centre. Bennett, the borough architect, soon found that he could not see eye to eye with Cook regarding many aspects of the city centre redevelopment plan. In this he was joined by F.L. Wooldridge, the new borough engineer, appointed in December 1944. In June 1945, Bennett and Wooldridge submitted a new plan to the planning committee.

As early as March 1944, in his letter to Bennett, Cook expressed his strong suspicion that it seemed that 'you prefer to work out your own scheme independently'.[68] Although they did try to collaborate, they moved farther apart as Wooldridge supported Bennett rather than Cook. In May 1945, the planning committee asked the three officers to report to the June meeting, in order that the committee might 'make a decision on the points outstanding in respect of the layout of the Central area'.[69] Bennett and Wooldridge submitted a joint report and plan at the June meeting. Councillor Lane, chairman of the committee, claiming that the new plan had been put forward to them 'without any prior notice or knowledge',[70] argued that 'the Council would make more progress by going ahead with the original scheme, which appeared to be good and acceptable, and obtain Ministerial approval of the plan'.[71]

The man who was mostly responsible for the new central area plan was F.L. Wooldridge, the borough engineer.[72] He argued that:

> ... the basic matters which will influence design are economics, and not engineering or planning principles. Unless the plan is sound economically it is useless no matter how fine it may be. To be sound

economically it must be capable of execution in several stages and there must be no insuperable difficulties in these stages. There is no need to emphasise the present state of the Country and the present lack of men, materials and money. Of course all these will become available in the near future but when they do, not for profligate use.[73]

One difficulty in the replanning of the central area was that it 'must be based on plain and simple common sense and yet sufficiently bold to our ever increasing traffic problems'. Bearing this in mind, Wooldridge could see that 'sufficient of the old plan of the town can still be utilised to build up the lines of the new'. For instance, it was intended to interfere as little as possible with parks or historic buildings, which 'still show us the dignity, tradition and characteristics which make Southampton such a homely and friendly town, a characteristic which in turn contributed in no small measure to its fame and prosperity as a shopping centre'.[74]

Two circular roads were proposed as the main features in a new road system. First was the 'Circular Road' – an outer or external traffic system girdling the 'shopping area' based on Above Bar/High Street. The primary purpose of this road was to improve direct access from all points of the compass, and to discourage any traffic from entering the main shopping street unless it had business therein. The main traffic from the south, i.e. from the docks, would be routed directly north, east or west along this road, rather than using a north–south route running parallel to Above Bar/High Street.[75] In the main, the route of this 'Outer Ring Road' followed existing roads. Another circular road, the 'Inner Ring Road', was to surround the Above Bar/High Street area starting at the civic centre and following the existing lines of Portland Terrace, Bugle Street, Canal Walk, Palmerston Road and East Park Terrace, then finally turning due west along the new road axial with the civic centre. The main purpose of this road was to allow for Above Bar/High Street to be treated as a shopping precinct in the future. As the borough engineer's report stated:

> In the first years bus services will probably use the Above Bar Street– High Street route but bus services must be made to circulate prop- erly and the ideal circuit for this purpose is the 'Inner Circuit Road' already mentioned. The advantage of this road as a circular bus route is that passengers can be put down or taken up along the whole length and breadth of the Shopping Area, and so build up an interest in the Shopping Area as a whole with consequent more uniform and sustained rateable value.[76]

The prime consideration when designing the main shopping area was to preserve as much as possible the existing layout and to enhance the importance of the original main shopping area of Above Bar/High Street. It was also proposed to provide a covered retail market on a site south of Bargate which would accommodate those small traders unable to establish themselves in new buildings with high rents and rates. With such a move, it was thought that there would be greater shopping interest in High Street and rateable values in this area would be immediately assured.[77] At the end of the report, Wooldridge emphasized again the importance of practical economics:

> In conclusion the guiding principle in the preparation of the scheme has been the extent to which existing roads, services and buildings can be preserved without perpetuating past defects in the layout of the town. In the main streets the rebuilding of the shops and business premises can be carried out merely by setting back to the new building lines. Utopian ideas have therefore been restrained by practical economics and an endeavour not only to plan a completed scheme but one which can be built up in successive stages without any insuperable difficulty.[78]

At the special July meeting it was resolved that the officers concerned should confer with the Ministries of Town and Country Planning and of War Transport to obtain their advice on the two plans.[79] But the proposed conference did not take place until November as the question of land acquisition policy became the most controversial point in the local elections.

In April 1945, following a conference with the Minister of Town and Country Planning in February, the borough council considered the planning committee's recommendation to advertise that the redevelopment of the city centre as a whole was being considered. While the recommendation was adopted by the council, discussion centred around the question of land acquisition policy. The Labour Party claimed that the local authority should acquire the whole of the area under consideration and should remain its owner as the minister had advised them in February. The Ratepayers' Party maintained that this advice did not mean that the council had to acquire all of the land.[80]

The planning committee had now to decide what area should form the subject of an application for a declaratory order under the 1944 Planning Act. A special meeting was fixed for 13 June. Before that date, the case of Canterbury City Council was made public. The Local Government Act 1933 laid down that any member of a council who had an interest in the properties affected or in contracts was unable to discuss or vote on matters such as the acquisition of land. In Canterbury, only six council members out of 26 could vote on the question of land acquisition. Most of the members of the Ratepayers' Party had to be disqualified in this respect. Accordingly, the special meeting for 13 June was cancelled and a way of avoiding disqualification was hastily sought.[81] By July, it was found that the Portsmouth City Council had applied to the Minister of Health for dispensation, and the planning committee resolved, upon a show of hands, to follow the same line.[82]

At the council meetings, however, the Labour Party was fiercely opposed to dispensation.[83] The local press strongly criticized the council's delay in deciding their post-war scheme. What Southampton needed was 'a "Get on with it" plan', but in order to get such a plan, the question of land acquisition had to be settled as soon as possible, for the principal cause for the delay was 'undoubtedly that there has been too much concentration in the Borough Council on making points for party at the expense of progress'.[84] The *Southern Daily Echo* soon revealed its own political stance on the question of compulsory acquisition by stating that the rebuilding would take twice as much time as it would without it:

> Those who favour wholesale acquisition will say that this is the view of 'vested interest.' Those who examine the facts dispassionately will recognise it as a view based on plain common sense.[85]

The dissatisfaction of local traders with the lack of a decision regarding the reconstruction of the town was also made clear to the council.[86] Moreover, the Ministry of Town and Country Planning became very concerned about the lack of progress in Southampton. As L. Neal reported to the minister in August 1945:

> ... there are strong political influences which are delaying any further formal action, and which are unlikely to be resolved until after the November elections. The Corporation, both elected members and officials, are divided into two camps. The more Conservative element, led on the elected member side by the Chairman of the Planning Committee and the Planning Officer, and the more Left Wing view led by the Deputy Chairman to the Planning Committee who supports the technical views held by the Borough Architect. It is therefore possible that after the November elections the present plan, which was prepared by a predominantly Right Wing Council, will be scrapped.[87]

In September, the ministry wrote to the council, saying that at the meeting in February it was understood that Southampton was in a position to submit an application for a declaratory order under the 1944 Act:

> The Minister notes with some anxiety that although more than six months have elapsed since that date, no such application has yet been submitted by the Town Council under the Act.[88]

At the adjourned special meeting of the council on 11 October, Labour put forward their amendment seeking to disqualify all council members except those whose interests were only nominal. In their view, dispensation simply meant that the vested interests of members of the Ratepayers' Party would be safeguarded. The amendment was lost by 23 votes to 32. It was a straight party vote. As Alderman Lewis, leader of the Labour Party, observed:

> The air is full of this question of the reconstruction of Southampton, and whether the views of the Ratepayers' Party, plus one member

of the Independent Party, are to rule or whether the considered, sensible views of the Labour Party are to prevail. That is the issue. I can quite see that some people want to get the municipal elections over first.[89]

Certainly, the question of land acquisition became the most controversial issue in the local elections. The Ratepayers' Party maintained that the council should purchase only as much land as necessary to carry out the replanning scheme, i.e. land for the widening of roads and other improvements, and the bottom part of the town.[90] Leasehold of 99 years was also criticized because it was 'not a long time in the life of a business'.[91] The importance of the February meeting with the minister which had been emphasized repeatedly by Matthews was rather cynically denied. As one Ratepayers' Party member said:

> But it was extraordinary that he [Matthews] put so much reliance on what was said then. The Government, by words only, had been encouraging the bombed towns to plan boldly, and acquire property. Councillor Matthews seemed to have swallowed that lock, stock and barrel.[92]

In their words, what the Labour Party was trying was 'to attach to the rebuilding of Southampton the opportunity of putting into operation what is nothing more or less than nationalisation of land'.[93]

The Labour Party showed no hesitation in stating that what the city needed was for the local authority to have the powers to plan the central area as its large-scale owner. As their manifesto for the local elections put it, public ownership would give the council continuous control of development, and would enable the increased values created by public expenditure on reconstruction to fall into public funds instead of into private pockets. As it went on:

> Reconstruction of the central area can in the long run be a reasonable financial investment for the people of Southampton, but only if the area is publicly owned. It has long been profitable to those who privately owned it. The Ratepayers' Party are not willing to adopt the policy recommended to it by the late Minister of Planning, who was a Conservative. They want to minimise acquisition and in so doing will add substantially to the long run cost of reconstruction, and make the plan itself ineffective.[94]

The result of the election was a sweeping victory for the Labour Party, gaining 13 seats out of the 16 previously retained by the Ratepayers' Party.[95] With this result, Councillor Matthews said confidently that the question of wholesale acquisition 'has been clearly settled by the electorate'.[96]

Quite apart from this issue, however, there remained a further problem, in that the city council still had to choose from one of two plans for the city centre, the original one prepared by the town planning officer and a new one prepared by the borough engineer and borough architect. Councillor Matthews was now entirely inclined to the new plan, despite his earlier efforts at bold replanning. There were some obvious explanations for his change of mind. First, given the expected shortage of labour and materials after the war, the first priority had to be housing. Secondly, the loss of rateable value with regard to houses and shops through war damage was extremely severe for Southampton, even compared to other cities which had been heavily bombed, such as Coventry and Bristol, and financial assistance from the government would be restricted. The local Labour Party's land policy – the wholesale acquisition of those areas under the replanning scheme – further confirmed the need for economy. Moreover, Matthews was concerned about the intimation of the Ministry of War Transport that they were not prepared to pay a full grant to the ring road in Cook's plan which consisted in the main of grandiose new roads.[97] These factors were certainly in line with the argument for a more practicable and economic plan based on the existing layout, so as to revive and possibly enhance as quickly as possible the rateable value of the main shopping street.

There was another factor which reinforced this argument. As Matthews told the city council in early 1941, the first consideration in replanning was the future of industry, which would be governed by national policy. In this connection, he made a comprehensive survey of Southern Hampshire for the Nuffield College of Social Reconstruction Survey in 1941–42. His conclusions regarding Southampton's industrial future were not at all promising. For one thing, he predicted that possible industrial expansion in the Southampton area would be related to industries linked with shipping services, local service industries and some miscellaneous industry which might be attracted to the area. Although he was acutely aware of the danger that Southampton's dependence on shipping might bring, he had to admit that 'The major issue for the town is the restoration and continued development of shipping.'[98] The future of other important industries such as aircraft manufacture and engineering was 'very uncertain', while there was 'in fact, little doubt that Southampton will revive as a premier port'.[99] At the same time, it was also expected that, in view of rationalization and the decrease in the numbers of insured workers in the shipping service that had taken place in the inter-war years, 'a large number of dock and shipping traffic could be carried out with a diminished labour force and that compensating industrial expansion would not necessarily be dependent on an increase of population'.[100]

The Ministry of Town and Country Planning Advisory Panel agreed with Matthews, adding that Southampton faced other possible adverse factors. First, those seaports in the north which had had traffic diverted to them from the south during the war might retain such business. Secondly, those large modern factories erected for war production in other districts would stay there after the war. It was generally agreed that 'the prospect of substantial industrial development in Southampton is not very bright', except that 'there is every possibility of people desiring to live in or near a town coming here to retire'.[101]

Hopes were raised again however in late 1944. In October, Cook reported to the planning committee that a number of applications and enquiries for modern factory buildings or sites had been received during the last few weeks, and told the committee that the fullest advantage and initiative should be taken to absorb such new industries into the town.[102] As he also stated in public around this time, 'if an enterprising policy is pursued, we shall get all the diversification of industry we need in this area'.[103] At the same time, as the White Paper on Employment Policy in 1944 indicated, it was widely thought that the Board of Trade would take action to control the location of industry after the war with the prime objective of revitalizing the 'Development Areas', i.e. the areas of the old staple industries which had suffered massive unemployment before the war. It was thus generally understood that the first priority with regard to the location of new industries would be given to these 'Development Areas'. Accordingly, in November, Cook approached the Board of Trade asking if the Board could give any assurance that new industries would be allowed to settle in Southampton. The Board, trying hard to commit themselves as little as possible at that time, stated that 'Southampton's needs were not regarded as of the same immediate urgency as the regions which have previously been drawn up as Development Areas'.[104] Cook pressed harder referring to the firms in London and Manchester who would like to move to Southampton, only to be told that the first priority in these cases should always be for one of the depressed areas. All he could get from the Board was that 'if the Development Areas appeared to be receiving a satisfactory number of new industries to absorb their post-war labour surplus, consideration would be given to further assistance to Southampton'.[105]

Although in 1945 the Southampton Labour Party still believed that extensive new industries could be located in the Southampton area, it was recognized that this would depend on the government accepting that 'a blitzed area should have equivalent treatment to the special areas which are being singled out for the establishment of new factories'.[106] In early 1946, Matthews complained about the government's attitude towards industrial development in Southampton, stating that 'Southampton appears to be regarded as an area whose prosperity and full employment is secure, and no great encouragement is so far being given to new industry to locate itself in the area'.[107] Nevertheless, with his knowledge that the city's industrial prospects were not bright, it is understandable that he favoured economy in the reconstruction plan.

Cook, being well aware of Southampton's grim industrial future, still maintained that the city centre required a certain amount of surgery. He was quite critical of the borough engineer's argument that economic considerations, rather than planning principles, should be the basic consideration when replanning the area:

... since to prepare a planning scheme on the basis that planning principles are a secondary consideration to any one of the many to be taken into consideration, can only result in the production of a plan lacking in balance to the detriment of some of the essential requirements of a good scheme.[108]

A good plan, as he argued, had to be economically sound, not only in first cost but in maintenance of the enhanced rateable values in the future.[109]

However ideal the plan might have sounded, the time factor was of importance in the redevelopment of Southampton city centre. The replanning scheme was intended to be self-supporting under the 1944 Planning Act, but what the town was able to rely on in regard to its future prosperity was not its industry but its badly damaged shopping facilities. It is therefore not surprising that Matthews had to opt for the plan for the future city centre that was based on the existing layout, and thus less expensive and protracted. On the other hand, Coventry, led by its Labour leader G. Hodgkinson, did adhere to their dream plan with a drastic new road system, shopping precinct and a civic centre with ample provision of open spaces, despite strong pressure from central government to redraw it. Coventry was in a sense rather fortunate, for the question of its industrial future did not preclude bold planning, as it did in the case of Southampton. It had been widely acknowledged that there was in Coventry 'a general alertness and enterprise among its citizens and readiness on the part of both management and labour to change to a new product or job if an old one failed'.[110] This led the Ministry of Town and Country Planning to be of the opinion that they 'should be optimistic about its post-war industrial development'.[111] The ministry's view was soon confirmed by the Board of Trade, who implied that 'in the long run the B.O.T. would expect expansion of Coventry, rather than contraction'.[112] While there was a certain apprehension about problems during the change-over process,[113] especially that of the city council with regard to the future use of shadow factories,[114] its industrial expansion in the long term was indisputable. As the city council told the Ministry of Town and Country Planning Advisory Panel, they were even making provision for a post-war population of 400 000, almost double that in 1943.[115] In Southampton, the population was expected to increase from 180 000 to 250 000, a figure based on the assumptions that new industries would diversify the city's industrial structure, and that further development of the south coast as a tourist resort would have some repercussions on the town.[116]

Apart from the question of their industrial futures, there was something else that served to contrast Southampton with Coventry. One of the main reasons why the ministry were unable to undermine the Coventry plan was the fear of possible public reaction to such an attempt. In Southampton, it was the Labour councillors who decided to dilute the ambitious plan. For Matthews in particular, it was extremely embarrassing having to give up the ideals he had pursued with such determination.

However, the Southampton Labour Party were not unduly anxious, because – rather ironically – the public as a whole were not particularly interested in replanning, even when the original 1942 plan was put to them. The Civic Society, for instance, organized an open meeting to discuss the new Southampton in May 1942. The meeting had been well advertised and several hundred notices sent out, but fewer than 100 people attended. The *Southern Daily Echo* reported that 'the old charge of apathy so often levelled at Southampton is being substantiated over replanning'.[117] The Civic Society continued their fight against 'the two vested interests', i.e. 'apathy and indifference'.[118] The society's efforts, however, did not bear much fruit. Ultimately, their main concern did not go beyond the question of how to increase public support for their aims if they were to exert any influence.[119]

Thus, in Southampton, the financial difficulties caused by the blitz, insufficient government financial and other assistance for reconstruction, and pessimistic prospects for the city's industrial future, all forced bold planning ideas to yield to economy and expediency. Professor Adshead, the ablest town planner of the day, had fallen a victim to this process. As we shall see, it did not take long for Southampton's need for economy to claim its next victim.

six

Replanning the city centre: Bristol 1940–45

The replanning of Bristol city centre during the war gives us a rather different picture from that of Coventry or Southampton. First, the preparation of a redevelopment plan took a considerable time, mainly because of the approach adopted by both the elected members and the officials of the local authority responsible for the task. The planning committee insisted in the early years that they should concentrate first on preliminary research, despite pressure to get down to replanning as soon as possible. In drawing up the reconstruction proposals following the research, the method adopted by the city engineer, who acted as chief planning officer, was to hold extensive consultations with the interested parties. This method proved to be very time-consuming. The plan was submitted to the city council in March 1944 for the first time and, after further consultation, was approved by the council in July 1945, with certain modifications. The council itself, which was divided equally between representatives of Labour and the Citizen Party – a coalition of Conservatives and Liberals – was not divided with regard to the replanning of the city centre; nor was there any particular planning expert or enthusiast, comparable to Coventry's Hodgkinson or Southampton's Matthews. Because of these factors – the rather late start at replanning, the lack of an enthusiastic expert councillor in planning and, ironically, the absence of party or personal conflict over the matter – it seems that Bristol failed to attract as much attention as it might have deserved at the national level, in view of the bold nature of its replanning proposals. The city was not paid any particular attention by the Ministry of Town and Country Planning until quite late in the war.

At a local level, however, the city council's replanning proposals brought about bitter conflict between the corporation and the interests concerned – local traders and a number of eminent architects and surveyors, widely known in the country. Of particular importance was the keen interest that the local chamber of commerce took in the replanning of the city. In early 1941, the chamber set up an organization representing the various interested bodies and undertook a comprehensive study of a wide range of subjects related to the matter. However, as the Ministry of Town and Country Planning observed in 1943, the chamber was 'active but tactless, ... and its relations with the Corporation are not too good'.[1] The chamber wished to be directly involved in the preparation of a reconstruction plan. They proposed to the council the co-option of their members onto the corporation committee responsible for planning, and the employment of an eminent town planner as a planning consultant. The council, for fear of possible loss of their replanning powers, would not take up the chamber's suggestions.

As these suggestions had failed to be adopted by the city council, the negative feelings towards its official plan became all the more acute. One particular area of controversy with regard to the corporation's plan was over the proposed transfer of the old shopping centre in the Wine Street/Castle Street area to a new site. Many small traders who wanted to re-establish themselves as soon as possible on their original sites, feared that a severance from the past would do them harm. The fact that the multiple stores, whose growth had been felt to be a threat to their existence, were in favour of a new site stiffened their objections still further. The attitude of those who opposed the official plan became almost uncompromising.

* * *

When the Bristol Chamber of Commerce met the government inspector of the test case survey in early 1941, he emphasized the importance of appointing an advisory body of the interested parties to make recommendations to the city council. The chamber of commerce took this advice, and in February set up a Special Advisory Committee (hereafter the SAC). The SAC included, in addition to traders, representatives of the Bristol Society of Architects, the Chartered Surveyors' Institution (Gloucestershire, Somerset and North Wiltshire branch), the Building Trade Federation; the Bristol Property Owners' Association, and the Multiple Shops Federation. In April 1941, the SAC forwarded their memorandum to the town clerk with a request that the Planning and Public Works Committee (hereafter the PPWC) should receive a deputation from the SAC. The memorandum, emphasizing the need for the earliest possible consideration of a long-term scheme for the replanning of the city, set forth two recommendations to the city council. First, the council should arrange for the co-option to its PPWC of experts in planning and architecture and others with particular knowledge of the city. Secondly, the council should immediately employ a chief officer, possibly an architect by profession, to whom should be given full power to collate the views of all interests and to prepare a replanning scheme in conjunction with the augmented PPWC.[2]

A deputation from the SAC led by Colonel Mark Whitwill, president of the chamber (by profession a shipping agent), was invited to meet the PPWC on 7 May. They stressed the importance of the co-option and of a chief officer, and urged the need for prompt action before any national policy was dictated. Such action was, as the deputation pointed out, all the more important, for the city had been selected for the government's test case survey and numerous announcements had appeared in the press that the ministry had asked the city council to submit a draft preliminary scheme of a bold nature. In reply, the chairman of the PPWC pointed out that new legislation to deal with replanning problems would be absolutely necessary, and that, until the government gave a lead in this matter, it would be futile to spend time which could ill be spared from the war effort in preparing any detailed scheme based upon the existing legislation. It was also pointed out that, contrary to recent press reports, the council had received no request from the Ministry of Works and Buildings to submit a draft replanning scheme. In fact, the PPWC had been embarrassed when the press reported in April 1941 that Lord Reith, Minister of Works and Buildings, had told the three test case survey cities – Birmingham, Coventry and Bristol – to plan for reconstruction boldly and comprehensively.[3] *The Bristol Evening Post* even reported that plans of a drastic nature were actually being prepared.[4] The PPWC responded quickly, making it clear that no communication had been received from the ministry instructing the council to plan for reconstruction as stated in the press. When a government inspector attended the PPWC's meeting on 19 February, all he said was that he had been sent to Bristol to enable the government to consider the legislative and administrative difficulties which would arise in the redevelopment of areas damaged by enemy action.[5] As Alderman Winchester (Labour), vice-chairman of the PPWC, revealed, this inspector told the committee that 'I have not come down to advise you, but only to listen.' Indeed, Winchester complained that, while they asked him if they could prepare plans, he would not answer even that question. As Winchester went on: 'We tried to get some indications of how we should go on, but he was dumb.'[6]

The PPWC told the SAC's deputation that they were thus of the opinion that the present time was most inopportune to submit a draft scheme to the ministry. The SAC's two recommendations – co-option and the appointment of a chief officer – were not welcomed by the PPWC. As regards co-option, the chairman of the PPWC said that it might not be convenient nor possible to co-opt members onto the PPWC by reason of the numerous interests which would need to be represented. As for the appointment of a chief officer, the PPWC promised that they would give it careful consideration,[7] but this request was never met by the PPWC.[8]

The chamber of commerce was very disappointed because, as it stated, the meeting with the PPWC 'gave no grounds for satisfaction'. The chamber went on to state that 'the Deputation gained the impression that no substantial action was yet contemplated' by the PPWC with regard to the actual preparation of replanning proposals.[9] Interestingly, the chamber's criticisms of the PPWC's rather inactive attitude were supported by some Labour council members. Alderman A.W. Cox, a senior Labour member, stated at the meeting of the city council in May that the state of indecision and uncertainty made him wonder what was happening to the question of replanning. He argued that they should have an early opportunity to discuss the matter at length, for other cities which had been heavily bombed had already had their replanning schemes more or less approved:

> We in Bristol ought to be in a position to know roughly what it is we are going to do, and we ought to begin to inspire the people with what we propose to do, what Bristol's going to look like, where roads are likely to be, etc. But in this question we seem to be sheltering behind something the Ministry has not said.[10]

The vice-chairman of the PPWC, Alderman W.H. Winchester (Labour), replied that they could only live from day to day in the present circumstances, and because of the many other more pressing problems, it was not possible for them to sit down and draw up a scheme for the redevelopment of the city, even if it were possible given the uncertainty as to what the ultimate problem would be. Yet at the same meeting, another Labour alderman, W.H. Hennessy, who tended to be vocal and a maverick, said that the committee had spent too much time on 'pettifogging' matters, but were not allowed to discuss major issues such as the replanning of the city. He received support from a few other members, and Winchester had to indicate that he intended to raise the matter at a later date. To this Hennessy gave a sharp reply: 'You are all avoiding the real issue.'[11]

The PPWC's first report to the city council on the replanning of damaged areas, submitted in July 1941, was little more than a reassurance of the position taken by the committee. Although the report drew attention to 'a unique opportunity for replanning the City' brought about by the destruction, it pointed out that in view of what other damage might be done before the war ended, it was considered 'inexpedient, if not impossible, at present to proceed in any detail with a definite scheme of replanning'. What the PPWC wanted to concentrate on for the present was preliminary survey work – the production of maps showing existing users and the extent of war damage, both of which were already well under way.[12]

Although the PPWC's report was eventually adopted by the city council,[13] there was strong pressure on the committee immediately it set to work. The City of Bristol Traders' Association, for instance, expressed their opinion that the general layout of the city centre as a whole should be completed as soon as possible because, contrary to what the PPWC maintained, it would not necessarily be affected by further bombing.[14] The Bristol Round Table sent a letter to the PPWC attacking the committee's '"wait and see" policy with regard to replanning'.[15] At the same time, a number of proposals and suggestions with regard to the replanning were being forwarded to the PPWC. In order to deal with these suggestions efficiently, the committee decided, upon the suggestion of the city engineer, to adopt a procedure by which such proposals would in the first place be forwarded to the engineer and then be considered in detail by a joint technical sub-committee (the 'Conference of Chief Officers') consisting of the town clerk, the city engineer, the city architect, the city valuer and the town planning officer. This conference would eventually prepare a report for the PPWC.[16]

The chamber of commerce tried to establish a close relationship with this conference of officers. In September 1941, the chamber sent a letter to the PPWC asking it to endorse the setting up of an enlarged representative organization to replace the existing SAC. This new body should have, through the medium of its liaison committee, close personal contact with the conference of officers, for, as the letter stressed, such contact would be the only way in which competent external opinion could be effectively presented to the corporation.[17]

At the meeting of the PPWC, some Labour members expressed their concern about the chamber's proposal. Alderman F. Bicker said that the conference of officers was most suited to deal with the matter, and if the committee attempted to bring everyone else in, they would have a jumble before anything could be done. Alderman Hennessy suspected that the chamber were trying to get representation on the executive. He went on to say that they were only anxious to secure restoration of the old city streets and not replanning.[18] In the end, however, the PPWC resolved to inform the chamber that they were generally in agreement with their proposals, provided that the committee would 'not delegate or in any way part with their replanning powers'.[19]

The chamber regarded this as a satisfactory reply and in October they formed an enlarged advisory committee, now renamed the Replanning Advisory Committee (hereafter the RAC), with their president and vice-president as chairman and vice-chairman respectively. The RAC represented more than 150 organizations and interests in the city, and was divided into 12 groups dealing with the arts, the churches, commerce, distributive trades, education, entertainment, industry, medical affairs, social welfare, sports, technical aspects and transport. An executive committee was set up consisting of the representatives of each group, and from this committee a liaison committee of five was appointed to maintain contact with the corporation's conference of officers.[20]

In the end, not much contact seems to have been made between the conference of officers and the liaison committee of the RAC. In December 1941, they met for the first time, and the liaison committee asked, among other things, whether the corporation had formed any ideas regarding the re-establishment on their original sites of those industries which had been damaged by bombing. They were also anxious to know the extent of the area which the corporation would propose to consider under any new planning scheme. The conference of officers insisted that very little could be done in connection with replanning until particulars of the impending legislation were known, and the liaison committee, although reluctant to do so, had no choice but to accept this.[21] In April 1942, the RAC approached the conference of officers again and asked if the town planning officer might accompany their proposed deputation to the Ministry of Works and Buildings. The PPWC replied that this request could not be granted.[22]

*   *   *

Meanwhile, the question of the reconstitution of the PPWC came under review. In August 1942, the chamber of commerce sent the interim report of the RAC to the conference of officers. The report recommended, among other things, the immediate setting up of an *ad hoc* planning committee for the region for which the city council was responsible. The report also stated that such a committee should co-opt up to 30 per cent of its membership from representatives nominated by the RAC. This suggestion called the attention of the conference of officers to the fact that the PPWC had 'a multitude of responsibilities' which were interlocked to a very considerable degree, thus preventing it from functioning efficiently. The PPWC had been set up in 1933 by merging the town planning committee and the sanitary committee. The dual function of planning matters and maintenance works, however, was not as compatible as had been hoped. As the town clerk put it, all matters were considered by the full committee of 18 members and, consequently, it spent a considerable amount of time discussing minor matters and the officers were detained for long periods. The officers' recommendation was that the duties of the PPWC should be carried out by two smaller committees, one dealing with planning matters and the other responsible for maintenance works. If the duties of the PPWC were divided on the lines suggested, then co-option onto the proposed *ad hoc* planning committee would be possible, especially for those review matters that were not normally considered by a corporation committee.[23]

While the PPWC had no objection to the officers' proposal to set up two smaller committees, they were unable to come to any conclusion on the question of co-option, and decided to refer it to the city council without making any recommendation.[24] However, the council also failed to come up with a satisfactory answer. At the council meeting in December 1942, Alderman R.L. Lyne, a member of the Citizen Party, argued that a planning committee would ensure that matters which concerned Bristol on a much wider basis would be properly co-ordinated and that their interests would be represented and authoritatively stated, the point made by the

RAC's interim report. Not surprisingly, one Labour member questioned if the motive behind the amendment was directed at co-option. Although this was categorically denied by the Citizen Party, a feeling of uncertainty and suspicion prevailed in the council chamber.[25]

A hint of conflict between the Labour members and the Citizen Party appeared in appointing the first chairman of the Planning and Reconstruction Committee (hereafter the PRC). Labour recommended Alderman Cox, while the Citizen Party pushed for Alderman Inskip, and the matter could not be settled at the first meeting in December 1942.[26] After a month, however, the PRC unanimously decided to appoint Inskip as chairman and Cox as vice-chairman.[27] As the city engineer urged the PRC, they had to settle down as soon as possible to the question of the officers and the committee itself.[28] The officers were 'firmly of the opinion that planning is essentially a matter which calls for team work and the fullest co-operation between the various officers concerned',[29] and claimed that the existing machinery (the conference of officers) would be most conducive to practical research and good planning.[30] The PRC, also emphasizing the importance of team work, stated that at the same time the new committee should appoint a 'chief planning officer' who would lead and co-ordinate all of the corporation's planning activities. The question was whether the post should be filled by the city engineer who was responsible for planning matters under the existing system, or by someone totally new. The PRC were 'satisfied that a new appointment from outside the service would not at the present time be in the best interests of the Corporation', and decided unanimously to appoint the city engineer as chief planning officer.

This decision enabled the city engineer to give the PRC his preliminary planning proposals for such matters as highways, the layout of the city centre,[31] housing and the siting of industry.[32] While these proposals were settling into shape nothing was done about the question of co-option and the chamber of commerce became impatient. They told the PRC that they had arrived at a point where they could be of no further service to the corporation unless they were brought into the committee's counsels and were informed of the corporation's plan.[33] In reply, the PRC told the chamber that:

> ... as and when this Committee are tentatively agreed upon any proposals affecting the principles of replanning the Committee will give an opportunity to the Chamber of Commerce or others who are directly interested to discuss the proposals.[34]

In this way, the chamber's insistence on co-option was virtually turned down and the preparation of replanning proposals for the city centre progressed without any particular intervention from outside bodies.

In May 1943, the city engineer submitted his road proposals to the PRC. The main objectives of the proposals were first to divert regional and national traffic from the city centre and, secondly, to deal with that traffic that would reach the city centre. The first objective was to be met by two ring roads – an 'outer ring' of 34 miles and an 'inner ring' of 21 miles. The second objective would be met by an 'inner circuit' of two miles, half of which was already completed as Redcliffe/Temple Way. Consultations with regard to the road proposals had already taken place with various interests, including the Ministry of War Transport, the regional planning officer of the Ministry of Town and Country Planning, the county surveyors concerned, the chief constable, the city architect and the Bristol Tramway Company. While the proposals met with fairly general approval, there was one particular point of discussion – whether public service vehicles (i.e. buses), should be allowed to use any or all of the roads within the inner circuit road. The city engineer maintained that buses should be excluded from the confines of the inner circuit, but many others argued that some streets within the inner circuit should be used as omnibus routes for the sake of public convenience.[35] A month later, the PRC approved the three ring roads, but the inner circuit was agreed in principle only and consideration of the question of exclusion of buses was left to the city engineer after further consultation with any interested bodies.[36]

Meanwhile, the PRC began to consider the city engineer's zoning plans for the city centre.[37] One member suggested that a progress report on the replanning should be submitted to the city council as soon as possible. Others maintained that before a satisfactory report could be presented, they had to come to a decision with regard to the planning of the area within the inner circuit, especially that of Castle Street/Wine Street. In this connection, the town clerk informed the committee that the Advisory Panel of the Ministry of Town and Country Planning was to visit Bristol in September to discuss the matter with the PRC and the officers concerned.[38]

The advisory panel found the case of Bristol rather difficult, but in a quite different way to that of Coventry. The local authority had made a late start with post-war reconstruction plans. Although the city engineer was said to be preparing a reconstruction plan, nothing particular was yet known of his proposals apart from those regarding the road system.[39] At the meeting between the panel and the local authority, the city engineer explained that, although there was not much to show on paper, his method was first to consult with interests on the basis of a rough sketch plan and then to base the plan on the results of the consultations. The panel expressed some concern about the size of the reconstruction area which the local authority might purchase. Some of the suggested 600 acres, such as those areas owned by the Dock Authorities, the Cathedral and the University, would not necessitate acquisition.[40] Back in London, the panel tried to figure out the salient planning issues for Bristol. The most they could discover was that, because the damage was more scattered than thought at first, the area of reconstruction might have to be large. It was also pointed out that Bristol was larger than any of the other six cities selected by the panel, and this would make the problem more complex.[41]

Although not much was achieved as a result of the discussion with the panel, the PRC carried forward the consideration of the planning of the areas within the inner circuit. In October 1943, an important suggestion was put forward by the Multiple Traders' Federation (hereafter the MTF), whom the city engineer had already met and was 'glad to find ... in agreement with his views on a number of points'.[42] Their suggestion was that the Castle Street/Wine Street area, the shopping centre before the war, should become a 'civic' area, i.e. an open space with perhaps a conference hall or other buildings of a similar character, and that the shopping centre originally in this area should be transferred to the north, i.e. to the Broadmead and Lower Union Street area.[43] The plan was soon prepared by the MTF. Their suggestion was then considered by the Retail Distributors' Group of the RAC, who told the PRC that, although they could not commit themselves until more detailed plans were available, they needed more information from the MTF on costs as a basis for further discussions with the PRC and conference of officers.[44]

The PRC in turn regarded the retailers' request for the estimate of cost as their virtual approval of the plan for a civic area, and decided to agree in principle to replan this area as an open space. The final question was where to site the new shopping centre – the city engineer had suggested either in the Broadmead and Lower Union Street area, or in Victoria Street.[45]

*   *   *

In February 1944, the city engineer completed his report on the proposals for the planning and reconstruction of the city centre. The area covered by the plan amounted to 774 acres, all of which had been affected by enemy action. As the engineer proudly put it, this 'Master Policy Plan' had been 'thoroughly well considered and should serve to form a useful basis of discussion in order that the tragic destruction of the war years may result in the replanning of a still better Bristol City'.[46]

Among the policy proposals, particular emphasis was placed upon the road system, for, as the city engineer maintained, in a commercial city such as Bristol 'neither efficiency nor amenity can be obtained unless very adequate arrangements are made to deal with the control of traffic'.[47] The most important proposal regarding roads was for the inner circuit, designed with 'an absolute control of access points to it'. Vehicular traffic would be allowed to gain access to, and exit from, the inner circuit only at controlled roundabout intersections. Outside the inner circuit, some important proposals included the possible widening of Park Street to give an adequate link between the inner circuit and the area west of it, and for the exclusion of traffic from Queen's Road in order to make it a shopping cul-de-sac.[48]

The inner circuit would enclose an area approximately three-quarters of a mile in diameter, an area that would be divided into enclosures or precincts by other major roads only secondary in importance to the inner

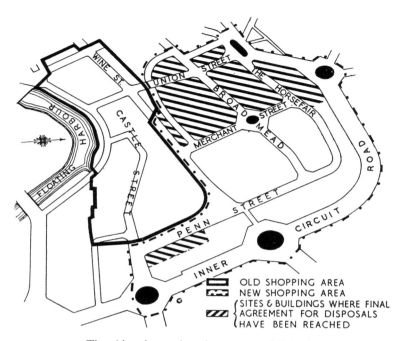

The old and new shopping centres of Bristol
Source: W.A. James, 'Redevelopment of the Central Shopping Area of Bristol',
Royal Institute of Chartered Surveyors' Journal, April 1954, 742.

circuit itself. Each portion thus divided would be planned in detail to
discourage heavy traffic, through traffic and public service vehicles travel-
ling across the area bounded by the inner circuit. At the same time,
although it was at first hoped to exclude altogether public service vehicles
from this area, as had been pointed out during consultations with the
interested bodies, this was 'practically unlikely without trespassing unduly
on public convenience'. It was therefore suggested that the minimum
number of public service vehicles should be routed across the area bounded
by the inner circuit, although most should travel via the inner circuit itself.[49]

In order to control the type of user that would be permitted in the various areas covered by the report, the zoning proposals included the following: a site of approximately five acres at the junction of Victoria Street and
Temple Way to be used as a central wholesale and retail market; a municipal civic centre in the College Green area; and a 60-acre precinct for
extensions to the university and medical area. Two particularly important
proposals were for a shopping zone and for enhanced public open space,
which had been duly commended by the Multiple Traders' Federation. The
pre-war shopping centre around the Wine Street/Castle Street area,
stretching between Bristol Bridge and Old Market Street, was now
reserved as a public open space with a limited number of buildings, such as

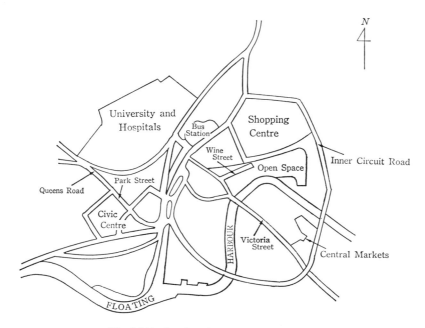

The 1944 plan for the central area of Bristol
Source: *Bristol Evening Post*, 15 March 1944.

a conference hall. A considerable area below this open space could be used as an underground car park, accommodating 2000 of the 4500 cars scheduled for sites provided by the city council. In the Broadmead area, to the north of the pre-war shopping centre, a new main shopping precinct of approximately 35 acres was proposed. Its pivotal point would be circular in shape, with arcaded shops, and the surrounding area was to consist of larger blocks, built to the most modern and approved description. No through traffic roads were allowed, but back service roads would be provided. Other areas zoned for shopping purposes included the frontages to Park Street and Queen's Road, which was a continuation of pre-war use.[50]

In concluding his report, the city engineer stated:

> Some of the proposals are new and possibly rather revolutionary, but your Engineer feels that the spirit of adventure is abroad in connection with post war developments, and that Bristol would not wish to be behind in this direction.[51]

Although the PRC decided that the city council should consider the city engineer's report 'in private',[52] the local press was quite pleased to see that the secret was eventually out. The new Bristol envisaged by the PRC was, as the *Bristol Evening Post* put it, 'bold beyond the wildest dreams of most people, but it is conceived through the telescope of 50 years ahead – to meet the needs of the Bristol of 2,000 A.D.'. One important question was 'who should pay for the cost'. The *Bristol Evening Post* expressed the concern that 'From the plans it would appear to have been designed on what is regarded as desirable, regardless of other considerations.' However, the paper went on to argue:

> The Government should pay, and there is a rightful expectation that it will. In any case, the scheme should prove to be economic, so that in the process of years increased values should reflect themselves in a balanced budget. If neither of these expectations could be realised it is still necessary that the blitzed areas should be restored, and the fear that the rates will reflect this necessity in an increased financial demand should not be allowed to paralyse an endeavour to worthily recreate our treasured city.[53]

At the same time, it was expected that there would be widely differing opinions on the city engineer's proposals, especially those relating to the new shopping precinct and the fate of its predecessor. However, when the PRC and the conference of officers met representatives of various interested bodies to discuss the report, they found – rightly or wrongly – that no serious criticism had been made.[54]

A month later, the city engineer told the PRC that he had given careful consideration to the alternative schemes allowing for the reinstatement of traders in the Castle Street/Wine Street area, but that he did not believe such a scheme would provide a shopping centre worthy of the city. The city valuer also stated that the ideal unit for shop sites should have a frontage of 25 feet and a depth of from 85 to 100 feet, and that the National Fire Service was asking that a fire break of at least 50 feet should be provided between blocks. The fire in November 1940 caused by the blitz had spread very rapidly because of congestion, and it was duly suggested that any reconstruction should have ample fire breaks to reduce the chances of the same thing happening again.[55] Because of these factors, it would have been impossible to reinstate all the traders in the old shopping centre. For example, the old shopping centre had a shopping frontage of 6000 feet compared with the 9600 feet proposed for the new site. The city architect also intimated that he was in agreement with the views expressed by the city engineer and the city valuer, adding that he regarded the proposal to have an open space in the central area as of prime importance. On these comments, the PRC stated that up to that moment they had received no practical information or proposals suggesting that there was any chance of all traders formerly carrying on business in the Castle Street/Wine Street area being reinstated there, although they also added that they would be prepared to consider any further proposals along these lines.[56]

* * *

In fact, criticisms and alternative suggestions to the city engineer's replanning proposals were flooding into the city council. In regard to the civic centre at College Green, the chamber of commerce maintained that the area should be retained as a shopping area in view of its past history.[57] In this connection, Bristol Rotary Club produced a plan for a new civic centre in Victoria Street, even scrapping the existing official proposal for College Green where a new Council House was already under construction. The merits of their idea were, first, that it was the only really level site in the city where extensive reconstruction could take place and, secondly, that it would provide a dignified approach for visitors to the city from Temple Meads Railway Station.[58] The proposal to convert Queen's Road into a shopping cul-de-sac and to ban traffic from it and Park Street also met considerable opposition, especially from the traders concerned.[59]

The most contentious issue with regard to the city engineer's replanning proposals was the re-siting of the shopping centre. There were two main grounds for the opposition to the proposed open space where the old shopping centre had stood. First, there was acute concern about the economic and social effects of the sterilization of too large an area of importance in the heart of the city.[60] Secondly, the majority of traders were anxious, *inter alia*, that this site should again be used for the shopping centre. Although this argument was perhaps understandable in the light of the old adage that 'better the devil you know than the devil you don't know',[61] most traders had become, as the city engineer told the PRC, adamant in their refusal of the council officers' contention that the area was not large enough to accommodate adequately all the traders who had formerly carried on business there.[62]

Thus the main criticism of the proposed new shopping centre in the Broadmead area was that it was geographically unsuitable, particularly because it was 'off the beaten track' of pedestrians who habitually walked through the centre of the old city – Wine Street and Castle Street. It was argued that the fact that these streets had provided a direct link between east and west Bristol made them a popular and valuable shopping centre.[63] Moreover, there was a concern that the Broadmead area, the low-level area on the bed of the River Frome, was 'waterlogged',[64] and the bearing qualities of the sub-soil were not sufficient to carry heavy buildings. Reference was made, for instance, to the flooding of 1889, even though improvements had been made since then to the River Frome to prevent the repetition of such an event.[65]

Not surprisingly, most of the alternative proposals to the city engineer's plan suggested the retention of the Wine Street/Castle Street area as the principal shopping centre. In general, it was understood that further development of this area might well take place northwards in the Broadmead area. In May 1944, the Bristol Re-planning Association – which was effectively a renamed RAC – put forward a scheme drawn up by eminent local architects for the replanning of the old shopping centre.[66] It had been thought that the association was generally in favour of the plan endorsed by the multiple stores which envisaged the new civic area based on the pre-war shopping centre. They had made it clear, however, that they were in fact of the opinion that it was open to serious objection.[67] In June, another suggestion appeared in the local press drawn up by a local architect on the instructions of certain Wine Street traders.[68] The Western Counties Branch of the Incorporated Association of Architects and Surveyors suggested a generous replanning of the old site with a traffic-restricted shopping boulevard between Old Market Street and The Centre.[69] Bristol Rotary Club, with the help of E. Button, vice-president of the Bristol Society of Architects, also produced a plan for the shopping centre based on the old area, with an extension northwards.[70]

This flood of alternative suggestions opposed to the official proposals for moving the shopping centre led the Lord Mayor to state strongly in public around this time that a final reconstruction plan should satisfy most, if not all, of the interests clamouring for recognition and adoption of their own ideas.[71] At the same time, there were some encouraging signs for the PRC in relation to their proposal for the new shopping centre. As the chamber of commerce admitted, it was generally understood that the multiple traders were favourably inclined towards the new site for a shopping centre in the Broadmead area.[72] It was stated by the MTF themselves that two-thirds of the traders were in favour of moving to the Broadmead area.[73] The Co-operative Society also informed the PRC that they had no objection to the removal of the shopping centre.[74] Some traders also showed their qualified support for the official proposals. The Bristol Retailers' Advisory Committee on Town Planning of the Chamber of Commerce, while regarding the re-planning association's plan as best, intimated that a civic centre in the Castle Street/Wine Street area might be acceptable on the understanding (a) that the redevelopment of this area as a civic centre was the only option to building a new shopping centre in the Broadmead area; (b) that the city council should be responsible for safeguarding the Broadmead area against flooding; and (c) that provision should be made as soon as possible for temporary shops to be erected in the Wine Street/Castle Street area during the building of the proposed new shopping centre.[75] In October 1944, the *Bristol Evening Post* also commented that a larger site than the original was needed for the new shopping centre. First, many of those who had traded on the old site indicated that they wanted more space; secondly, many well-known firms who had previously not been represented in Bristol were said to be keen to establish themselves there, particularly in the new shopping centre. As the *Bristol Evening Post* went on:

> While understanding the desire of the former traders in the old site to conserve their interests, the public would, doubtless, welcome newcomers as adding to the variety of goods displayed and the delight that shopping gives to womenfolk.[76]

Meanwhile, the PRC continued to consider the city engineer's reports on all criticisms and observations of the corporation's plan of March 1944, and on all alternative suggestions and plans put forward to the city council. In September 1944, the committee decided to make important modifications to the original proposals by accepting alternatives to (1) the original proposal to convert Queen's Road into a shopping cul-de-sac and to ban traffic from it and Park Street, (2) the development of a civic centre at College Green and (3) the proposed open space in the Wine Street/Castle Street area.[77]

The PRC now decided that both Queen's Road and Park Street should remain as two-way thoroughfares for traffic, with Park Street being widened by 20 feet so as to adapt it for modern traffic. It was this decision which forced the committee to look elsewhere than the College Green area for a site for the civic centre, because as the chairman of the committee later put it, 'It would never do to have a main traffic street running right through the civic area.'[78] As an alternative, the Rotary Club had proposed turning Victoria Street into a site for civic buildings. However splendid their plan might have looked, Victoria Street did not commend itself to the PRC, for they thought that the new shopping centre should be in close proximity to the civic centre, and not separated from it by the river.[79] At this point, the city engineer expressed the view that much of the opposition to the proposed new shopping centre in Broadmead would fall away if the Castle Street Wine/Street area could be satisfactorily developed instead of it being reserved as an open space. In view of these proposals, the PRC came to the conclusion that the Castle Street/Wine Street area, the most important and most valuable area in the city, should in the long term house such buildings as a museum, art gallery, guildhall, municipal buildings, concert hall and conference hall. Moreover, this decision then opened the way to a further concession – the request that the College Green area should be used for shopping purposes in continuation of pre-war practice.[80]

The amendment to the zoning of the College Green area provided a further opportunity to accede to the traders' request. It at first brought about the question of the future use of the Council House, the construction of which was nearing completion. In January 1945, the PRC decided that the building should be completed as quickly as possible in order to provide accommodation for the activities of the council, since the suggested layout of the Castle Street Wine/Street area as a civic centre should be adopted as a long-term policy. At this point, the city engineer suggested that the pre-war shopping centre might be used, pending its final layout for public purposes, for the erection of temporary shops until such time as the shopping centre in Broadmead was developed.[81] Requests on these lines were forwarded from the Retailers' Advisory Committee on Town Planning and the City of Bristol Traders' Association.[82] By June, negotiations with all those interested had begun, and the PRC decided to provide 100 temporary shops in the Castle Street/Wine Street area in the first instance.[83] Taking care of the industrialists who were affected by the city centre plan was also of major importance, and in June 1945 the city council approved the joint recommendation of the PRC and the docks committee to set up a trading estate at Avonmouth at an initial expenditure of £275 000.[84]

Meanwhile, the Ministry of Town and Country Planning, which had not been well acquainted with the redevelopment plans for Bristol city centre, became fairly impressed by them. In April 1945, the ministry suggested that the PRC submit the city centre plan to them informally for comments before submitting it to the city council for approval. The city council had been reluctant to apply for a declaratory order for compulsory purchase under the 1944 Town and Country Planning Act. The aim of the ministry's suggestion, therefore, seemed to be to encourage the council by telling them that their plan which had to accompany the application for a declaratory order was favourably viewed by the minister.[85] In June, the city engineer reported to the PRC that Professor Holford, technical adviser to the ministry, had inspected the draft plan for the city centre, and intimated that he was 'broadly speaking' in sympathy with the main proposals.[86] In fact, Holford held a very high opinion of them. As he wrote to the regional planning officer of the Ministry of Town and Country Planning around this time, 'It is very satisfactory to see that the basis for a really effective plan is being so well laid in Bristol by discussion between the Council and the various interests.' For instance, a new proposal for siting civic buildings on the old shopping centre would, as he put it:

> ... have the advantage of preserving the area from becoming 'dead' and, since the civic buildings will not be built for some years, of allowing a very valuable site for temporary shops while those in Broadmead are being built. I am, therefore, inclined to the view that if a suitable layout is agreed for public buildings on the former shopping area, there could be little objection to the proposal.[87]

As for the proposed new shopping centre, he pointed out that:

> ... the trading interests, and in particular the multiple stores, had shown considerable interest in this scheme, and were sufficiently well organised to be able to give what amounts to a satisfactory assurance to the Council that if it were developed in the way proposed, they would take up leases.[88]

*   *   *

In July 1945, the city council considered the PRC's plan for the city centre, with a view to applying for a declaratory order. The significant difference between the original and new plans was the modifications to the proposals with regard to the Wine Street/Castle Street area, College Green, and Queen's Road and Park Street. But the site of the new shopping centre was not changed. In fact, the PRC's strongest emphasis was placed upon their adherence to the new shopping centre in the Broadmead area. As Alderman Sir John Inskip, chairman of the committee, told the council, the question of the main shopping centre had been 'the most contentious and the most difficult'. There had been considerable opposition

A view of the heart of the proposed new shopping centre of Bristol
Source: Bristol Evening Post, 13 July 1945.

to the idea of transferring it from the Castle Street/Wine Street area to Broadmead. He asked the council, however, to grasp what a modern shopping centre would require:

> It is all very well to say Castle Street and Wine Street have served the city well over all these years, and why not put the shops back there? The fact that they have been there, and, therefore, should remain, is surely the worst of all possible reasons.[89]

Regrettable as it was to break a link going back many years, the PRC were convinced that it was impracticable to rebuild shops in such a re-stricted area. For example, the PRC estimated that only 60–70 per cent of the previous traders could be accommodated there again when taking into account the larger shop frontages they required. Also, there were the new businesses, large and small, which it was hoped would be attracted. The argument for the northward extension to Broadmead proposed in many of the alternative plans was also dismissed because the two areas were on different levels. The city council approved the plan unanimously. However, there was a certain concern regarding the proposal to erect temporary shops in the Castle Street/Wine Street area, for it was thought that this might reinforce the feeling that the area should be retained as a shopping centre.[90]

W.S. Palmer, chairman of the Retailers' Advisory Committee on Town Planning, pointed out in the press that the new proposals appeared to take into account certain important suggestions put forward by interested parties following the lines of the MTF's plan. For example, the re-siting of the civic centre to the Castle Street/Wine Street area would probably affect those opinions held regarding the redevelopment of Broadmead as

Proposed conference buildings in the Wine Street – Castle Street area of Bristol
Source: *Bristol Evening Post*, 13 July 1945.

the new shopping centre. Palmer pointed out that a large number of people had not liked the idea of an open space on the old shopping centre. He also expressed the view that traders would welcome the proposal to provide temporary shops as quickly as possible. Describing the new proposals as 'a bold scheme', he stated that they 'would certainly receive the early and most careful consideration – of which it was worthy – of the retailers'.[91]

To many others, however, the new proposals related to the shopping centre were far from being acceptable. Eustace Button, vice-president of the Bristol Society of Architects and one of the five members of the liaison committee of the replanning association, for instance, was strongly opposed to the new civic centre and the shopping centre. As he put it:

> It is interesting to note that the civic buildings are going to be moved within the Inner Circuit to the business heart of the city. It is curious, however, that the most difficult and expensive site for these buildings has been chosen, in the Castle Street and Wine Street area, when a much finer site is available in the Victoria Street boulevard.
>
> Now that the Castle Street and Wine Street area is to be built over, it is all the more necessary to hear what are the over-riding reasons for displacing the successful shopping centre from its original position, at vast expense, and reinstating it in an area that has always been 'off the map'.[92]

Bristol Rotary Club soon made representations regarding the passing of the new proposals for the city centre. The PRC's argument that only 60–70 per cent of the present tenants in the Castle Street/Wine Street area could be accommodated was, as one member pointed out, never convincing, because the same area was going to be a civic centre with any extension that would be necessary. In fact, in the corporation's proposal, the civic buildings were to be scattered over several different sites. It was also said that the new shopping centre would never succeed, because people wanted it sited as before in the heart of the old mediaeval town. As one member said, the corporation's scheme had 'one fundamental unsoundness', the lack of an expert's advice to judge it: 'The people who devised it are the judges of their own work – the plaintiffs are their own judge and jury.'[93]

Against this the PRC and the conference of officers could argue that they had considered very carefully the criticisms of and the alternative suggestions to their original proposals in 1944 and in certain respects acceded to them: 340 comments and criticisms of the original proposals plus 20 alternative plans had been put forward, and 25 associations had been consulted. As the city engineer told the local press confidently, 'We believe we have done the best possible to meet the many difficulties involved and the wishes and representations expressed to us.'[94] Thus, as the chairman of the PRC told the council, their officers and the committee were convinced that the Broadmead shopping centre was 'the right and only practicable proposal' and, therefore, that 'there could be no letting the traders go back to the sites they occupied before'.[95]

*   *   *

In October 1945, a joint meeting was held of the chamber of commerce, the replanning association and the Rotary Club. In view of a pending public inquiry, prescribed under the Town and Country Planning Act 1944, into the city council's application for a declaratory order with the city centre plan as supporting evidence, they agreed to make a joint submission of the objections of the three organizations to it.[96] The strong objection in some quarters to the corporation's plan for the city centre had, however, very little if anything to do either with the municipal election in November 1945 or with the city council's attitude towards the plan. The only difference between the Labour Party and the Citizen Party with regard to the question of reconstruction seemed to be the former's hostility to, and the latter's sympathy for, traders. As the Labour Party's municipal programme read:

> To us now is given a chance that is truly priceless – the chance to plan and build a city that will be worthy of the ancient traditions of Bristol and its glorious future. If this chance is to be utilised to the full no vested interest, no selfish profit-making clique must be allowed to endanger it. The Labour Party serves no private vested interest. It is only concerned with the greatest good of the majority of the people. We believe shopping interests should serve the people and not the people the shopping interests.[97]

The Citizen Party, stating their reconstruction policy, said:

> We realise fully the struggle of the small private traders and all those who have to re-establish themselves after the ravages of war, and it will be our earnest endeavour to help them and to so order the plan-

ning and reconstruction of the city that both the largest and smallest trader shall find himself re-established on a suitable site at the earliest possible moment.[98]

This did not mean, however, that the traders' plea for the re-establishment of the old shopping centre might be accepted by the city council. As the Citizen Party's programme went on to say:

> Nothing will be allowed to hinder the planning and reconstruction of Bristol. The city should be the cultural and artistic centre of the West. We believe that the proposed layout of the destroyed centre of the city is a good one, and we shall actively proceed to carry it out, and especially that part of it which provides for new public buildings, including a conference hall and concert hall.[99]

Thus both the Labour Party and the Citizen Party were confident of the corporation's plan for the city centre, and were keen to proceed with the matter as quickly as possible. At the same time, it should also be noted that both parties made housing their first priority, and as Alderman Inskip, leader of the Citizen Party, admitted, there seemed to be no particular issue which divided the two parties.[100] If anything, the Labour Party placed more stress on public ownership and control in various matters, whereas the Citizen Party sought room for the private sector to take part in, and keep abreast of, the local authority. The result of the November election was a sweeping victory for the Labour Party, with a majority of 18 councillors.[101] Declaring victory, Labour stated that they were determined to initiate the programme as quickly as possible, with their 'sleeves rolled up for action', but that the two most important issues were the provision of housing and the municipal ownership and control of the city's bus service; the reconstruction of the city centre was not placed centre stage.[102] This was not surprising, as the city council had always been united in supporting the city engineer's approach to the replanning of the city centre. They were also confident that they had given enough consideration – and in some cases even concessions – to the suggestions of those with a vested interest. At the same time, it was agreed by all the parties that housing should be given priority, and that, in view also of the shortage of labour and materials, the redevelopment of the city centre would not be at the fore-front; indeed, it might take years to materialize.

In the case of Bristol, there was not much enthusiasm for the re-development of the city centre. On a city council of 112 members, neither party seemed to have any acknowledged planning expert. There was no response to the electric atmosphere of the early days of the war, and a rather late start was made to the replanning of the city centre given that Bristol was one of the test case survey cities. The approach of the council, however reasonable it may have been, being based upon extensive consultation with those having a vested interest, did not allow for rapid progress. By the time the council approved the fairly bold replanning scheme for the city centre, it did not attract the attention of the nation as the plans of other cities – notably that of Coventry – had done earlier. The general public in the city did not seem to be particularly interested either. When local organizations were expressing their opinions one after another about the city council's original plan in 1944, one local paper observed:

> The problem has, in fact, received considerable publicity, but the impression remains that the people of Bristol have not displayed any signs that they are fired with holy zeal to design the 'shape of things to come.' It may be that the general public, so well schooled in the primary necessity of first winning the war, prefers to leave the minor conflict of city planning 'till the boys come home.' The boys themselves, being now almost solely occupied with the grim and necessary task of wiping out cities, have had little time or opportunity to express their views on the future plan of what they have been fighting for.[103]

When the war was over, however, the people's main concern was housing. The existence of the RAC (later the replanning association) and some of the other organizations might give the impression that the replanning of the city centre had been widely discussed, and that objections to the city council's plan were rife among the population. However, it must be emphasized that these organizations only represented a small number of interest groups, notably traders and such professions as architects and surveyors. There was also considerable overlap of membership among these bodies and, as the city engineer's exhaustive list of comments and suggestions with regard to the city centre reconstruction scheme shows, keen interest in the matter came in the main from these limited sources.[104] Moreover, as the larger traders were inclined to be in favour of the corporation's proposals, the small traders felt more worried about their futures.[105] As for the architects, Bristol was said to have been endowed with a long tradition and eminent figures.[106] Both the traders and the architects were attempting to establish themselves in the redevelopment of the city centre through such recommendations as co-option and the appointment of a planning consultant. However, the PRC never let them in on the decision-making process. It is not difficult to understand why the threatened traders and the frustrated and possibly offended architects were so opposed to the main features of the corporation's plan – the re-siting of the shopping centre.

seven

City planning in the immediate aftermath of war: 1946

During the immediate post-war period, local authorities became confident in proceeding with reconstruction work thanks to encouragement from the new Minister of Town and Country Planning, Lewis Silkin. Both in Bristol and Coventry, the councils showed that they had confidence in their city centre plans, and in Coventry public support for their plan was overwhelming. In Southampton, however, there was some controversy, for by the end of the war there were two competing city centre plans – the original one as supported by the Ratepayers' Party and a new one endorsed by Labour. Moreover, incidents prior to the public inquiry were seemingly casting a big question mark over the wisdom of the council's replanning policy.

Lewis Silkin, the Minister of Town and Country Planning in the new Labour government of 1945, was known to want to make rapid progress as regards the rebuilding of heavily bombed city centres.[1] In the first instance, he expected those local authorities concerned to submit an application for a declaratory order for the compulsory purchase of war-damaged areas, with a replanning scheme as supporting evidence for such an application. The procedure laid down by the Town and Country Planning Act 1944 required the minister to call for a public inquiry into such applications, at which objections could be lodged. After examining the objections at the inquiry, the minister might confirm the order as a whole or with possible modifications, which would then entitle the local authority to purchase the land covered by the confirmed order under the powers of the 1944 Act, compulsorily if necessary.

Towards the end of 1945, however, Silkin became 'seriously concerned' about the lack of progress, especially 'the absence of applications by blitzed cities'.[2] Ministry officials reported[3] that there was a combination of obstacles which made local authorities hesitant to make a move. First, there was the question of 'war-damage payment' to bombed-out owners. An owner of war-damaged premises was entitled to a 'cost-of-works payment' (i.e. full cost of actual rebuilding) under the War Damage Act 1943. However, if his or her premises were included in the local authority's replanning scheme and thus were to be compulsorily acquired, then, according to the Town and Country Planning Act 1944, he or she would be entitled only to a 'value payment', equivalent to the March 1939 value of the premises (plus, in the case of owner-occupiers, a supplementary addition of up to 30 per cent of such value). With regard to the soaring building prices prevailing at the time, there was a strong feeling of injustice that owners of war-damaged premises affected by the replanning scheme would be unable to afford to rebuild their premises on new sites. The local authorities for their part feared that if such owners did not receive enough to cover the cost of building on new sites, then essential rebuilding by private enterprise in the bombed areas would not take place – or if it did at a very slow rate – and consequently the authorities themselves would have to shoulder the financial burdens of rebuilding.

The financial provisions of the Town and Country Planning Act 1944 were heavily criticized as inadequate, especially by those local authorities like Coventry who were not sure whether their replanning schemes would prove entirely self-supporting within 10–15 years, as presupposed in the Act.[4] The local authorities were also concerned about the acute shortage of labour and materials. Because of the pre-eminent importance of housing, it was feared that there would inevitably be a considerable delay in acquiring the labour and materials necessary for the redevelopment of city centres. Thus, as Bristol told the ministry in April 1945, large-scale purchase of such an expensive area as the city centre with little possibility of an early start on actual redevelopment would 'land them in a loss over a long period and put their finances in Queer Street'.[5]

Finally, the absence of developed schemes for the city centres was, for many local authorities, an obstacle to an early application for a declaratory order. Officially, the schemes had only to be 'skeleton' proposals presented as supporting evidence in the authorities' applications. At the local level, however, it was generally assumed that the public inquiry would be an important – and possibly final – opportunity for those with vested interests to object to the scheme as a whole. Understandably, many authorities were 'a little timid of facing a local inquiry until they have assured themselves fully that their proposals are unassailable'.[6] This was particularly the case where the replanning of the city centre had become a serious political issue, which was often complicated by the competing plans of the various technical officers of the local authority. In such cases, the authorities often pressed – as Southampton did in late 1945 – for the ministry to pass judgement on them.

Ministry officials were extremely cautious about this matter. They pressed the minister to adhere to wartime practice, i.e. to continue assistance and guidance to the authorities on technical matters, but to refrain from any direct intervention which might have political repercussions. For the moment, any articulate comments on, let alone final judgements about, the plans were out of the question, until the ministry's patient education programme produced much improved plans acceptable to most of the interests concerned.[7]

Bearing these points in mind, Silkin proposed to meet the local authorities concerned individually in early 1946, in order to encourage them to proceed, especially as regards early applications for declaratory orders.[8] As far as Bristol, Coventry and Southampton were concerned, they had all virtually decided to make formal applications when they met the minister in early 1946. Nevertheless, these meetings were quite significant as far as the three authorities were concerned, for they were each uncertain as to whether they would be able to proceed with reconstruction in view of the various obstacles mentioned above. The minister tried hard to persuade them not to take too gloomy a view. He maintained, for instance, that the local authorities were exaggerating the problem of cost by assuming that present-day building prices would continue. He himself expected them to fall in a few years' time to approximately 30 per cent above pre-war levels, once greater stability had been achieved, in which case the alleged difference between 'value payment' and 'cost of works payment' would not be appreciable.[9] He was particularly anxious to impress upon them that he took a fairly liberal view of the financial provisions of the 1944 Act, which had been regarded by the authorities as inadequate. If there was eventually a substantial deficiency in respect of government grants, he promised that the matter would be duly taken up with a view to remedying it by amending legislation, adding that no government would be able to resist the pressure of the local authorities on such an issue.[10] Moreover, with regard to the difficulty in attracting building labour for city centre redevelopment, the minister intimated that there would have to be some preference given to blitzed towns.[11]

The most striking encouragement by the minister was his praise for Bristol City Council's replanning proposals, particularly since his officials had suggested he refrain from any public comment. Silkin told a local newspaper reporter on his visit to Bristol in March 1946, that the corporation's central area plan was 'a scheme I can support in every way', adding that he saw 'no reason why the Ministry should not be able to give its word "Go" to Bristol in "a matter of months"'. He continued:

> If no serious objections are forthcoming, I may consider the possibility of saving time by not holding a public inquiry. You will appreciate that in this sort of thing we are in a sense creating the appropriate procedure as we go.[12]

Although objections to the corporation's application for a declaratory order necessitated a public inquiry in June 1946,[13] the planning and reconstruction committee decided to ask, along with a declaratory order, for a more expedited procedure with regard to the new and old shopping centres by applying for two compulsory purchase orders: one dealing with the Castle Street/Wine Street area for the provision of 112 temporary shops, and the other in the Broadmead area for the siting of permanent shops and the inner ring road. It was essential that once these compulsory orders were confirmed, all of the properties covered by them would be vested in the corporation in one go, rather than individual properties coming before it as in the case of a declaratory order.[14] It was hoped that these compulsory purchase orders would greatly facilitate an early start on the development of the new shopping centre and, at the same time, while preventing the rebuilding of any of the shops in the old centre, provide funds for redevelopment in the new centre.[15]

While the city council was thus determined to proceed quickly with the redevelopment of the city centre, local interests hardened their stance against the corporation. In March 1946, a draft statement of objections to the corporation's application for a declaratory order, drawn up by the chamber of commerce, the replanning association and the Rotary Club, was approved by the interested bodies.[16] Significantly, one of the main reasons for the objection was that these bodies would not approve the corporation's reconstruction proposals, especially those related to the resiting of the shopping centre.[17] Moreover, as the ministry's regional planning officer observed in early 1946, 'whilst in the early days there seemed to be very considerable support to the Corporation's proposals ... that agreement is weakening and doubts are rising in some of the interested parties' minds'.[18] For one thing, the Bristol Retailers' Advisory Committee on Town Planning, whose chairman had made a sympathetic comment on the city council's revised plan in July 1945, was now making a number of objections to the proposed new shopping centre at Broadmead. As corporation officers reported to the PRC in December 1945, they had held a number of conferences with this advisory committee, only to find that they were unable to make any further progress.[19]

The public inquiry into the city council's application for a declaratory order was held in June 1946. A total of 356 objections were lodged, 191 of which were objections to the principle of compulsory purchase, the remainder to parts of the council's replanning proposals.[20] At the inquiry proceedings, however, it was made clear that the majority of the objections to the corporation's plan, especially to the resiting of the shopping centre, were in effect based on a hatred for compulsory purchase, notably because of the loss of freehold and traders' goodwill, and the injustice to owners involved in compensation proceedings.[21] It was also argued by the objectors that the council's application covering an area of 771 acres was outside the scope of the 1944 Act, because its replanning proposals were for the sake of 'a long term planning policy, and not the laying out afresh and the redevelopment of war damaged areas alone'; the only way war damage had entered into the application was that it afforded the corporation 'an excuse to do all these other things that they wish to carry out'.[22] Thus the anti-compulsory purchase feeling was particularly strong when it came to undamaged properties including cinemas and churches.[23]

There was also grave concern about the uncertainty relating to finance, especially the terms of compensation, the possible cost of the replanning scheme and the extent to which government grant would cover it. As M. Rowe, KC, who appeared for the MTF put it:

> I wonder what you would say about a man who asked an architect to design a house and then told him to go ahead and build it without asking how much it would cost. You would say the fellow was stark raving mad, and yet that is really the position in which we are in this matter of rebuilding Bristol. We all want to get the best possible plan, but how can you tell what is the best plan unless you have some idea if it is financially possible?[24]

At the same time, he did not hesitate to admit that his clients, multiple shops, were in agreement with the corporation as to the location of the new shopping centre. However, they kept 'coming up against a brick wall', because they did not know exactly what the government had in mind as regards financial help towards reconstruction. His attention was then focused on the government:

> We do very earnestly beg the Minister of Planning to put an end to this apparent policy of keeping everything up his sleeve and telling nobody what he really has in mind. If it were not for this policy of silence, if we really knew what was in the Minister's mind, and had been given an opportunity of discussing it, half the objectors in this room would not be here, and a very good deal of time and money would have been saved.[25]

The corporation's defenders – T.J. Urwin, deputy town clerk, and H.M. Webb, city engineer – first of all stressed that there had been urgent need for the comprehensive replanning of the city centre. Most of the buildings in the area covered by the application would be ripe for redevelopment in the quite near future. There were also three main defects in the area from a planning point of view: considerable traffic congestion in the main streets; the haphazard cheek by jowl mingling of all kinds of property; and a lack of the amenities one would expect in a city like Bristol. The corporation was definitely of the opinion that they had a splendid opportunity to rebuild the area, and it was determined to take the fullest advantage of it.[26] The allegation that the corporation's application was outside the scope of the 1944 Act was flatly dismissed. As the deputy town clerk stated, the prime purpose of the 1944 Act was to deal satisfactorily with what was called extensive war damage, and Bristol was a city in which the war damage had been extensive, for there was 'nothing in this area which cannot be described as near or neighbouring on war damage of one kind or another'.[27] What was more, there was 'no satisfactory way of dealing with it [war damage] in this city, except as part of a comprehensive scheme of redevelopment as a whole'.[28] Thus any individual undamaged property should not be omitted from the application, otherwise an island of freehold would be set in a sea of leasehold interests, which could not be touched when the surrounding leaseholds became due for redevelopment.[29] With regard to the cost of the scheme (i.e. cost of the acquisition), the corporation stressed that they were expecting a large government grant, for 'A blitzed city like Bristol should have some claim for national help.'[30]

The public inquiry made it clear that the corporation's replanning proposals – especially that of the resiting of the shopping centre – could stand against the objections made to them. The local authority demonstrated its determination to redevelop the city centre in a comprehensive way. At the same time, the objections lodged by those with a vested interest were shown to be based on a narrow interpretation of the 1944 Act, hostility to compulsory purchase and strong concern about the ambiguity of government reconstruction policy. But they failed to bring to the inquiry any alternative schemes to the corporation's proposal for a new shopping centre at Broadmead.

The inquiry also made it clear that future progress would depend on the clarification of government reconstruction policy. First, would the government uphold bold planning by – as an initial step – confirming the large-scale declaratory order and the two compulsory purchase orders? Secondly, would they give the local authority generous financial help to offset the cost of acquisition, without which there was going to be a heavy burden on the rates? And, thirdly, as Bristol intended that most of the actual rebuilding should be carried out by private interests rather than by the corporation itself, would the 'cost-of-works' question be solved as soon as possible by the government, so that the traders could be totally confident of rebuilding for themselves in the new shopping centre? Although some suspected that there was 'undue optimism on the part of the City Council as to what they may expect from that quarter' (the government),[31] the corporation's confidence in their proposals was fairly justifiable, considering the endorsement of them made by the minister in March 1946. Immediately after the Bristol inquiry, the ministry held another into the case of Coventry, to which we now turn.

* * *

Ministry officials were never contented with Coventry's replanning scheme, despite the fact it had gone through important modifications. As Doubleday, the RPO, stressed in early 1946, there was one outstanding point still left unresolved in the reconstruction scheme, namely the amount of land devoted to the proposed civic centre. He continued:

> I have never been satisfied that this area of the Scheme is sound. I still feel that the Redevelopment Committee should be asked to

produce some evidence that the Civic Centre is on the lines required for the area. In other words that it is not merely wishful thinking on their part of what buildings are needed.[32]

The CRC thought differently. To them 'the time has arrived when it is appropriate to initiate steps for a definite start on the Coventry Redevelopment Scheme'.[33] Accordingly, they resolved in January 1946 to issue a public notice announcing their intention to apply for a declaratory order. It was also hoped that a start on the scheme itself would be made during 1946, the first stage of which would be the development of the Broadgate area.[34] In February, it was decided that the equestrian statue of Lady Godiva, designed by the sculptor Sir Williams Reid Dick, should be erected in the centre of the new Broadgate, directly in line with the cathedral vista.[35] In March, the CRC decided to organize a 'levelling stone' ceremony on the forthcoming Victory Day, 8 June, as a suitable 'advance work' to mark the official inauguration of the redevelopment scheme. The site would be near the top of Smithford Street, within what would eventually be one of the gardens of the shopping precinct.[36] Lord Kenilworth, who had met the cost of the model of Gibson's city centre in 1941, again offered help to cover the cost of the levelling stone, and the preparation for the ceremony proceeded rapidly.[37]

These two projects – a site for the Lady Godiva statue and the levelling stone ceremony – were originally suggested by Gibson, the city architect, who had frequently been exposed to fierce criticisms from ministry officials as well as his fellow corporation officers. It seemed that Gibson was now in a stronger position than ever to encourage the CRC to make an early start on his scheme. One of the main reasons for this was that he eventually found that he had 'allies' among his fellow corporation officers.[38] F. Smith, the town clerk, who had been the most adamant opponent of his scheme during the war, decided in early 1946 to retire, stating significantly that this would be convenient given the redevelopment scheme the council had in mind.[39] C. Barratt, deputy town clerk, who was to replace Smith, and Dr A.H. Marshall, city treasurer since 1944, were said to be determined to get on with Gibson's plan, just the opposite to their predecessors.[40]

In May 1946, Coventry City Guild, which had been active in the replanning of the city centre before the war, expressed its general approval of the city council's scheme and pressed them for prompt action.[41] The relationship between the city council and the chamber of commerce had also been greatly improved since the compromise amendment was made to Gibson's plan in July 1945. The CRC's decision in early 1946 to erect temporary shops with the five-year interim development permission, as opposed to the one-year permission during the war, was welcomed by traders.[42] A conference was arranged between the corporation and those with vested interests likely to be affected by the redevelopment scheme in order to discuss the resettlement arrangements of such interests.[43] As Hodgkinson observed in June 1946, what the city council needed most had been:

... the sympathy and earnest co-operation of the citizens, and perhaps more particularly those who subsequently conduct their businesses on this central site ... We have, I believe, passed through a delicate negotiation stage with much credit to all concerned, for there is now general agreement that the major plan is acceptable.[44]

The city council were also encouraged by the firm confidence of the general public in Gibson's scheme. In early 1946, the city council arranged the 'Open Ideas Competition' in association with the *Coventry Evening Telegraph*, to obtain the views of citizens as to what redevelopment should be carried out. About 2500 individual suggestions were made, but though they were mostly related to the need for the provision of such welfare facilities as children's playgrounds, nurseries and community centres throughout the whole city, a significant number expressed their approval of Gibson's city centre plan.[45] In fact, it seemed that the public were also very understanding of the difficulties the council had been facing with their city centre plan. As the *Coventry Evening Telegraph* put it at the beginning of 1946:

> For a long time the re-development scheme was almost bogged down, and the ideal of 1940 ... looked rather like an embarrassment in later years ... We are still a long way from the stage of big building operations, but the perseverance and latterly the adaptability of the local planners has produced a result from which we can derive encouragement.[46]

The CRC's determination to proceed with their city centre plan was also reflected in their choice of the optimum area for the declaratory order application. It should be noted that a few reputedly radical Labour councillors were rather critical of the committee's attitude to severely damaged areas other than the city centre. An area of 452 acres was proposed to be included in the application for a declaratory order based on the city centre as defined by the inner ring road plus the run-down Spon Street neighbourhood immediately to the west of it. In February 1946, the CRC was asked to consider the desirability of applying for a declaratory order for the Hillfields area to the east of the city centre as well. This area, admittedly severely damaged during the war, was 513 acres in size. The CRC argued that it would be 'mistaken policy to attempt at this stage, when so much effort has to be devoted to the completion of the preparatory work for Area (of Extensive War Damage) No. 1, to commence work on another and larger area'. They maintained that 'good and useful changes can be made in suitable parts of the suggested area' by using the general powers of the Town and Country Planning Acts, a course which they thought 'more advantageous ... than to attempt at this juncture formally to prescribe a second Area of Extensive War Damage'.[47]

The CRC's decision was vigorously challenged at the city council meeting in March. Mrs Allen, one of the Hillfields councillors, moved the resolution that the CRC should prepare a report regarding other blitzed areas of the city outside Area No. 1. As she told the council:

> It was time they knew where they were going in the other 'blitzed' areas of the city as well as in the centre. This was especially the case as people in those other areas were forced to live amidst the debris, whereas in the centre of the city people were not having to live amongst it.[48]

While observing that there was no lack of sympathy in respect of Hillfields or any other damaged areas, Hodgkinson argued:

> ... they could only bite off as much as they could chew, and a very big programme was involved in the central area. There seemed to be a view in the Council that areas were going to be left behind because of prior attention somewhere else. They would look foolish if they went on prescribing areas of development when they already had one iron in the fire concerning the central area. It was a question of how much they could carry.[49]

In the end, the council's application was formally lodged with the ministry on 4 April, in respect of Area No. 1 only as had been initially intended.[50]

The laying of the levelling stone ceremony on Victory Day, just about a fortnight before the public inquiry, played quite an important role in strengthening public acceptance of the city centre scheme. As Hodgkinson declared:

> To-day, we hitch our minds and hopes to a conception of new and better things. For many of us there will be only a glimpse of the final creation, but there is a bounden duty on those who have responsibility to-day, to ensure that Coventry takes the splendid opportunity to build worthily of a people who have made so great a sacrifice and contributed so much to the nation's survival.[51]

A *Coventry Evening Telegraph* editorial gave whole-hearted sympathy and encouragement. Noting that 'the Coventry reconstruction scheme, which broadly commands the support of the majority of the citizens' would eventually bring 'the solid results ... when the strain of these times is eased', the paper observed:

> ... if to-day's ceremony is an act of faith in the future, it is also a fitting reminder of what has already been achieved. The men and women who have brought the scheme to this stage deserve the city's thanks. They have done well to mark their achievement and their faith in public manner on this Victory Day. Another generation will see the end of the labour and the fulfilment, but as long as the stones of the new city stand, what Coventry did on Victory Day in 1946 will be remembered.[52]

The public inquiry into the city council's application for a declaratory order was commenced on 25 June 1946. In all, 259 objections were lodged, but only six held that the scheme was not good planning.[53] One of the points at the inquiry was, therefore, 'to what extent the Corporation could meet these objections without seriously upsetting the plan'.[54] In fact, opposition to the scheme as such lost much weight at the actual inquiry. For instance, one objector, who represented himself as a planning expert, described the appearance of new Broadgate as 'diabolically German and Fascist in character', and declared that 'it was planned largely for architectural need at the expense of Coventry considerations', and thus would not be taken to by 'all the poor people of Coventry [who] have suffered at the hands of these wretched Nazis'.[55] Cross-examined by the new town clerk, however, the same objector agreed that the style of Trinity Street was satisfactory and eventually admitted that the corporation responsible for that development might be trusted to make a satisfactory job of further planning.[56] Criticism was also made that the proposed civic centre was 'laid out extravagantly to satisfy the aesthetic standards of one or two town planners or even the Redevelopment Committee', irrespective of cost. The contender argued that the corporation should concentrate on 'the planning of a new city, not a Utopia', and thus 'must come down from the clouds down to the realms of hard cash', for the 1944 Act did 'not contemplate, much less authorise, a dream city'. In reply, Gibson, the city architect, stressed that the public buildings of the present day were quite inadequate, and that, in view of the phenomenal population growth the city had experienced, the proposed centre was essential to meet future needs.[57]

Strong concern about the financial effects of the scheme as a whole, considering the uncertainty of government help, were also dismissed by the corporation. M. Rowe, KC, appearing for the chamber of commerce and the Multiple Shops' Federation, intimated that there would be a considerable burden on the rates. Although he had been told at the Bristol inquiry that the government would be generous in making good most of the likely financial shortfall in the replanning scheme, he was extremely suspicious of such promises. In reply, E. Ford, the city engineer, stated emphatically:

> If we are unable to meet all liabilities, we shall expect – and I think have a right to expect – the Exchequer will meet what was a loss to the city caused by a national disaster. It was not Coventry's fault. It was a national matter, and should be spread over the whole of the nation.[58]

Most objections, as in Bristol, reflected the strong criticism of government policy on such matters as the 'cost-of-works' payment and the basing of compensation on 1939 prices. One counsel, disapproving of the provisions of the 1944 Act on these issues, declared:

> There is injustice. There is differentiation. It is the first duty of a Government to administer social justice, and see all people are treated equally and fairly.[59]

At the same time, he told the inquiry that the substance of his contention lay in a belief that 'by reiteration of protests at inquiries like this remedies could sometimes be secured'. The difficulties involved in the matter were 'not all of the Corporation's making but of a policy dictated at higher level'. In fact, he warmly appreciated the manner in which the corporation had treated objectors, and went on to say that 'Coventry's scheme revealed a great deal of careful thought and consideration'.[60]

All told the corporation showed very little difficulty in carrying through the inquiry. The main reason for this was their conviction that they had public support for their replanning scheme, shown, as the new town clerk pointed out, in events like the 'Future Coventry' exhibition held in October 1945 and the 'Open Ideas Competition' in early 1946. The vast majority of people in the city were convinced that the scheme was 'worth while and to the ultimate benefit of Coventry', and with this support, the corporation 'would not allow themselves to be deflected from their goal by mere personal interest' put forward to the inquiry.[61] The 259 objectors, representing approximately 1000 interests, accounted for only one-tenth of those affected by the scheme.[62] And as the *Coventry Standard* noted, even those interests themselves gradually realized that the necessity of the local authority's wholesale control of the city centre was incontrovertible.[63] A *Coventry Evening Telegraph* editorial made assurance doubly sure:

> We believe that the Corporation is right in seizing an opportunity created by misfortune, an opportunity which may never occur again to rebuild the centre of the city so that it provides for the needs of this age. There would be no wisdom in a policy of timidity at this time, and the Council has approached the matter from the point of view of the whole city.[64]

Thus, the importance of the Coventry inquiry lay in the fact that it reinforced support for the corporation's replanning scheme, and that such support made the case for the local authority's control of land indisputable. At the same time, it was once again made clear that further progress in the matter would all depend on the government; how to ameliorate the aggrieved feeling of private interests and how to respond to the local authority's high expectation for genuine assistance in the implementation of the scheme. We finally look at the remaining case, Southampton, where the replanning of the central area had become, unlike the previous two cities, a critical issue of local politics.

*   *   *

Immediately after the municipal elections in November 1945, Southampton Borough Council, now led by Labour, decided to make a formal application for a declaratory order. They also sought judgement from the ministries concerned on the relative merits of the two alternative schemes for the city centre as prepared by Cook, the town planning and development officer, and Wooldridge, the borough engineer. Two conferences with the Ministries of War Transport and of Town and Country Planning were held hastily in the same month. As Alderman Matthews, now chairman of the planning committee, told the ministries, the council was most anxious to make a decision on the matter as soon as possible so that they should be able to submit a formal application for a declaratory order. Moreover, while he was in favour of the Wooldridge plan, it had not yet been before the city council for approval. It was thus obvious that his real intention was to obtain *de facto* authorization for the Wooldridge plan from the two ministries.[65]

These conferences, however, proved to be of little use. Whereas the Ministry of War Transport was generally in favour of the Wooldridge plan, the Ministry of Town and Country Planning described it as little more than 'a series of road proposals',[66] which needed 'more detailed examination than they have received'.[67] In particular, there was a fundamental difference between the ministries in their opinions as to the precinct treatment of Above Bar/High Street proposed by Wooldridge. It was understood that while private cars were allowed to use the street, any public transport service would be excluded from it and have to use an inner ring road. The Ministry of War Transport supported the idea strongly, but the Ministry of Town and Country Planning 'expressed the opinion that it would be impracticable to take public service vehicles out of the main shopping street, and that, if this were done, it would seriously disturb the values of land and property in that street'.[68] The conferences thus reached an impasse, and the only joint recommendation made to the planning committee was 'to suggest that the matter is clearly one on which your Committee must definitely make up their own minds'.[69]

In January 1946, the committee made the decision to take Wooldridge's plan as the basis for a final plan, which should be completed jointly by Cook, Wooldridge and D. Winston (the new borough architect) by March.[70] As Matthews observed at the council meeting:

> Where experts differ the layman has to make a decision ... and having made it the officers must loyally accept it and get to work on the details so that the reconstruction of the central area can proceed rapidly.[71]

Cook, however, would not give way. He was unable to accept any plan which placed greater emphasis on economy rather than planning principles.[72] Accordingly, the planning committee decided to submit Wooldridge's plan to the council for approval.[73] At the March council meeting, it was carried by 40 votes to 1 – the solitary dissenter being Alderman Kimber.[74]

The council's adoption of the Wooldridge plan was the last straw for Cook. Within a month he had resigned his appointment as town planning and development officer.[75] He was soon welcomed as secretary and technical adviser to the newly formed Central Area Association of

Southampton.[76] The association was set up in April 1946 to represent some 200 business and industrial interests in the city centre and to facilitate their rehabilitation.[77] Cook emphasized the unique advantage of the association, having in view the public inquiry to be held in September into the corporation's application for a declaratory order. While individual traders might find it difficult to object in very broad terms to a replanning scheme, an organization like this was obviously better placed to put forward objections dealing not only with individual properties but the whole policy and general proposals envisaged by the council. Moreover, such an inquiry would possibly be the only opportunity for the public to put forward their views, after which it would be entirely a matter for the corporation and the ministry to decide what was to be done in the area.[78] How much Cook was motivated by a grudge against the corporation in his activism in the association is not clear, but he was certainly strongly opposed to the principle of wholesale acquisition, not to mention the Wooldridge plan.[79] The setting up of the association was welcomed by other organizations[80] which had declared their disapproval of the corporation's acquisition policy since November 1945,[81] and in May 1946 it was duly proposed to form 'a united front' of the central area association, the chamber of commerce and the Property Owners' Protection Society, in objecting to the corporation's scheme at the forthcoming public inquiry.[82]

While it was not unusual for the interests concerned to express their objections vigorously before the inquiry, things were moving in the wrong direction for the corporation. First, as Alderman Lewis, the Labour leader, admitted, there was a hint of regret about the fact that 'the original grandiose scheme could not be operated and had to go by the board'.[83] When it came to the Wooldridge plan, because it had to be adopted rather hastily in connection with the application for a declaratory order, there had been little time for the corporation to consult with those interests concerned about it.[84] Furthermore, Cook's resignation as planning officer did not reflect well on the corporation. Alderman Kimber and former Councillor G.E.H. Prince (Ratepayers' Party, member of the planning committee during the war, who was not returned at the municipal election in November 1945) did attempt to make Cook's departure look scandalous by asserting that Cook had been forced to resign by Matthews.[85]

Whether the accusation was true or false, Matthews, who had been responsible for the creation of the town planning and development department in 1941, had now to propose its abolition. In May 1946, the borough council adopted the planning committee's recommendations that the planning department should cease to exist as a separate entity. Its duties were to be distributed between the borough engineer, architect and valuer; and a technical panel of these officers plus a principal planning assistant was established to co-ordinate the implementation of the Wooldridge plan as well as the preparation of any further planning schemes.[86] At the council meeting, Matthews admitted that for some years they had had to face 'a nightmare' – inadequate co-operation between departments. The recommendations would lead to better co-ordination of departmental action than had been possible in the past, thus facilitating rapid reconstruction. Alderman Lewis supported Matthews by adding that the total situation was 'due to a set of circumstances over which we have no control'. As he went on:

> I agree he [Cook] did excellent work, but this is not a question of his work, but one of working together. When he left we said that we must have a different method to get all the co-operation we can.[87]

Whether the new arrangement was the result of the unforeseen or not, the fact that Cook joined the objectors' camp caused strong concern about the corporation's handling of reconstruction policy, for which Matthews was most responsible. There was thus the possibility that the forthcoming public inquiry into the declaratory order covering 514 acres would be a considerable blow to the adoption of the Wooldridge plan.

In fact at the inquiry, which began on 24 September 1946, the corporation were accused of neglecting those with vested interests when adopting their scheme. The ubiquitous M. Rowe, KC, this time appearing for the central area association and a number of individual firms, observed that the Southampton inquiry differed deeply from other recent inquiries. Elsewhere there was a certain measure of agreement upon the basic principles of the schemes. This was due to the fact that there had been prolonged consultations between the local authorities and the principal local interests. He continued:

> Here that is not the case ... there has not been the slightest real effort to obtain from any important and representative section of the public their views upon this plan. That is an extraordinarily unfortunate thing, because I am sure it must have impressed itself on the inspector [of the inquiry] that Southampton has taken an interest in the plan, and many of the owners and those principally concerned would not have been backward in trying to co-operate with the Corporation in getting something satisfactory to both parties.[88]

Little information was thus available in respect of such matters as alternative accommodation and the conditions of lease.[89]

Severe criticisms were made of the Wooldridge plan, and some alternative proposals – including Cook's 1944 plan – were submitted to the inquiry. Especially strong concern was expressed about the future of Above Bar. For one thing, the introduction of precincts was not favoured. As A.E. Lees, appearing for Marks and Spencer, put it, if public service vehicles were to be banned from a main shopping street, the importance of the street would be quickly destroyed.[90] For another, the excessive use of Above Bar for shopping purposes was called into question. In this connection, T.S. Dulake, a town planning consultant from Mayfair, proposed that it should be developed as a new Regent Street with cinemas, hotels, restaurants, offices and shops,[91] rather than a 'dreary terrace of shops'.[92]

The substance of the objections, however, differed very little from other inquiries. An analysis of the 370 objections put forward at the inquiry showed that the majority were associated with the inequity and hardship involved in compulsory purchase – the 1939 basis of compensation and the 'cost-of-works' payment.[93] Loss of freehold was never popular among owners who would rather have rebuilt their businesses themselves on their former sites.[94] Hysterical criticisms were made of the leasehold system, which was described as 'unEnglish', 'nothing short of nationalization of land' and 'a despicable act on the part of the Corporation to attempt to cash in on the citizens' misfortunes'.[95] Representatives of Edwin Jones, a multiple store and the second largest ratepayer in the borough, asserted that 'The Corporation have gone completely mad on this fetish of no freeholds.'[96] The proposed redevelopment of 514 acres was regarded as 'a grandiose scheme, municipal self-glorification, and nothing connected with war damage'.[97] Concern was once more expressed that the corporation had no idea of the cost of the redevelopment and that it was relying too heavily on government.[98]

On balance, the corporation managed to defend its case. N.C. Scragg, senior assistant solicitor in the town clerk's department, who conducted the case for the corporation, dismissed the alleged lack of consultations between the corporation and the principal local interests. To begin with, those with the greatest interest – such as the Southern Railway, the Harbour Board and the churches – had been consulted, and there was a considerable measure of agreement.[99] Moreover, the traders had been consulted extensively since 1942, and the new plan 'was built up after taking into account all the major trading issues which have been so forcibly ventilated during the past four years'.[100] As circumstances permitted, the corporation would discuss such matters as alternative accommodation and rents, and they would not let the traders down.[101]

Cook's 1944 plan was categorically described by Scragg as 'far more expensive than the plan we have to-day',[102] while other proposals were partial alternatives to the Wooldridge plan intended to redevelop the original sites themselves.[103] Regarding the criticism of a shopping precinct in Above Bar, the corporation argued that it would obviate serious traffic congestion, and thus enhance rather than destroy its value as the main shopping street. The suggestion from a Mayfair planning consultant to develop Above Bar like Regent Street did not represent the views of local traders, who preferred a continuous shopping frontage. As Scragg went on: 'Members of the Council, as representatives of the public, are far more qualified to know what the public of Southampton require.'[104]

The mere dislike of leasehold was 'not a good and valid reason against this Order', without which there would still be 'a jumble of user, traffic congestion and other difficulties'.[105] While the corporation was sympathetic to owners regarding compensation at 1939 values and loss of 'cost-of-works' payments, their objections were objections to the 1944 Act for which the council had no responsibility.[106] The corporation was unexpectedly encouraged by the evidence of an objector, R.W.H. Collier, war damage and valuation expert. He argued that the area covered by the Order was within 80 yards of war damage, thus within the scope of the 1944 Act, and that the scheme would be a success financially.[107] Failing this, the corporation was, as Scragg argued, justified in expecting large additional government grants 'as some compensation to the loss and sufferings of the towns which, owing to their situation or importance to the national effort, experienced savage bombing from the enemy'.[108]

Thus the objectors failed to halt the corporation in their adoption of the Wooldridge plan. Had there been any serious challenge from the Ratepayers' Party at council level before the inquiry, the situation would have been more critical. Previously, the Ratepayers' Party had opposed both wholesale acquisition and the Wooldridge plan advocated by Labour before the municipal elections in November 1945. But the election results brought significant changes. First, former Ratepayers' Councillor Lane, who as chairman of the planning committee had consistently supported Cook's plan, was not re-elected. The Ratepayers' Party continued their opposition to wholesale acquisition, but now supported the Wooldridge plan, on the grounds that it could be implemented more quickly and economically than Cook's plan. It was obvious that the party, especially its leader Alderman Woolley, had changed its mind, in view of the still serious loss of the town's rateable value,[109] and the urgent need for the rapid rehabilitation of the town's trade.[110] Not only did Woolley praise the new plan,[111] but he even supported the abolition of the town planning and development department, a move for which Matthews expressed genuine gratitude.[112]

This bipartisan support for the Wooldridge plan made it look as if the council were also united in their support for the wholesale acquisition policy. This was, on the one hand, a logical conclusion, for the importance of the plan was its role as supporting evidence for the declaratory order at the public inquiry. On the other hand, the Ratepayers' Party, demoralized by its minority position, could do nothing to prevent wholesale acquisition being adopted by the council. In November 1945, immediately after the municipal elections, Woolley seconded Matthews' recommendation to apply formally for a declaratory order. Although at that time Woolley still maintained that the question of wholesale acquisition was quite another issue and threatened that 'we shall have something to say about it later',[113] in the event no effective opposition was made at council level before the public inquiry.

It was not until the council meeting following the public inquiry in October 1946 that Woolley once more asked the council to withdraw its application for a declaratory order. His speech at the council meeting was pathetic in its inconsistency. He stated that he had always been in favour of Cook's plan, to the amazement even of Alderman Kimber. He also observed that a declaratory order was essential to the speedy purchase of land, but because he believed piecemeal rather than wholesale acquisition should be adopted, he asked for the withdrawal of the application altogether. In the end he stated: 'I submit the resolution, knowing that it will not be carried.' This resulted in a straight party vote, eight for his resolution and 38 against.[114]

Before the municipal elections in November 1946, the Ratepayers' Party hastily tried to object to compulsory purchase. At a public meeting, the corporation's acquisition policy was denounced as confiscation of freehold property, which would cost £50 million and increase the rates by 25s.[115] This rather extravagant statement was denounced at the council meeting by Labour Councillor Parker, chairman of the finance committee, as 'arrant nonsense'.[116] At the same time, despite knowing that they had 'reduced the opposition to impotence',[117] Labour nevertheless seemed to experience some anxiety about the elections. As the Labour candidate with the largest majority told an after-the-poll party meeting, they had 'had a difficult election to fight, because the past year had been one in which foundations had been laid, but the fruits were not evident yet, and some people were disappointed'.[118] The results of the elections – another Labour gain increased their majority to 28 – were, as Alderman Lewis confidently stated, 'a complete endorsement by the people of Southampton of Labour's policy and administration during the past twelve months'.[119] Labour were thus able to feel more confident about their reconstruction policy, already well established by the success of the public inquiry.

*   *   *

The analysis of the three public inquiries has shown certain important points about the replanning of these city centres. First, and perhaps most importantly, it was quite an institutional affair: the inquiries provided a battlefield for head-on confrontation between owners – especially local traders – and the local authority. The interests concerned often closed ranks to air their objections to compulsory purchase and, to a lesser degree, to the corporation's planning proposals. Although in Bristol and Southampton the corporations' replanning proposals were controversial and could have been in jeopardy, the selfish motives behind the objections did not pose a serious threat to the legitimacy of official plans approved by the councils as duly elected representatives of the public. As Wooldridge emphatically told M. Rowe at the Southampton inquiry, 'no evidence you can bring will change my opinion [about the plan]. If you want to change it, get elected to the Council.' This finally silenced Rowe, who replied: 'In view of what you have said, I will accept your hint and will sit down.'[120] In this respect, Coventry is worthy of special mention. The corporation there cited the support of the general public for the city centre plan as the principal reason for acquisition. Local newspapers, which were not necessarily pro-Labour, consistently endorsed the council when it came to the replanning of the city centre.

The objectors were not only self-interested but behind the times. The reason behind their objections – an abhorrence of the loss of freehold – was totally against the principle of the Town and Country Planning Act 1944, passed by the coalition government. As many counsel admitted at the inquiries, objections were often made as a plea to the government to show mercy. Yet city centre redevelopment based on bold plans, with local authorities acting as ground landlords, was the demand of the day, endorsed since the early years of the war by the ministers responsible for town and country planning. Those councillors who represented the objectors were either quite content with this principle, or, as in the case of Southampton, simply incompetent.

The success of the public inquiries led the local authorities to conclude that their city centre plans had in general been accepted. With encouraging signs coming from Lewis Silkin, the new Minister of Planning, of positive government assistance, the local authorities had every reason to believe that an early start and rapid progress could be made in the redevelopment of their own city centre.

eight

The fate of planning after the war

After the public inquiries of 1946 Bristol, Coventry and Southampton held high hopes about the ministry's backing for city centre redevelopment through early confirmation of the declaratory orders and subsequent approval of the city centre plans. These hopes were, however, ill-founded. First, there were considerable delays and curtailment to the minister's confirmation of declaratory orders. His early confirmations, such as the case of Plymouth, ran into High Court appeals, and he had to wait the outcomes until around mid-1947.[1] Moreover, his confirmation of a declaratory order was consequent upon the Treasury, whose interest was, as he told the local authorities in October 1947, 'naturally to cut down'. As he continued: 'we are perhaps, if I may say so within these four walls, rather too closely tied up [with the Treasury] in the 1944 Act – [they] have perhaps too big a say in these matters'.[2] Consequently, the confirmation of orders involved considerable reductions in scale.[3]

The new town planning legislation did not offer much help either to the local authorities. The Town and Country Planning Act 1947 consolidated the number of planning authorities from 1441 to 145 county and county borough councils. Every planning authority had to carry out a survey of its area and to prepare a development plan. By this means, it was expected that broad planning principles should first of all be established over a wide area, with the detail being filled in when the development was about to take place.[4] But the crucial question regarding city centre redevelopment was how smoothly local authorities could proceed with acquisition of land covered by the declaratory order. In this connection, the government grant or acquisition was to last for as long as 60 years, commencing with up to 90 per cent for the first five years, but then scaling down. However, the grant system made the local authorities extremely cautious when proceeding with acquisitions, because they had no guarantee that actual redevelopment would follow in the immediate future.[5] The economic crisis only helped to worsen the situation. Those local authorities badly affected by the blitz had been very concerned about the shortage of building labour and materials; now, building operations were prohibited unless a strong case could be made that it was essential to the export trades; and even compulsory acquisition of land, which had to be pursued in a miserable piecemeal manner, was further limited by the ministry's Circular 39 in March 1948 restricting capital expenditure.[6] As Silkin observed in October 1947:

> At the moment we are concentrating on such measures of reconstruction as will enable us to improve our economic position. Housing, the rebuilding of our blitzed towns, even the building of new towns, are for the moment regarded as luxuries, or rather as irrelevant in the rebuilding of our economic position, and only such building as will further our economic position will, for the time being, be permitted.[7]

In the face of these difficulties, as the construction of housing continued apace, no permanent shops or other buildings were being erected in war-damaged city centres.

The effect of such an extremely grim prospect for city centre redevelopment was all too obvious. As the *Architects' Journal* observed as late as 1952 (when a token start had been made):

> Since the war everyone has been waiting for the priority work – houses and schools – to be finished, and for the economic crises to end, so as to allow the rebuilding of the blitzed and decaying centres. What is being slowly forced on us is the realization that there is no foreseeable end to the priority work, or to the economic crises. If the country's wealth does not markedly increase there may be no possibility of rebuilding the town centres and we, or our children, may watch, for a change, not the growth but the galloping decay of a city, in terms of property, not from the outside in, but from within outwards to the perimeter.[8]

Whether this prediction proved to be true or not, pessimism could only give rise to doubts about any city centre plan. This was all the more reason why the minister's approval of a plan was necessary in the remaining years of the 1940s when no visible progress was expected, in order to instil confidence in the local authorities that what they envisaged was along the right lines. Yet here again the local authorities soon realized that obtaining the minister's approval was almost out of the question.

A striking change was taking place within the ministry after the war:

most of those officials active during the war had gone, and the local authorities would have to deal with new faces. As Silkin put it, this change was imperative because, understandably in the case of a newly created ministry in 1943, 'our original staff consisted of people who could be spared from other Departments', and 'inevitably they have not all been good'. For new officials, however, 'it does take a little time to get into the atmosphere and to get going, to understand the complexities of town planning, and especially town planning legislation, and we have suffered from the fact that we are a new Ministry and that we have practically a new personnel'.[9] In fact, these new officials began to impose further restrictions on local authorities and even attempted to deny the legality of 'planning boldly'; they were overwhelmed by their planning responsibilities, and less inclined to give authorization or approval of a city centre plan. The odds were against those councils that needed to reconstruct.

*   *   *

Things did not look particularly favourable for the speedy redevelopment of Southampton city centre. The housing problem there was formidable. In March 1947, the permanent housing programme for that year envisaged completing 1087 houses and starting another 1318.[10] By June, the council had erected 1014 prefabricated temporary bungalows out of the 1750 allocated to the city.[11] Yet in May, it was reported that there was a vast amount of overcrowding throughout the borough, with 11 810 applicants on the corporation housing list as of 6 April. Additional applications were being received at an average rate of 60 per week.[12] The borough council also had to face an acute shortage of building labour of which, as Alderman Lewis observed, there was no immediate prospect of any improvement.[13] The financial prospects of the town were also gloomy. The rates, which had to be increased in March 1946 for the first time for five years by 2s. 10d. in the pound,[14] were further increased in March 1947, this time by 3s. 5d., or by 52 per cent over a period of two years.[15]

Nevertheless, both the local traders and the corporation wanted the speedy redevelopment of the city centre. The fear of loss of trade to such neighbouring towns as Salisbury and Winchester began to prey heavily on Southampton's traders' minds.[16] They also complained about the increasing number of street traders operating in the town, particularly those in the main shopping thoroughfares.[17] The corporation's determination was reflected in their policy with regard to the allocation of building labour between housing and other work. The general practice throughout the country was that 60 per cent of the labour force was funnelled into housing and 40 per cent into other building. However, as Councillor Barnes, chairman of the housing committee, observed, the corporation were 'compelled by force of circumstances and their own common-sense' to pay regard to the urgent need for getting shops and commercial and industrial buildings going again, and thus came to the conclusion that there should be a 50–50 division of labour rather than a 60–40 split.[18] Moreover, Matthews was convinced that the time had come to consider the reconstruction of permanent shops in Above Bar as well as temporary shops. Despite a warning from the ministry of taking premature action before confirmation of the declaratory order,[19] in June 1947 the council adopted Matthews' resolution to apply for a compulsory purchase order in respect of five acres in Above Bar for permanent shops, with expedited procedures.[20]

The relationship between the borough council and the local traders was not good. The traders pressed the council to inform them of the precise sites for redevelopment and allow them to proceed with their rebuilding plans.[21] They further argued that it was essential to such speedy rebuilding to have immediate and frequent discussions between the planning committee and themselves.[22] The committee, however, avoided seeing the traders on a regular basis, maintaining that such consultations should start only after the ministry had confirmed the corporation's declaratory order, and thus the uncertainty in government policy was clarified.[23] The central area association managed to see the committee only once before the confirmation of the order, and made a request for further discussions.[24] While the committee left it to Matthews to arrange further consultations,[25] there was no sign of such meetings taking place, and the association became very frustrated.[26]

Apart from awaiting confirmation of the declaratory order, the planning committee had another reason for avoiding close contact with local traders. Under the new Town and Country Planning Bill 1947, it became obligatory for the local planning authority to prepare a plan for the area for which it was responsible within three years from the appointed day. Moreover, while the 1944 Act was basically an Act for land acquisition with a redevelopment scheme as an appendage to the application for a declaratory order, under the new Bill the designation of land for such application would form part of a 'development plan', the minister's approval of which was now the most important target for the local authority. As far as the city centre plan was concerned, the council wanted to go ahead with the existing plan discussed at the public inquiry. In May 1947, the council gave general approval to the detailed layout of the area around the civic centre – the Guildhall Square section; the East Park terrace section, consisting of such buildings as a six-storey health centre, an indoor bath with a gymnasium, a museum, colleges and a municipal office block; and the large-scale commercial development west of the civic centre between the law courts block and the central station.[27] It appeared that many local interests realized that the corporation's city centre plan would be approved by the minister in some shape or form, following his confirmation of the declaratory order, and that there was little chance of upsetting it.[28] But others, like Cook, still argued:

> The present is an opportune time to suggest that a plan for the future of an area of such importance should be the subject of discussion between all the interests concerned. Even at this stage

much time and energy could be saved by following a policy of consultation and collaboration in the true sense of the word.[29]

Thus it became all the more important for the council to obtain not only
the minister's consent to the declaratory order but his early approval of the
replanning scheme for the central area. However, the relationship between
the council and the minister was no better than its relationship with the
local interests. In June 1947, when the corporation became frustrated at
the declaratory order not being confirmed, Silkin stated that much of the
responsibility for the delay in the replanning of badly damaged city centres
should lie with the local authorities themselves. They had been very slow in
putting their proposals to him because they were so 'nervous of taking the
plunge', despite his consistent encouragement. Matthews angrily replied
that the minister's statement was unfair to Southampton, because the
corporation had gone 'as far ahead as could reasonably be done', only to be
held up by the government's restriction on labour and materials and by the
minister's own indecisiveness as to the corporation's declaratory order and
the city centre plan. The planning committee decided to ask the minister
to receive a deputation 'to clear up any misunderstandings'.[30] Indeed, the
local Labour Party became so furious that they wrote to Silkin and to the
National Executive Committee of the Labour Party in July urging that
'responsible Ministers of the Government should refrain from making
irresponsible statements'. They went so far as to say that, when 'it is
becoming increasingly difficult to keep the people with the Labour Government and, in Southampton, with the Labour Council' because of the
increasing cost of living, austerity, etc., they could not understand why the
minister 'should go out of his way to provide political opponents with
substantial ammunition to castigate Southampton Labour Party'.[31] Within
a week of this letter being sent, the local Labour Party received a reply
from the minister, in which he wished to make it clear that what he said
was not to be taken as criticism of the approach made by Southampton or
any particular authority, but as a general observation. The letter also
stated that the borough council would now receive his decision on the
declaratory order.[32]

This long-awaited confirmation covered approximately 270 of the total
514 acres in the application. Those portions excluded embraced the area to
the north of the civic centre (a residential area) and the Northam and
Chapel districts (a proposed industrial area alongside the River Itchen).[33]
Officials at the ministry had wondered why the demarcation in the application appeared to have been decided in relation to Cook's plan. For one
thing, the northern half of the area in the application would have been
required for the northern portion of the ring road, but it was no longer
required for this purpose in the new plan. When it came to the Northam
and Chapel districts, war damage was not extensive enough for them to be
included in the order.[34] The council's reaction to the confirmation was one
of relief. Matthews said at a Labour Party meeting that although the

exclusion was substantial, he was 'pleased and satisfied' with the order after waiting 11 months since the public inquiry. Among other things, it included the whole of the area south of Commercial Road, 'the very important core area'. Moreover, the confirmation opened up the way to consultation with the ministry about any necessary modifications to the plan for its final approval. When it came to actual redevelopment, however, Matthews warned that 'miraculous advances' would not be produced automatically. There were 'still many hurdles' to clear, and redevelopment would necessarily be 'a step by step process'.[35]

In August 1947, a meeting was held between the council and official of the ministry as to future action following confirmation of the declaratory order. Alderman Matthews wanted to obtain, first and foremost, the ministry's view of their plan, and possibly their final agreement. The ministry maintained that the matter should be considered in the light of the new Planning Act 1947, and should be left, for the moment, to discussion of detailed technical points. Assuming that agreement could be made quickly on the technical points, much of the discussion at the meeting focused upon how best the local authority could proceed with the actual acquisition of land in view of the fact that it had to be a piecemeal process.[36] Thus in October, when the council was invited to the minister's 'blitzed towns' conference, with a strong determination 'to put up a powerful case for blitzed towns to be allowed to go ahead, even under crisis conditions',[37] the question of the minister's approval of the city centre plans was not touched on at all.[38]

Ministry officials had not been entirely averse to the Southampton plan. For one thing, during the examination of the declaratory order, they were impressed with the plan's proposed layout as a whole in that 'to a considerable extent the existing road system has been incorporated in the new plan and the present predominant use of zoning has been adhered to wherever possible'. At the same time, they were critical of some important proposals in the plan. First, they were concerned that the areas set aside for shopping and business were 'too large and too widespread'. The council's intention to revive High Street as an important shopping street was especially questioned, and it was suggested that a large portion of it should remain as warehousing and for similar purposes, considering the marked northward move of shopping concentrated in Above Bar. With regard to the new road system, it was observed that the construction of the western arm of the proposed inner ring road would require further examination with a view to confining any portion of it within the existing Western Esplanade. The reason for this was to disturb the historic character of the area as little as possible, especially the old town wall around St Michael's Square. It was also proposed that, instead of widening Cumberland Place and Brunswick Place to form the main east–west route, it might be advisable to widen Commercial Road and to continue it eastwards even across East Park to join the improved Six Dials roundabout. The ministry officials maintained that this would be a more direct link for east–west traffic, and would result in relieving the congestion at the junction of Civic Centre Road/Above Bar/New Road, the middle of the central shopping area. Another point they were concerned with was that the north–south route for heavy dock traffic (via the line of St Andrew's Road, St Mary's Place, Threefield Lane and Latimer Street) would cut an existing desirable residential area into two.[39]

However, the meeting between corporation officials and the Ministry of Town and Country Planning (plus the Ministry of Transport) in September did not bear fruit,[40] and as time went by the council became extremely impatient about the lack of official response to their views on the city centre plan. Eventually, as a kind of ultimatum, the two ministries were invited in March 1948 'to talk quite plainly' about their views of the plan, i.e. 'whether they could accept it broadly as it was, or ... if they could not, what kind of revision should be undertaken'.[41] In reply, Buchanan, a Ministry of Town and Country Planning official, first outlined in general the ministry's attitude at that time towards city centre plans, a great many of which had been examined. These general points were not only discouraging for the council, but were also illustrative of the ministry's acknowledgement of a full retreat from bold planning. Buchanan explained:

> ... they had been gradually forced to realise that in considering central area plans they were undertaking a very much more difficult task than was at one time contemplated ... The plan of a blitzed town before destruction was the product of perhaps 1,000 years of development, and so it could hardly be expected that the best plan for reconstruction could be produced in the twinkling of an eye. It seemed, in fact, to be impossible to arrive at the perfect plan. A second general point in considering a central area plan was whether the plan got the most out of what was there already.[42]

Regarding the technical points, the council were once again faced, as in November 1945, with conflicting views from the two ministries on one key issue. The Ministry of Town and Country Planning duly recommended extending Commercial Road straight across East Park as the main east–west traffic route. Against this, the Ministry of Transport observed that east–west traffic should not be taken through the park, but should be kept to the north of it, i.e. the Cumberland Place/Brunswick Place route. In the end, the corporation were unable to obtain a single recommendation on the matter. Other points put forward to the council included the western arm of the inner ring road, the north–south route for dock traffic (as an alternative, the East Park Terrace/Palmerston Road/Strand/Canal Walk route was suggested), and the need for economy in such matters as width of roads and size of traffic islands. The Ministry of Town and Country Planning were pleased to see that the corporation had changed its mind regarding over-provision for shopping, business and industrial purposes, as in the treatment of the High Street area.[43]

With these points in mind, the revised plans were quickly prepared.[44] Concessions to the views of the two ministries were made by realigning the inner ring road, so avoiding passing through the old part of the town, and by economizing on the layout of some roads and traffic islands. At the same time, the planning committee made it clear that the suggested extension of Commercial Road was 'wholly unacceptable', and thus the east–west traffic route should be the improved Cumberland Place/ Brunswick Place route as proposed in the 1946 plan. The north–south route for heavy traffic was also to be unchanged.[45] Thus the revised plan did not include any radical change from the 1946 plan, but rather 'a refinement of the 1946 zoning by a more detailed sub-division of the areas into their respective use zones'.[46]

In May 1948, the borough council considered the revised plan. The Ratepayers' Party pleaded without success to defer the matter until the plan had been discussed with the interests concerned, and it was approved by a straight party vote of 32 to 20.[47] Repeated requests from the central area association to be involved in the creation of a new plan had not been met,[48] and the proposals in the comprehensive development plan for the central area under the 1947 Act, eventually submitted to the ministry in 1954, 'relate closely to those in the Plan produced by the Council at the Declaratory Order Inquiry in 1946'.[49] However, it should be stressed again here that Southampton's city centre plan was by no means a bold one. It was primarily aimed at the quick recovery of the existing shopping street, and at relief of traffic congestion by means of, *inter alia*, an inner ring road system based on the existing road layout. It was inevitable that the plan would be criticized for its lack of imagination, given that a great opportunity had been provided by the wartime bombing.[50] A typical example was the Guildhall Square scheme, one of the few bold proposals in Southampton's plan. As the corporation's development plan itself admitted in 1954, when the scheme was finally approved by the ministry, the proposed 400-feet gap between the north and south frontages had been reduced to a mere 164 feet.[51] Temporary landscaping was then carried out which still survives, awaiting implementation of the scheme.

In particular, the early redevelopment of the main shopping area was severely criticized. Generally, blocks of two-storey retail shops, simply erected along both sides of the street, had been designed as a complete set of units with rear access and unified treatment. First, they were criticized for their lack of height; instead, as was pointed out, crowning the shops with tall blocks of offices or flats would have been preferable.[52] Only in 1984 was it noted that the traders were 'reaping the fruits of the lack of foresight and are developing the upper floors'.[53] This 'block development' was a product of the change in the council's land purchase policy – admittedly forced on it by the government – to avoid, wherever possible, compulsory acquisition. It was true that unified architectural treatment was required, and that developers were encouraged to co-operate to ensure co-ordinated planning and building, and to agree wherever necessary to adjust site boundaries in order to improve the building layout. However, the resulting architectural expression was rather poor, for, as specialists commented in 1953, the ultimate responsibility did not lie in the council alone.[54] Inevitably, the new shops in Above Bar appeared 'unnecessarily pretentious'.[55] Somewhat ironically, it was the construction of multiple stores and department stores, such as Tyrell and Green, Edwin Jones, C & A Modes, and Plummers that offered the opportunity to produce a more completely integrated design than was possible in a block of smaller shops.[56]

Overall, the case of Southampton is dominated by a timid approach to planning. Alongside the council's obsession with economy and quick rehabilitation, the government departments were most to blame. The Ministry of Town and Country Planning especially was most unwilling to authorize the local authority's plan. The points that the ministry raised were mainly technicalities regarding the layout of roads, and the ministry did not show much enthusiasm for settling such minor problems and boosting the confidence of the local authority. Moreover, the ministries concerned – the Ministries of Transport and of Town and Country Planning – were far too often unable to see eye to eye, which was of little help to the council. In the end, it seemed that economy was not even really the object, for whether it was modest or extravagant, the ministry's authorization was most unlikely to be given, and the feeling that the replanning of the city had been dictated by Whitehall continued to grow.[57]

*   *   *

In contrast, Bristol's very bold city centre plan received praise from the planning minister in early 1946, with his promise to give it the go ahead very soon. Following the public inquiry, the local authority expected early authorization of the plan.

In Bristol itself, the prospects for actual reconstruction were as grim as in any other heavily bombed city. In July 1946, the housing committee complained that, while bricks were available, the shortage of bricklayers meant that house building was moving slowly.[58] It was noted that the labour required for industrial building alone in 1946–47 would be about three times greater than that available.[59] In November, the housing committee reported that there were about 19 000 applications on the waiting list,[60] although the completion of 1023 temporary and 198 permanent houses by the end of that month was regarded as satisfactory, placing the city in fifth place behind Birmingham, Hull, Plymouth and Sheffield on the 'temporary houses list'.[61]

When it came to the question of the city centre, the minister dealt a hard blow to the council in December 1946. In confirming the declaratory order, the minister had made drastic modifications, designed to limit the land affected to that which had been extensively damaged – just 245 of the 771 acres applied for. While the confirmed area included the new Broadmead shopping centre and the Castle Street/Wine Street public buildings zone, the council's planning committee observed with alarm that the modified order did not cover the land necessary, *inter alia*, for the completion of the inner ring road and the redevelopment of the Park Street area.[62] As Alderman Bicker, chairman of the committee, said:

> The committee are disappointed, there is no question about that, very disappointed, at the Minister's decision. What has caused him to take that decision must be left to conjecture, I do not know.[63]

In fact, this set the tone for the extremely hard times the council would face before actual redevelopment commenced. The PRC were at a loss, both about how to proceed with reconstruction work in general and acquisition in particular, and about whether the ministry still supported their city centre plan. In February 1947, the city engineer met with officials from both the Ministry of Transport and the Ministry of Town and Country Planning in a meeting that lasted for more than six hours. He was told, *inter alia*, that the Ministry of Town and Country Planning were not in favour of the proposal to use the old shopping centre – the most valuable area – for public buildings, but would prefer the construction of buildings that would bring in a direct return, because it would be difficult to satisfy the Treasury on the question of finance. They also felt that the Broadmead shopping centre was far too large – in their opinion, an adequate plan could be prepared retaining the Castle Street/Wine Street area as a shopping centre.[64]

The ministry were also doubtful as to whether the corporation would be granted compulsory purchase powers with a special expedited procedure in the immediate future. First, the 100-acre area covered by the orders was too large; because of pressure from the Treasury and of the new grant system under the 1947 Planning Bill, the ministry's recent acquisition policy stated that individual sites should be acquired by piecemeal application when the land became immediately needed for redevelopment. Moreover, if the council adhered to the Broadmead shopping centre plan despite the ministry's opposition, then the proposed compulsory order for the Castle Street/Wine Street area for the erection of temporary shops would make it extremely difficult to transfer shopping activities to Broadmead at a later date.[65]

Not surprisingly, the city engineer's report to the PRC on this conference was very pessimistic. The ministry's earlier guidance 'to plan boldly and to take broad steps to bring land for redevelopment into public ownership was no longer the policy to be followed'; Treasury interests rather than planning interests were 'going to control any action that could be taken locally in the immediate future', and 'because of this there would be no great enthusiasm at London level to approve any plan for the central area at this stage, but rather to play a delaying action by raising point after point, each involving further research, further plans, and further discussions'; moreover, all of the London representatives of the ministry were entirely new appointees who 'had given very little thought to the Bristol proposals, [and] apparently knew very little of Bristol local conditions, and quite frankly ... seemed to know very little of local government administration and requirements'. The city engineer thus concluded that, unless further discussions changed the ministry's opinions:

> ... any material progress ... will be put in cold storage for an indefinite period, leaving the Planning and Reconstruction Committee with the hopeless job of dealing with interim development applications meeting by meeting with no understanding as to what is finally going to be approved and therefore with no certainty that the decisions they may make are right or wrong.[66]

No particular progress was made, however, between the officials of the corporation and the ministry, and the latter insisted on holding a public inquiry into the two compulsory orders despite the corporation's request for expedited procedure.[67] Officers of the corporation wondered why a further inquiry into the area covered by the confirmed declaratory order was necessary, only to come to the conclusion that it was due to pressure from the Treasury so as to delay the spending of the money, and to ministerial opposition to the council's proposal for the old shopping centre.[68]

Several difficult decisions had to be made. First, should the PRC adhere to the original proposals for the Broadmead area and the Wine Street/Castle Street area? If so, the ministry had intimated that temporary shops should definitely be built on the Broadmead area and not the old shopping centre. Local traders, however, agreed to the new shopping centre on the conditions that the acquisition of the old centre should proceed quickly and that the latter area should be developed for temporary purposes. The idea of municipally controlled temporary shops in the Wine Street/Castle Street area could meet the traders' second condition very well. If, however, the PRC were to accept the ministry's proposal of temporary shops in Broadmead, in view of the ministry's recent policy with regard to land acquisition, the Wine Street/Castle Street area would have to be left sterilized for a long time, unless appropriate temporary use other than shopping was proposed. Moreover, should such a situation arise, many traders might make planning appeals directly to the minister against the council's refusal of permission for interim development, which in theory could only be dismissed by him on the grounds that the land was to be acquired by the local authority. Such private 'temporary' shops could easily be constructed in permanent form, thus obstructing the area's ultimate use. In any case, the willingness of the interests concerned to support the council's plan was 'now suffering a very distinct setback', being replaced by a 'mood of bewilderment and frustration' with a feeling that 'there is such a complete lack of confidence between the local planning interests and the Minister that nothing practical is likely to emerge for some considerable time'.[69]

The PRC, anticipating the need to abandon the Castle Street/Wine Street temporary shops proposal, still decided in July 1947 to adhere to the principle that the old shopping centre should be reserved for the ultimate provision of civic and semi-civic buildings. A deputation was also appointed which, together with local MPs, was to meet the minister.[70] At the meeting, the minister tried hard to encourage the council. On the one hand, he had to emphasize the difficulties that he was facing, such as the High Court appeals, Treasury influence and traders' appeals against the council's refusal to permit interim development. Although the council had repeatedly asked for his approval of the city centre plan, he could not give it at present. At the same time, he stated that on broad issues he supported the council, and that with regard to the location of the shopping centre in particular, if the council were determined, 'then he would bow to their view'.[71]

Overall, the PRC seemed to be fairly encouraged, for, soon after the meeting, they decided to submit formally to the minister the city centre plan for approval, and to request him to proceed with the proposed public inquiry into the compulsory orders.[72] In August 1947, the committee decided to abandon entirely the Castle Street/Wine Street temporary shops proposal. Instead, temporary shops would be built on the new Broadmead shopping centre site. The old shopping centre was to be used in the short term for such purposes as car parking, temporary warehousing, offices and motor repair garages.[73] It was thought that those using the area for such temporary purposes would bring in an appreciable financial return pending that time when the area could be used for more permanent purposes, and would be of considerable assistance in supporting the committee's refusal to allow shops in the area.[74]

By this time, local objections to the city centre plan seemed to be confined to a few particular interest groups and the council were confident that the majority of traders supported their plan.[75] At first sight, this looked justifiable. The multiple traders' agreement to the new shopping centre had long been known. The public inquiry in August 1947 into the compulsory orders reassured the PRC that 'the traders were generally disposed to support the City Council' as to the Broadmead shopping centre proposal.[76] The support of the retailers' advisory committee on town planning for the new shopping centre had gradually been restored,[77] and in October 1947 the advisory committee appointed a panel to discuss the layout of the Broadmead shopping centre with the PRC.[78] Furthermore, two decisions were taken by important interest groups at this time which worked in favour of the council. In June 1947, the chamber of commerce decided not to proceed with its proposed High Court appeal against the whole declaratory order of 245 acres, in the main due to a fear of delaying still further the rebuilding of the city.[79] In the same month, the replanning association, appeased by the reduced declaratory order and suffering from tight finances, decided to disband itself and amalgamate with the civic society.[80]

There was, however, one particular group of traders whose persistent objection to the new Broadmead shopping centre proposal continued to cause the council trouble, i.e. the Bristol Retail Traders' Federation, a group representing the small traders and which had resigned from the

Bristol Retailers' Advisory Committee on Town Planning as the latter moved towards acceptance of the corporation's plan.[81] In October 1946, the federation put forward to the PRC their alternative proposal based on the Wine Street/Castle Street area – a riverside shopping centre with tiers of some 281 shops bounded at different levels by three new roads for traffic and pedestrians.[82] When the PRC rejected it in January 1947,[83] the federation organized a poll on the question of the shopping centre, which showed some 13 000 people preferred the reinstatement of the old shopping centre, and only 400 wished to have the new centre.[84] Labour, provoked to anger by this, made a strongly worded public statement attacking the federation. It read:

> The so-called poll is without any official sanction and can carry no weight. The slipshod, inefficient and utterly undemocratic methods by which it is being conducted are reminiscent of Hitler's early efforts in political demagogy.[85]

The federation held on, and in August 1947 met a sub-committee of the PRC. They insisted that the PRC should hold a poll to decide the site of the shopping centre, only to be told by Alderman Bicker, the committee's chairman, that the decision had been made and that it would be abided by.[86]

Meanwhile, the minister had failed to respond either to the corporation's application for compulsory orders or its submission of the city centre plan. By the spring of 1948, there was a growing feeling that the city had had a 'raw deal', in that reconstruction had been delayed by the minister and much shopping trade had been lost and initiative been discouraged.[87] A Bristol MP, W. Goldrick (Labour), asked Silkin if he was aware of the anxiety felt in the city at the lack of progress in reconstruction.[88] In May 1948, Alderman Bicker remarked in front of Miss E.A. Sharp, deputy secretary of the ministry, that town planning 'has been a nightmare' and deplored the suspicion among the blitzed local authorities that others had found favour with the ministry while they had 'gone away with a barren bone'.[89] In fact, the minister granted a token confirmation of the compulsory orders – for a mere four and a half acres in the Broadmead area. As Alderman Bicker reminded the council 'in a sudden and effective burst of cynicism ... Christopher Wren's plan for London had been defeated by expediency, and that – briefly – they had learned that lesson'.[90]

Moreover, the traders had become tired of waiting for the Broadmead shopping centre plan to materialize and were increasingly anxious about the volume of trade being funnelled away from the city to Bath. In July 1948, the retailers' advisory committee on town planning, who had been in support of the new shopping centre, eventually advised all its members formerly in the Wine Street/Castle Street area to apply at once to the council for temporary shops.[91] This compelled the PRC to ask the minister to back the council.[92] The council had refused the traders' applications for temporary shops on the grounds that it would prejudice the development of the Broadmead shopping precinct.[93] The traders then made planning appeals to the minister, which he dismissed one after another. It was regarded as a clear indication of his approval of the new shopping centre.[94] The minister's refusal resulted in the traders serving notices on the council to buy their land in the former shopping centre. Section 19 of the Town and Country Planning Act 1947, said that an owner of land who proved to the minister that refusal to allow him to develop his land had rendered it incapable of reasonably beneficial use could compel the corporation to buy it. By July 1949, the minister had confirmed six of 58 such notices, and it was expected that he would ultimately confirm them all.[95] Although the financial implications of the purchase of the whole area were considerable – it was estimated that it would cost about £5 million – the PRC were 'still unanimous in their belief and determination to go ahead with the Broadmead scheme', and the council adopted the committee's recommendations to borrow £1.75 million in the first instance from the Ministry of Health towards the purchase and to use the land for a car park, temporary offices and warehouses, etc., but no temporary shops.[96]

In October 1949, the PRC decided to begin negotiations with the traders regarding the terms of leases in the Broadmead shopping centre,[97] and in December it was announced that the first steel allocation from the government would enable them to erect the first shop in that area,[98] which was eventually built by the corporation itself and opened in 1951. Multiple shops and department stores such as Woolworth, Marks & Spencer, and John Lewis's followed, and with them as magnets, individual traders as well as shoppers were gradually attracted to this new centre. The re-siting of the shopping centre was later described as 'the most radical movement of a shopping centre proposed in the post war years' and 'undoubtedly a clear success' from the planning and commercial viewpoints.[99] Some credit for the success should go to the council's determination. As the Labour mayor proudly claimed in 1949:

> ... it might have been that some weaker-minded Councils, faced with grievous difficulties and frustrations, might have deviated from their bold plan. But we have felt it better, in spite of all criticism, to wait until we could re-develop our city in the way we wanted. Members of the present City Council are dogged pioneers, just like the Bristol pioneers of old.[100]

To Alderman Bicker, chairman of the PRC since 1945, it was a quite different story. As a result of municipal elections in May 1949, representation in the council was again split between Labour and the Citizen Party.[101] Consequently, Labour had to drop three aldermen, and Bicker was one of those not renominated.[102] He reckoned that this decision revealed the party's opinion of his 'independent' attitude and opposition to the government's reconstruction policy and he resigned from the Labour Party in protest. As chairman of the PRC, he went on, he had had every reason 'consistently to attack Whitehall' for causing delays and difficulties, but:

> I have had little or no support from the Labour members on that
> committee. Their docile attitude was to me alarming. I believe
> protests such as mine have been justified by the results of the recent
> council elections throughout the country.[103]

It seemed that his critical attitude towards the Ministries of Town and
Country Planning and of Transport[104] was too much for the majority of the
local Labour Party who, admittedly patient on town planning issues, chose
to put housing, education and health services at the top of the list.[105] Even
in 1961, when the Broadmead shopping centre was thriving, there was
persistent concern among local interests about the future of the Wine
Street/Castle Street area, which had served largely as a car park for the
past 20 years, and the call for an outside planning consultant of national
standing remained.[106] Thus, although the minister's dismissal of traders'
planning appeals for temporary shops in the original shopping centre acted
as his *de facto* approval of the council's proposals, it clearly was not as decisive as it could have been, had he granted the *de jure* approval which the
council longed for, and Silkin himself at one time very much wanted to
give. It seemed that the approval of a city centre plan was out of the question. We now turn our attention to Coventry's plan, which the ministry had
always wished to curtail.

*   *   *

Coventry's determination to go ahead with its city centre plan continued
after the successful public inquiry in the summer of 1946. The situation
faced by Coventry was no better than that of other cities – the corporation's housing list had nearly 11 000 applications in April 1947,[107] while
the acute shortage of building labour was repeatedly pointed out.[108] Yet
the council once again quickly responded to an opportunity to celebrate
symbolically the start of reconstruction. In October 1946, the Dutch
National Committee offered the city flowering shrubs as an expression of
the Netherlands' gratitude for their liberation in 1945. Although the Dutch
were extremely anxious that the flowers should be in bloom the following
summer, the CRC jumped at the chance to commence the Broadgate
garden, an island square 212 × 140 feet at the top of the shopping precinct,
which until now existed only on paper.[109] Corporation officers worked with
enthusiasm[110] in the face of opposition from the government departments
concerned,[111] and in May 1947 the Dutch Embassy officially handed over
8000 bulbs and shrubs. Unfortunately, the garden island was still under
construction, but the ceremony only served to strengthen the expectation
of completion.[112]

A week later, the city was informed that the minister would confirm the
declaratory order. The local reaction to this news reflected the hopes and
confidence so far raised in the city centre plan after the war. Even though
it was nearly a year since the public inquiry,[113] and the area to be developed had been reduced from 452 to 274 acres,[114] the council were, as the

town clerk put it, 'highly pleased with the outcome of years of negotiations with Government departments'. The fact that the order covered the core area including the shopping, business and civic centres, was regarded as 'The City's Charter of Reconstruction' in that 'the "Dream City" of Coventry, which up to now has been a matter of drawing-board plans executed by Town Planning experts will, after all be translated into bricks and mortar'.[115] The right-wing *Coventry Standard*, agreeing that there should be 'no physical handicap to the building of the modern city visualised by idealists', also reaffirmed (as they did at the public inquiry of 1946) that:

> In some respects it will mean a serious and maybe unpalatable infringement on the rights of private business and individual desires, but it is impossible to conceive a new Coventry without this concession being made to communal development.[116]

In May 1948, the Broadgate garden was completed and Princess Elizabeth laid the foundation stone of the shopping precinct. As she observed at the opening ceremony:

> ... if the spirit which the citizens of Coventry showed on the night of November 14th, 1940, can be reborn in the hearts of our people today, then we shall indeed see the fruits of peace. They will be far richer and far more plentiful than we have found the fruits of victory to be ... The old Broadgate was the heart of Coventry, and, as is usual with things we have always known, I am sure you had a great affection for it. But in this century new and prosperous industries have found their homes in Coventry, and the town had outgrown its ancient centre. I hope that before many years I shall come back to this place where we now stand to find a new Broadgate, as fine as modern taste and craftsmanship can build it, and worthy of the great city of which it will be the centre ... Let us be sure that in ourselves, and in the personal effort which the times demand from each one of us, there is to be found the same spirit of enterprise which is rebuilding Coventry and the other towns of Great Britain, a spirit alive to the great opportunities of our day.[117]

As the *Coventry Evening Telegraph* put it, 'Royal recognition to Coventry's post-war achievements and aspirations' was thus given.[118]

Around this time, the council decided to make a start on the first phase of reconstruction in the shopping precinct. The construction of five blocks was proposed on the understanding that the main prospective tenants were to act as the developers, to whom leases would then be offered by the council. The city architect was given the final say as to the designs, elevations and materials to be used. At the same time, the council reserved the power to carry out development themselves in cases of difficulties.[119] As negotiations with the developers progressed various difficulties indeed arose.[120] In the case of 'Block B', for instance, the development companies could not agree to build a connecting bridge over Hertford Street, which the council regarded as an architectural feature of prime importance, and in the end they decided to build it themselves.[121] In May 1949, the CRC authorized the compulsory purchase of land to form the first instalment of the College of Adult Education, a building the Ministry of Town and Country Planning had thought least necessary.[122]

It should be noted, however, that behind the firmly established general approval of the city centre plan, the assertion by civil servants that it should be drastically modified did not lie down and die. For one thing, they never took to the 'lavish scale' of the civic centre; it was 'out of proportion for the stated number and type of public buildings to be erected and wholly disproportionate to other uses within the central area', leaving a strong concern about the 'financial implications of such an extensive use of highly valued land'. What is more, the ministry maintained that the inner ring road should contain only the area to constitute the city centre proper. In this respect, the western section of the proposed alignment was 'too wedded to the idea of achieving a ring'.[123] Instead, it should follow the existing Queen Victoria Road so as to tightly circumscribe the shopping precinct, and until this matter had been settled between the corporation and the Ministry of Transport, general approval of the redevelopment of the city centre, which the council repeatedly requested, was out of the question.[124]

The council argued that the ministry's ideas for Queen Victoria Road would set too rigid a western limit to city centre redevelopment. It was planned as a main shopping street, with the likely future expansion of the shopping precinct into it.[125] Moreover, the Ministry of Transport had been of the opinion that they could not settle the question without the Ministry of Town and Country Planning and the local authority agreeing as to the final redevelopment plans for the city centre,[126] an argument which was, as one official put it, 'liable to get us nowhere'.[127] Eventually, in May 1949, the ministry agreed that if there were shops in Queen Victoria Road and if they were essential, then it could not be used as part of the inner ring road, and thus the council's proposed alignment had to be accepted. To the council's further satisfaction, the ministry at last decided to approve the city centre plan, 'so that Coventry could have some confidence that in proceeding with redevelopment they were on the right lines'.[128]

In July 1949, the council received a letter stating that the minister had agreed that their plan for that area within the proposed inner ring road should be accepted as the basis for redevelopment.[129] As Hodgkinson put it, they were 'glad' because 'some of the hesitations which might have marked our progress will disappear ... knowing that the Minister gives full approval' of 'the ambitious programme which Coventry has set for itself'. They were not, however, at all carried away at this news. As he went on: 'We must move forward step by step to avoid the financial problem which might arise if we were to take too big a bite at the task at one time.'[130]

While his comments reflect in general how difficult the first phase of city centre redevelopment after the war had been, what he did not stress (though he may not have realized) was that Coventry was almost certainly the only city to obtain the minister's formal approval of city centre redevelopment before the construction of permanent buildings commenced at the end of the 1940s. It was an extremely difficult period for those towns and cities which had experienced heavy bombing, for ministry officials were most reluctant to approve any plan. For Coventry, however, it seemed that its battle with the ministry was already over by the end of the war. The local authority in Coventry felt that it had made enough concessions, and that it would be able to use its experience of dealing with civil servants when undertaking the plan. The council knew how it should start the actual redevelopment in accordance with the minister's policy – shopping facilities and commercial enterprise.[131] While a comparatively good relationship held between the ministry and the council in terms of the replanning of the shopping centre,[132] the council took every opportunity it had to highlight the support of the general public for its city centre plan as a whole, which culminated in the visit of the Princess Elizabeth in May 1948, confirming that there was no turning back. Under such a situation, the minister's approval of the plan was inevitable.

As the implementation of the bold plan gradually took shape, its boldness was again praised as 'a feather in Coventry's cap'.[133] The buildings erected by the corporation itself – including the problematic 'Block B' and the public buildings in the civic centre – were regarded as architecturally the most interesting buildings.[134] Reviews by specialists in the early 1960s, after the sharp change in architectural fashion and standards, were still favourable to Coventry.[135] Commercially, the shopping precinct became a great success, especially with the advent of the multiples in the mid-1950s, such as Woolworths, Marks & Spencer, Owen Owen, and British Home Stores. There, Gibson's original idea of a traffic-free precinct was restored thanks to his no less enthusiastic successor, Arthur Ling.[136] This dream city, envisaged by imaginative and devoted planners and whole-heartedly supported by local leaders and the general public through difficult times, was built despite central government's attempts to impose restraint and modesty.

nine

Conclusion

War created both opportunities for, and obstacles to, the redevelopment of city centres. By comparing the experiences of Bristol, Coventry and Southampton, it has been possible to throw some light on these contradictory effects of the war. While all three councils recognized that the bombing had provided a golden opportunity for comprehensive replanning, their initial responses were strikingly different.

Coventry took the swiftest action. Established within a fortnight of the November 1940 blitz, the city's redevelopment committee sent a deputation to Lord Reith in January 1941. He told them to plan boldly. In March 1941, the city council rejected a rather conservative plan proposed by the city engineer, in favour of an imaginative one prepared by D. Gibson, the young city architect. The sheer speed of the council's action showed their determination – especially that of George Hodgkinson, Labour and council leader who initiated the deputation – to grab the opportunity and make the best of it. The city was further inspired by the nationwide publicity given to the plan, because it became a symbol of post-war reconstruction in general. At the same time, the ideas incorporated in the plan were not produced on the spur of the moment. Discussion about a new city centre had been going on both within and without the council before the outbreak of war. Gibson and his staff had produced an impressive model, a prototype of the 1941 plan, which had already attracted considerable attention before the 1940 blitz.

In Southampton, the Ratepayers' Party – with a majority on the council – was in favour of the quick redevelopment of the heavily damaged main shopping area. The loss of rateable value was indeed severe. Councillor Matthews, deputy Labour leader, was anxious to prevent rash action. First, the town's future had to be thought of in a wider context than merely aiming at a swift recovery of trade. Its industrial prospects were of prime importance, which had to be seen both from a regional and a national point of view. Secondly, the council's inadequate planning personnel had to be strengthened by outside consultants. In these respects, his efforts bore fruit fairly rapidly. An independent department and committee for planning had been set up by early 1942, while the council, on the advice of Lord Reith, decided in August 1941 to employ Professor Adshead as planning consultant. In February 1942, Adshead and H.T. Cook, newly promoted town planning officer – through the backing of Matthews – submitted their joint plan to the council.

Bristol City Council's approach to the replanning of the city centre was very different. First, they denied press reports in early 1941 that Lord Reith had told them to prepare a bold plan. Instead, they stressed the need for a preliminary survey, despite pressure from those interests who wished to get on with the job. Moreover, shaping the machinery for this task took a long time. The planning and reconstruction committee was set up in December 1942, and it was not until February 1943 that the ultimate responsibility for the preparation of a city centre plan was given to H.M. Webb, the city engineer. At the same time, particular emphasis was placed on the teamwork of those officers concerned, and any replanning proposals were considered through the 'conference of officers' system set up in August 1941. The plan for the city centre was finally submitted to the city council in March 1944.

The plans adopted by the councils during the war proposed drastic solutions to problems in city centres – traffic congestion, mixed usage, and the lack of social amenities or focal points of public life. An inner ring road would divert through traffic from the central core, which would be divided into sections according to function, so as to avoid the mixing of the various users. Both in Bristol and Coventry, the existing main shopping streets were to be replaced by a traffic-free shopping precinct, while in Southampton the second shopping centre, a shopping promenade, was proposed at the intersection of main traffic routes. In Bristol, the existing main shopping streets were to be reserved for public purposes; in Coventry, a civic centre was envisaged, combining administrative, cultural and educational buildings; and in Southampton, the new shopping promenade and the existing civic centre would constitute the town centre, a focal point of public life. In these plans, the planners were not too concerned about the existing layout or possible costs. The important underlying assumptions were that the defects in the city centres would be cured only by drastic surgery, and that the government would, as Lord Reith promised, do their utmost to facilitate such surgery.

*   *   *

These bold proposals, however, provoked opposition both from local interests and from the ministries concerned. The three councils reacted to this opposition in very different ways. In Southampton, local traders were particularly critical of the shopping promenade because it would be too competitive with the existing main shopping street. The Ministry of Transport also objected because it would be dangerous to pedestrians. The council, controlled by a coalition of Conservatives and Liberals, was receptive to these criticisms. The idea was abandoned in the revised plan of February 1943, which placed prime emphasis on the improvement of the existing main shopping street. The offer of Adshead to continue his service as a consultant was turned down by the council in January 1943.

In Bristol, the council, equally represented by the Labour and the Citizen Parties, took pains to conciliate the local interests concerned. On the initiative of the chamber of commerce, a replanning association was formed as early as February 1941 with a view to being directly involved in the replanning process. It included not only traders but also architects who had established reputations in the field. This body had considerable influence. Extensive consultation took place between the local authority and interested parties about various replanning proposals. The most controversial point was that the existing main shopping area based on Castle Street/Wine Street was to be reserved as a public open space, and to be replaced by a new shopping centre at Broadmead. Fierce objections were raised and the council compromised providing temporary shops in the Castle Street/Wine Street area and scheduling it as an area for public buildings rather than an open space. At the same time, the council adhered to its original proposal for a new shopping centre. The council stood resolute against opponents who wished to re-establish the old shopping centre. It should also be noted that the requests for the co-option of outside members onto the council's planning committee and for the employment of an outside planning consultant were successfully resisted.

The opposition of traders to the city centre plan did not cause Coventry City Council much concern at first. In fact, the council did not bother to discuss the plan with them for a long time because, as they argued, it had already been adopted and simply awaited ministerial approval. The ministry, however, turned out to be the council's most formidable opponent. Whitehall's criticisms were two-fold. First, the plan was made up in undue haste and there was a serious lack of consultation between the local authority and the local interest groups concerned. Secondly, certain proposals, especially the shopping precinct and the civic centre, were too imaginative to be brought into effect. The Ministry soon found that the town clerk was also rather hostile to Gibson's city centre plan. With his co-operation, immense pressure was placed on the council to begin consultation and to modify the plan along more modest lines. This pressure worked to some extent, and in early 1944, the first meeting was held between the city council and the chamber of commerce to discuss the scheme, focusing especially on the proposals for the shopping centre. The chamber maintained that the shopping centre should be constituted of the main shopping streets together with access for traffic rather than a traffic-free precinct, wiping out the existing layout. The council made some compromises in that the precinct should apply to a limited portion of the whole shopping frontages, and that a traffic route should be allowed to intersect the precinct. But the council insisted on the principle of a precinct, especially with regard to the Smithford Street area, the city's principal shopping street, and it claimed that the demands of the retail interests had been sufficiently met by these compromises. Although the Ministry wished to curtail what they saw as another extravagant proposal, i.e. the civic centre, the council never let them take the offensive in this matter.

In putting pressure on Coventry, the ministry had to keep a low profile. In face of the call for swift and positive action by the government, its response was very slow and evasive, causing doubts as to the genuineness of its early encouragement to plan boldly. Expert opinions were, as the fate of the ministry's panels showed, not utilized as much as had been initially intended. Decisions as to a central planning authority and the legislation for built-up areas were delayed and, when made, increasingly limited in scope and nature. Although the ministry, especially its officials, always maintained that the Coventry plan lacked public support, and wished to curtail its boldness on the grounds of practicability, their attack had to be made behind the scenes. Even the town clerk – the 'cat's paw' of the ministry – reported that the plan actually enjoyed substantial support among the citizens of Coventry. It would have been very embarrassing to the ministry if, by criticizing Coventry's plan explicitly, the impression was confirmed both within and without Coventry that the ministry and the government were really trying to suppress the aspirations of those authorities whose towns and cities had been severely damaged.

In contrast, progress in Southampton was along lines quite acceptable from the ministry's point of view. The local authority employed a consultant in the preparation of a plan, discussed it with the interest groups and ministries concerned, and modified it in order to meet any criticisms. Moreover, consideration in a wider context – among other things the town's industrial future – was given by Councillor Matthews' Nuffield Reconstruction Survey.

The rather pessimistic conclusions of this survey made him opt at the end of the war for a new plan prepared by the borough engineer, who had emphasized the economy and practicability of the plan, and thus, the full use of the existing layout. Following this retreat from bold planning, the local Labour Party concentrated on the quick restoration of the town's main shopping street and the municipal ownership of land in the city centre, which was opposed by local traders and the opposition party. Labour won the 1945 municipal elections, and the new plan was adopted by the council in March 1946. H.T. Cook, town planning officer, resigned and soon joined an opposition organization, the Central Area Association, set up in April 1946. Bristol did not present serious problems to the ministry during the war, partly because the plan appeared very late, but mainly because extensive consultations were undertaken with local interest groups and there was no real political conflict among councillors or corporation officials.

*   *   *

The first important phase of post-war city centre redevelopment consisted of public inquiries into local authority applications for municipal acquisition of war-damaged areas under the Town and Country Planning Act 1944. The plans were regarded as supporting evidence for such acquisition. In practice, it was thought that these inquiries held in 1946 would be a last opportunity to lodge objections to these plans. Generally, the councils managed to defend their plans. This was primarily because the substance of any objections – mainly from vested interests – was related to the local authority's acquisition of private property. However, this principle had been established by the coalition government in the 1944 Planning Act, and thus had very little to do with the councils. The argument that the plans should not be accepted because of the objection to the acquisition based on them was, therefore, easily ruled out by the councils. The three councils – all of which were now controlled by Labour – expected substantial and swift progress to be made in city centre redevelopment under a Labour government. But with the new planning minister, Lewis Silkin, it was becoming more and more difficult to meet such high expectations. Economic considerations now played a vital role in the country's reconstruction and priority had to be given to certain essential items in the context of the acute shortage of necessary building labour and materials. City centre redevelopment had to give way, for one thing, to the provision of housing and schools. Consequently, Silkin (who was not a member of the Cabinet) had to cut back considerably on the amount of municipal land acquisition – the foundation work for city centre redevelopment – largely due to Treasury pressure. Subsequently, the country's worsening economic situation as from the summer of 1947 virtually eradicated any hope of commencing any city centre redevelopment.

Such a gloomy prospect made those authorities who had already drawn up a plan desperate for ministerial approval. In Southampton, there were strong feelings among those who had not been consulted during the drawing up of the new plan. In Bristol, the opposition of some traders to the re-siting of the shopping centre continued – if not worsened – despite the fact that the plan had been praised by Silkin on his visit to the city in early 1946. In order to clear up any objections to their plans and uncertainties and doubts as to their practicability, and thus to commence the actual redevelopment with confidence as soon as circumstances permitted, nothing could be more persuasive than the minister's formal authorization.

Silkin, however, emphasizing how important it was to start planning under the new Planning Act 1947, looked as if he was about to shelve any consideration of these advanced cases, i.e. those plans awaiting his formal approval. Apart from economic considerations which had to be obeyed, there were other reasons for his rather cautious attitude. The enthusiasm surrounding city centre replanning in the early years of the war had gradually withered away. The motto was now 'first things first'. The most essential thing now was better housing, and not ultra-modern city centres for those towns and cities which experienced the blitz. In this sense, the question of city centres had become a victim of what the Labour government pursued most vigorously, i.e. a more egalitarian society, explicitly shown in their efforts to create the welfare state.

There was also a marked tendency among ministry officials, most of whom were newcomers after the war and thus somewhat ignorant of the authorities' early efforts, to sit on the fence when considering local authorities' replanning proposals. They admitted unashamedly that they were overwhelmed by the magnitude of the task. Thus even in the case of Southampton, whose plan was no longer a bold one, ministry officials were never able to pass judgement, and remained bogged down with detailed technical matters, often confusing the situation by disagreeing with officials of the Ministry of Transport. In the case of Bristol, the civil servants were critical of the new shopping centre proposals, and yet never lent themselves earnestly to helping the local authority, which was battling against the fierce opposition of some traders and therefore in desperate need of formal approval. Not surprisingly, the relationship between the ministry and local authorities such as Bristol became rather tense and often a little hostile.

Given the situation and the climate of the time, the fact that the ministry approved Coventry's city centre plan in 1949 was perhaps surprising. The ministry wished to consider plans under the 1947 Planning Act, rather than the 1944 Act confined to war-damaged areas, so that every plan could be placed on an equal footing, whether the areas covered by it had been blitzed or not. These plans generally appeared in the early 1950s, though it took several more years before the approval of the ministry was obtained. In other words, when the construction of new permanent buildings commenced at the end of the 1940s in the three cities, only Coventry was following an authorized plan, and thus could be confident that they were moving in the right direction. What accounted for this approval? First was the nationwide publicity and the unique status the city had enjoyed for being the first city to prepare a plan immediately after the blitz. The ministry – because of Lord Reith's legendary encouragement to Coventry to plan boldly – was unable to pressurize Coventry into curtailing the city centre plan's imaginative features. Secondly, the city council had actually gained experience and confidence through dealing with ministry officials since the plan was first made public in 1941. Bristol and Southampton were bitter in their expression of the unfair treatment meted out to the bombed cities and they showed anger, disappointment and distrust of the ministry after the war, while opposition from local interest groups was still smouldering, and often becoming inflamed. Coventry no longer blamed the government; instead, once the war was over, Coventry Council took every opportunity to explain to the public that the plan had met all relevant criticisms. A public exhibition and ceremonies to mark the start of the plan's implementation were organized, attracting wide and sympathetic attention. The city centre plan thus became generally recognized. In Bristol and Southampton, the local authorities were content with claiming that their plans should be supported, simply because they were approved by the elected representatives of the people. This argument, however, was not enough to convince the ministry. As demonstrated in the case of Coventry during the war, ministry officials were very sensitive to the political repercussions of city centre replanning. Their criticisms of any plan were therefore subject to the level of public support for it. But it could be argued that, in fact, ordinary people were rather indifferent. They were very concerned about housing, jobs and welfare – subjects which were more directly tangible, and tended to dominate controversy during the municipal elections. Whereas the people had directly experienced the blitz, they felt remote from a paper plan for the future city centre. It was very technical, and was, as shown in the local authorities' consultation process and the public inquiries of 1946, an affair for vested interests and those with specialized knowledge. What was needed to arouse public interest was, therefore, a start to reconstruction, as in Coventry.

*   *   *

As this study has demonstrated, it was difficult after the Second World War to reach a consensus out of the myriad views of the new world order and how to undertake reconstruction. Even on a local level in Britain, there existed differences of opinion between officials, which often worked to adverse effect. At the same time, the unease of drastic change dictated the pace of the decision-making process. All three cities suffered opposition from the propertied and retailing interests and the timidity of the ministry. Southampton exemplified the case most clearly. They sacrificed their original plan with its progressive ideas and drawn up by planning experts, for the quick restoration of trade. The fact that Labour concentrated on the land acquisition issue in the municipal elections shows how influential the opposition was. Bristol approached its replanning with deliberate steps, especially in terms of extensive consultation with the main interested parties. Yet when the plan was forwarded to the ministry, no final judgement was passed – merely a hint of scepticism. To these two cities, planning became a nightmare, and Whitehall began to dictate the proceedings.

In this sense, the efforts of Coventry to obtain public support were of utmost importance. From the beginning, the council was determined to grab the opportunity provided by the blitz to undertake extensive reconstruction. At the same time, however, it should be asked whether the blitz, and the war in general, provided the ideal circumstances for the replanning of city centres. The bombing had certainly destroyed those otherwise untouchable jumbles of buildings that had grown up in the heart of British cities, and it had drawn attention to the problems that existed there and which had hitherto been neglected. However, the opportunity seems to have presented itself too suddenly.

It became increasingly clear that people would find it difficult to accept the drastic changes proposed by town planning experts. The thoughts of the government, and of civil servants in particular, were coloured by convention. And the public at large had more mundane problems to worry about both during and after the war – and without being fully informed and given the opportunity for serious participation, they certainly would not commit themselves. However, neither the professional organizations associated with town planning nor the local authorities (except Coventry) made any particular efforts to involve the public at large. The experts' belief in technocracy and the local authorities' belief that they represented the public were, therefore, rather ill-placed.

Moreover, the war gave rise to too many reconstruction problems, which induced the government to restrict the influence of local authorities over the replanning process. In view of the strictly limited resources, and of the ever deteriorating economic situation of the country in the 1940s, it was essential to make priorities. Labour placed emphasis on an export drive – even if it were to harm balanced industrial development – and on the creation of the welfare state in accordance with its 'fair shares' philosophy. The implementation of the Beveridge Report became the litmus test for the government's achievements, and later attracted the warmest of public approval. At the same time, city centre redevelopment was brought to a standstill. It now became the priority of those local authorities whose towns and cities had been severely damaged by wartime bombing to have the ministry approve their plans; however, civil servants in particular were not prepared to do so.

The case of Coventry, therefore, was an exceptional one. To its credit, the local authority involved the public as much as possible; however, its serious lack of consultation with local interest groups in the early planning stages may have backfired if there had been an influential local traders' organization as in Bristol. In terms of industrial development after the war, Coventry Council had very little say. Coventry continued to grow in importance as an engineering city, thus complying with government post-war policy, especially in terms of the export drive and Korean War rearmament. This, in effect, exempted the council from taking the city's industrial future into consideration, in contrast with Southampton, where fears that the city's economic base would not be sufficient to sustain a bold plan for the reconstruction of the city centre came to play an important part.

At the same time, because of the pressure from Whitehall to enhance Coventry's existing industrial base, the city inevitably failed to diversify its industrial structure, or to control its population growth. Ironically, Southampton expanded its industrial base, mainly due to new developments in industries such as oil refining, telephone and cables, and the construction of light commercial vehicles.

There was no coherent national planning policy in the 1940s. City centre replanning proceeded largely independently of other considerations in reconstruction work. The decision-making process involved a three-way negotiation between local authorities, local vested interests and central government. Generally, the public at large played little part in the planning process, while the advice of outside experts was often not adhered to. By the time the war was over, city centre redevelopment was no longer given the high priority it once was, and it continued to suffer setbacks because of the difficult post-war economic climate. The war, it seems, created as many obstacles to the comprehensive replanning of city centres as it provided opportunities, before a more firmly established consensus on the need for such replanning could be made.

Notes

Series editor's introduction

1 A. Reid, 'World War I and the working class in Britain', in A. Marwick (ed.), *Total war and social change* (London, 1988), pp. 16–24.
2 M. Pugh, *Electoral reform in war and peace, 1906–1918* (London, 1978); S.S. Holton, *Feminism and democracy: Women's suffrage and reform politics in Britain, 1900–1918* (Cambridge, 1986).
3 H.L. Smith (ed.), *British feminism in the twentieth century* (Aldershot, 1990).
4 J. Stevenson and C. Cook, *The Slump: Society and politics during the Depression* (London, 1979).
5 P. Summerfield, 'Women, war and social change: Women in Britain in World War II', in A. Marwick (ed.), op. cit., note 1, pp. 95–118; P. Thane, 'Towards equal opportunities? Women in Britain since 1945', in A. O'Day and T. Gourvish (eds), *Britain since 1945* (London, 1991).
6 This is discussed in A. Marwick, 'Introduction', in A. Marwick (ed.), op. cit., note 1, pp. x–xxi; and H.L. Smith (ed.), *War and social change: British society in the Second World War* (Manchester, 1986).
7 Ibid.
8 J. Stevenson, 'Planner's moon? The Second World War and the planning movement', in H.L. Smith (ed.), op. cit., note 6, pp. 58–77.
9 C. Barnett, *The audit of war* (London, 1986).
10 N. Tiratsoo, *Reconstruction, affluence and Labour politics: Coventry 1945–60* (London, 1990).
11 Ibid.; B. Lancaster and T. Mason (eds), *Life and labour in a twentieth century city: The experience of Coventry* (1986).

Chapter 1: Introduction

1 See, for example, W.W. Ashworth, *The genesis of modern British town planning* (London, 1954); G.E. Cherry, *The evolution of British town planning* (London, 1974). Important background information is also to be found in J.B. Cullingworth, *Town and country planning in Britain* (London, 1982); P. Hall, *Urban and regional planning* (London, 1982) and *Cities of tomorrow* (Oxford, 1990); E. Reade, *British town and country planning* (Milton Keynes, 1987). S. Buder, *Visionaries and planners: The Garden City Movement and the modern community* (Oxford, 1990), gives an informative account of the subject. See also G.E. Cherry (ed.), *Pioneers in British town planning* (London, 1981), who presents a background to nine important personalities, including F.J. Osborn.

2 See, for example, L. Silkin, 'The nation's land', *Fabian Research Series* (1943), **6** (70); Nuffield College Social Reconstruction Survey, *Britain's town and country planning pattern* (London, 1943).

3 P. Abercrombie and J.H. Forshaw, *County of London plan* (London, 1943), pp. 3–5.

4 A. Marwick, 'Middle opinion in the thirties', *English Historical Review* (1964), April, p. 285. See also J. Stevenson, 'Planner's moon? The Second World War and the planning movement', in H.L. Smith (ed.), *War and social change: British society in the Second World War* (Manchester, 1986), pp. 58–77.

5 *Report of the Royal Commission on Geographical Distribution of the Industrial Population (The Barlow Report)* (Cmd. 6153, London, 1941).

6 See, for example, F.J. Osborn, *Transport, town development and territorial planning of industry* (London, 1934), esp. pp. 27–33 regarding a National Industrial and Commercial Siting Board.

7 For example, A. Tripp's ideas on precincts were published in *Road traffic and its control* (London, 1938). T. Sharp's influential work, *Town and country planning*, was already finished, although it appeared in 1940 (Penguin, London).

8 A. Ravetz, *Remaking cities* (London, 1980), ch. 1; L. Esher, *A broken wave: The rebuilding of England 1940–1980* (Pelican edn, Harmondsworth, 1983), ch. 1.

9 J.B. Cullingworth, *Environmental planning 1939–1969, Vol. 1: Reconstruction and land use planning 1939–1947* (London, 1975).

10 See, for example, P. Addison, *The road to 1945* (London, 1975); J.M. Lee, *The Churchill coalition, 1940–1945* (London, 1980); K.O. Morgan, *Labour in power 1945–1951* (Oxford, 1984); C. Barnett, *The audit of war* (London, 1986).

11 See, for example, K. Richardson, *Twentieth-century Coventry* (Coventry, 1972); G. Gregory, 'Coventry', in J. Holliday (ed.), *City centre redevelopment: A study of British city centre planning* (London, 1974); P. Johnson-Marshall, *Rebuilding cities* (Edinburgh, 1966).

12 Though see T. Mason and N. Tiratsoo, 'People, politics and planning: The reconstruction of Coventry's city centre, 1940–53', in J.M. Diefendorf (ed.), *Rebuilding Europe's bombed cities* (London, 1990) and N. Tiratsoo, *Reconstruction, affluence and Labour politics: Coventry 1945–60* (London, 1990) for two recent attempts to look at this thesis. These studies stress the importance of the local authority's efforts to mobilize public support for its city centre plan while under pressure from Whitehall.

Chapter 2: Development of reconstruction policy during the war

1 I.R.M. McCallum (ed.), *Physical planning* (London, 1945), p. 11.
2 Ibid., p. xi.
3 Ibid., p. xi.
4 This series was collected together in a book: F.J. Osborn (ed.), *Making plans* (London, 1943). The quotation in the text can be found on p. 10.
   The BBC approached the Ministry of Works and Buildings in January 1941 about broadcasting on reconstruction. An outline of a series was prepared by the BBC in July and, after intensive discussion between it and the ministry, broadcasting began in December 1941 and lasted 24 weeks. See HLG 71/1253, *Letter from A.H. Jenkins to E.S. Hill* (both officials of the ministry), 4 August 1942.
5 A. Ravetz, *Remaking cities* (London, 1980), p. 24.
6 Summarized reports of these conferences were published by Faber and Faber (London). See, for example: F.E. Towndrow (ed.), *Replanning Britain* (for the Oxford conference, March 1941); H. Bryant Newbold (ed.), *Industry and rural life* (for the Cambridge conference, March 1942); D. Tyerman (ed.), *Ways and means of rebuilding* (for the London conference, July 1943).
7 Published by Faber and Faber.
8 Published by Todd Publishing Co.
9 Royal Institute of British Architects (RIBA), *Rebuilding Britain* (London, 1943). The Architectural Press also published *Towards a new Britain* (London, 1943) for this exhibition. RIBA set up a reconstruction committee in March 1941; its first conclusions were published in *The Journal of the RIBA* (1942), **XLIV**.
10 F.J. Osborn (ed.), *Planning and reconstruction year book 1944–5* (London, 1945), pp. 238–47.
11 HLG 71/1570, Bombed areas – Redevelopment: Notes on Bristol, Birmingham, Coventry and Southampton by G.L. Pepler (Ministry of Health), 28 February 1941. This report was submitted to the third meeting of the Interdepartmental Committee of Officials on Reconstruction on 14 March 1941. See HLG 86/24.
12 J.B. Cullingworth, *Environmental planning 1939–1969, Vol. 1: Reconstruction and land use planning 1939–1947* (London, 1975), p. 59.
13 As for the Harrison Committee, see HLG 86/22 and 23, and CAB 117/114.
14 See A. Ravetz, op. cit., note 5, p. 20. As for this replacement, see also J.C.W. Reith, *Into the wind* (London, 1949), pp. 440–47.
15 As for personnel, see HLG 86/3, which contains a list of members.
16 The setting up of the panel was decided at the fourth meeting of the War Cabinet Committee on Reconstruction of Town and Country, 27 January 1941 (see CAB 87/21). However, John Anderson, Lord President of the Privy Council, insisted that the members of the Panel should be consulted individually and not as a body (HLG 86/5, *Letter to Lord Reith*, 5 April 1941). Despite the pressure, Reith, supported by his officials (see, for example, HLG 86/5, *Letter from Vincent to J.C.W. Reith*, 7 April 1941) was determined 'to choose the best method of working as we can go on' (HLG 86/5, *Letter to Anderson*, 8 April 1941) and held two meetings of the panel as a whole. As for these two meetings held on 23 April and 30 October 1941 and related papers, see HLG 86/8.
17 This developed into the suggestion to prepare a manual for local authorities on the technique of redevelopment in central urban areas, a draft of which was nearly completed by the panel's second meeting in October. See HLG 86/8, 'Note for the Minister before second meeting of 30/10/1941'.

18 While Vincent secured Lord Justice Scott as chairman of this group, he also proposed that it should be an independent committee rather than a group of the panel. See HLG 86/3, *Letter from Vincent to Whiskard* (Secretary of the Ministry), 4 September 1941. Accordingly, the Scott Committee was appointed in October 1941.

19 The decision was made as a result of a meeting of 1 August 1941 between Uthwatt and some other members of his committee, Sir Claud Schuster (Lord Chancellor's Office), T.D. Harrison and Vincent.

Outside members of the new group were L.H. Keay (City Architect and Director of Housing of Liverpool), H.J. Manzoni (City Engineer and Surveyor of Birmingham), D.A. Radley (Town Clerk of Leeds, and President of the Town Planning Institute), F.J. Osborn (Honorary Secretary to the Town and Country Planning Association), H. Chambers (Surveyor, acted for the Duchy of Cornwall), with J.W. Morris, K.C. as chairman. As for the group's two meetings and related papers, see HLG 86/27.

20 Argued by Manzoni.

21 Argued by Keay, who alternatively suggested pooling of ownership and a public redevelopment trust.

22 Argued by Chambers.

23 HLG 86/27, *Letter from G.L. Pepler to Vincent*, 29 October 1941.

24 HLG 86/27, *Letter from Vincent to Chambers*, 18 February 1942.

25 HLG 86/2, *Letter from Vincent to E.S. Hill*, 11 March 1942.

26 HLG 86/3, *Letter from F.J. Osborn to W.R.S. Harrison*, 23 March 1943.

27 HLG 71/1253, *Letter from A.M. Jenkins to E.S. Hill*, 4 August 1942.

28 Ibid.

29 *The Times*, 10 September 1942.

30 A special memorandum of the National Federation of Property Owners on the Uthwatt Report, cited in P. Pool and F. Stephenson, *A plan for town and country* (London, 1944), p. 42.

31 *Housing and planning after the war*, a report prepared for the party's annual conference of June 1943, p. 10. The report was based on an article by L. Silkin, 'The nation's land', *Fabian Research Series* (1943), **6** (70).

32 Later Herbert Morrison was to tell the party's 1945 conference the nationalization of land was not to be included in the party's immediate post-war programme. As he went on:

> Surely during this period – a period of first things first – as long as we have the power to purchase land at a fair price and expeditiously, as long as we can buy up the insufficient landowner in agricultural areas, that is enough for the time being, and the bigger project can follow later (*Labour Party Annual Report*, 1945, p. 91).

Some local authority representatives had been urging outright nationalization and often could not see eye to eye with the views held by the National Executive Committee (see, for example, *Labour Party Annual Report*, 1942, pp. 164–5; 1943, pp. 202–205; 1944, p. 201. As Lewis Silkin, the party's spokesman on town planning himself admitted at the 1945 conference, the party's policy regarding land was 'not altogether adequate', and said that he 'should therefore have welcomed a much bolder and more imaginative policy' (*Labour Party Annual Report*, 1945, p. 124).

33 *The Times*, 5 October 1943.

34 At the opening session of the National Housing and Town Planning Conference in London, 7 October 1943. *The Coventry Evening Telegraph* (hereafter *CET*).
35 See J.B. Cullingworth, op. cit., note 12, pp. 90–93.
36 HLG 88/8, *Letter from E.S. Hill to L. Neal*, 31 December 1942.
37 HLG 88/8, *Note from L. Neal to Whiskard*, 4 February 1943.
38 HLG 88/8, *Note by L. Neal* on a meeting held on 25 February 1943.
39 Members of the panel included:

> *Unofficial*: H. Chambers (Surveyor, acted for the Duchy of Cornwall), Col. M.D. Methven (North Eastern Trading Estate Ltd) and H.J. Manzoni (City Engineer and Surveyor, Birmingham).
> *MTCP*: G.L. Pepler, J.A. Stewart, H.W. Wells, A.M. Jenkins, with L. Neal as chairman.

40 HLG 88/9, 'Report of Advisory Panel on Redevelopment of City Centres' (hereafter 'Panel's Report'), 2 August 1944, para. 1. The terms of reference were based on Neal's note on the task of a Blitzed Cities Committee, 4 September 1942 (HLG 88/8).
41 HLG 88/9, Panel's Report, op. cit., note 40, para. 6.
42 Ibid.
43 For details, see J.B. Cullingworth, op. cit., note 12, ch. 4.
44 The minister in the broadcast on 19 November 1944, reported in *The Times*, 20 November 1944.
45 *The Times*, 25 October 1944.
46 G.D.H. Cole and R. Postgate, *The common people* (London, 1946), revised edn, p. 673.
47 HLG 88/9, Panel's Report, op. cit., note 40, para. 30.
48 Ibid., paras 50 and 78.
49 Ibid., paras 53–69.
50 Ibid., paras 81 and 82.
51 As for the panel's recommendations with regard to organization, ibid., section III, paras 83–109.
52 See letters from the local authorities and the ministry's regional planning officers to the ministry, HLG 88/15.
53 HLG 88/15, *Letter from H.J. Manzoni to L. Neal*, 13 April 1945.
54 See the debates over cottages *vs* high-rise flats in F.E. Towndrow (ed.), op. cit., note 6, pp. 91–111, 133, 155–64; D. Tyerman (ed.), op. cit., note 6, pp. 59–63; *passim* in the Minutes of the Housing and Town Planning Sub-committee of the Central Committee on Reconstruction of the Labour Party 1941–44.
55 See the acute criticism of planners in 'Report on propaganda for town planning (Report of talk given by Tom Harrisson at Housing Centre, London)', *Mass Observation File Report* (18 March 1942) no. 1162, pp. 4–6.
56 E.M. Nicholson, 'Democracy', in I.R.M. McCallum (ed.), op. cit., note 1, pp. 19–20. See also 'What people in Britain are thinking and talking about', *Mass Observation File Report* (March 1943), no. 1647, pp. 4–7.

Chapter 3: Bristol, Coventry and Southampton before the war and the impact of the bombing

1 The information under this heading is, unless otherwise stated, mostly derived from HLG 88/9, 'Notes preliminary to a visit to Bristol', 22 September 1943;

HLG 71/1270, Ministry of Town and Country Planning, 'Statistical register of 691 local authorities in England and Wales (A–K)', February 1946; HLG 82/28, Nuffield College Social Reconstruction Survey, 'Bristol area: Preliminary report on population and employment', October 1941, and 'South west area: Report on population and employment', November 1942. See also Bristol Corporation, *English city: The growth and the future of Bristol* (Bristol, 1945); B. Little, *The city and county of Bristol* (London, 1954); K. Brace, *Portrait of Bristol* (London, 1971); F. Walker, *The Bristol region* (London, 1972); C.M. MacInnes, *Bristol at war* (London, 1962); R. Whitfield, *The Labour movement in Bristol 1914–1939*, unpublished M.Litt. thesis, History Department, University of Bristol, 1982.

2 As for the election results, see e.g. *Western Daily Press*, 2 November 1938.

3 'Note of the Conference of Officers on Planning in Bristol and District and the duties of the officers engaged thereon', submitted to the Planning and Reconstruction Committee (hereafter PRC), 13 January 1943.

4 Report of the Special Sub-committee submitted to the PRC, 3 February 1943.

5 BRO 35510, Bristol Planning (No. 5) Scheme.

6 The information under this heading is, unless otherwise stated, mostly derived from HLG 88/9, 'Notes preliminary to a visit to Southampton', 9 June 1943; Nuffield College Social Reconstruction Survey, 'Interim Report on the Southampton area', June 1941, 'Summary of reports', July 1942, and 'Southampton regional report', December 1942. (HLG 82/13 and 14 and Nuffield College Library Box N.C.S.R.S., 'Area reports, Southampton reports'). See also A. Rance, *Southampton: An illustrated history* (Portsmouth, 1986); F.J. Monkhouse (ed.), *A Survey of Southampton and its region* (Southampton, 1964); B. Knowles, *Southampton – the English gateway* (London, 1951).

7 *The Southern Daily Echo* (hereafter *SDE*), 2 November 1938.

8 *SDE*, 22 February 1938.

9 D. R. Childs, 'Southampton', *The Architects' Journal* (1953), 16 April, p. 483.

10 HLG 88/9, 'Notes preliminary to a visit to Southampton', op. cit., note 6. For details about the civic centre, see also S. Kimber, *Thirty-eight years of public life in Southampton 1910–1948*, privately published (Southampton, 1949, ch. IV). Also, 'Civic Centre', a pamphlet at the Southampton City Records Office.

11 See H.T. Cook, 'Communications', in P. Ford (ed.), *Southampton: A civic survey*, a report of the Civic Survey Committee of the Southampton Civic Society (Oxford, 1931). See also HLG 88/9, 'Notes Preliminary ...', op. cit., note 6.

12 G.W.S. Robinson, 'The social pattern: The central district', in F.J. Monkhouse (ed.), op. cit., note 6.

13 SRO D/Mat/10/4, Reports of the Southampton Chamber of Commerce and the Southampton Civic Society, 'The re-planning of the lower part of the town', November 1934.

14 See, for example, SRO SC/EN/7/4/2, SRO SC/EN/13/5/2/1 and SRO SC/BA2/15.

15 See, *inter alia*: W. Lancaster and T. Mason (eds), *Life and Labour in a twentieth century city: The experience of Coventry* (Coventry 1986); F. Carr, 'Engineering workers and the rise of Labour in Coventry 1914–1939' (unpublished Ph.D. thesis, University of Warwick, 1979); K. Richardson, *Twentieth century Coventry*, (Coventry, 1972); J.A. Yates, *Pioneers to power* (Coventry, 1950); G. Hodgkinson, *Sent to Coventry* (Coventry, 1970).

The following materials of the Ministry of Town and Country Planning during the 1940s are also useful: HLG 71/1270, 'Statistical register of 691 local authorities', op. cit., note 1; HLG 88/9, 'Notes preliminary to a visit to Coventry', 2 July 1943.

16 *The Midland Daily Telegraph* (hereafter *MDT*), 21 December 1938.

17 *Coventry Standard* (hereafter *Standard*), 27 February 1937.

18 The city engineer pointed this out as early as 1912. See J.E. Swindlehurst, 'Town planning: A preliminary report', 26 February 1912, in the Local Studies Section of Coventry City Library.

19 For these two streets, see pamphlets in the Local Studies section of the Coventry City Library on the official openings of Corporation Street (1931) and Trinity Street (1937). See also *MDT*, 13 August 1937 and *Standard*, 18 September 1937.

20 *MDT*, 8 March 1937.

21 CRO Sec/CF/1/10625, report by the City Engineer and the Chief Constable to Traffic Joint Committee, 'Traffic in central Coventry', 26 January 1938.

22 See *The Coventry Herald*, 23 July 1938, about the overcrowded Council House.

23 See 'Report of Civic Centre Sub-committee', to the Estates and Parliamentary Committee, 30 September 1935. See also *Standard*, 24 April, 1 May and 5 June 1937.

24 The city's three major art groups urged the city council to provide an art gallery. See, for example, City Council, 26 February 1935. M.S. Garratt, 'The redevelopment of the central area of the City of Coventry 1924–1958' (unpublished manuscript, 1959, in the Local Studies Section of Coventry City Library).

25 'Report of Civic Centre Sub-committee', op. cit., note 23.

26 See, for example, the plan of R. Hellberg, C. Redgrave and H. Beney in *MDT*, 14 May 1936.

27 They, for instance, organized the exhibition of civic centres for 28 December 1936–2 January 1937, and formed a special sub-committee to prepare a scheme. For details, see 'Report of the Civic Centre Sub-Committee', in *The Annual Report for 1938 of Coventry City Guild*, CRO Sec/CF/1/7602.

28 See Alderman Payne's scheme, with the aid of R. Hellberg and C. Redgrave, in *MDT*, 26 January 1937.

29 The *MDT*, for instance, gave a series of interviews on the topic with leading local politicians in the summer of 1938.

30 F. Smith, 'The Town and Country Planning Act, 1932: Report of the town clerk', 5 April 1933, in the Local Studies Section of Coventry City Library.

31 HLG 79/130, E. Ford (city engineer), in H.R. Wardill, 'Bombed areas – Redevelopment of Coventry' (government test case survey), 21 February 1941.

32 *The Coventry Herald*, 14 January 1939.

33 *Standard*, 25 February 1939.

34 See HLG 7/188, the Note of the Ministry of Health on 'Deputation from the Coventry City Council on problems arising out of the erection of shadow factories in the City', 5 January 1940.

35 For the details of these factories, see HLG 79/131, *Letter from E.H. Doubleday to A.M. Jenkins*, 13 August 1943.

36 *Standard*, 10 April 1937.

37 *MDT*, 2 July 1938, one of the interviews mentioned in note 29.

38 P. Johnson-Marshall, *Rebuilding Cities* (Edinburgh, 1966), p. 292.

39 D. Gibson, 'Birth of the precinct idea', *The Birmingham Post*, 'Survey of Coventry', 10 July 1962.

40 Ibid.

41 Ibid.

42 P. Johnson-Marshall, op. cit., note 38, p. 293. See also P. Johnson-Marshall, 'Coventry: Test-case of planning', *The Listener*, 17 April 1958, p. 653.

43 D. Gibson, op. cit., note 39.

44 Ibid.

45 Ibid.

46 See, generally, T. Harrisson, *Living through the Blitz* (London, 1978); and, specifically, T. Mason, 'Looking back on the Blitz', in W. Lancaster and T. Mason (eds), op. cit., note 15; and, for Bristol, see also R. Winstone, *Bristol in the 1940s* (Bristol, 1961).

47 See HLG 711/1570, G.L. Pepler, 'Bombed areas – Redevelopment', summary of test case surveys, 28 February 1941. As for the individual case studies, only the Coventry one seems to have survived. HLG 79/130, H.R. Wardill, op. cit., note 31.

48 HLG 88/9, Report of Advisory Panel on Redevelopment of City Centres, August 1944, Appendix II.

49 See, for example, HLG 68/66, G.L. Pepler, 'Bombed areas – Redevelopment: Replacement of shops as a temporary measure', 24 January 1941.

50 HLG 71/1570, G.L. Pepler, op. cit., note 47.

Chapter 4: Replanning the city centre: Coventry 1940–45

1 HLG 88/9, 'Short notes on the seven cities', 25 May 1943.

2 HLG 79/130, 'Bombed areas – Redevelopment of Coventry', by H.R. Wardill, 21 February 1941.

3 HLG 79/132, *Letter from W.M. Fox to B. Gille*, 17 May 1944.

4 Ibid.

5 HLG 79/127, *Letter from E.H. Doubleday to A.M. Jenkins*, 1 October 1945.

6 City Council, City Redevelopment Committee (hereafter CRC), 10 December 1940.

7 CRO SEC/CF/1/7963, Ministry of Works and Buildings, verbatim note on 'Deputation to the Minister from the Redevelopment Committee of the Corporation of the City of Coventry', 8 January 1941.

8 Ibid.

9 At the city council meeting of 28 January 1941, as reported in *The Coventry Standard* (hereafter *Standard*), 1 February 1941.

10 Ford and Gibson could not agree, perhaps because Ford had never been able to accept Gibson's appointment and the political move it represented. HLG 79/130, op. cit., note 2, p. 11.

11 CRO SEC/CF/1/9464, 'Report on the Redevelopment of the central bombed areas, or "core" of the city', by E. Ford, submitted to the CRC, 31 January 1941.

12 HLG 79/130, 'Redevelopment of city centre – Coventry', by D. Gibson, submitted to the CRC, 1 February 1941.

13 As for the debate at that city council meeting, see *Coventry Evening Telegraph* (hereafter *CET*), 25 and 26 February 1941; *Standard*, 1 March 1941; *Midland Daily Telegraph* (hereafter *MDT*), 25 February 1941.

     The plan with architect's impressions is included in HLG 79/130, op. cit., note 2. See Also *MDT*, 13 March 1941. Councillor Payne, active in city centre replanning before the war, described Gibson's plan as 'a very good and noble one'. In early 1940, Payne questioned whether the council needed to keep the city architect's department which cost the city quite a lot of money (*Standard*, 6 January 1940). Initially critical of the department, a year later he revised this opinion, adding that Gibson's plan surpassed his, which he had taken 'the trouble and expense to prepare some time ago' (*CET*, 26 February 1941).

14 See, for example, *MDT*, 20 February 1941; *The Daily Herald*, 26 February 1941; *The News Chronicle*, 26 February 1941; *Reynolds News*, 2 March 1941; *Everybody's Weekly*, 15 March 1941.

    Around this time, Gibson expressed the council's determination to plan boldly on various occasions: on 4 December 1940 in London an address made to the Royal Society of Arts (see *The Times*, 4 and 7 December 1940); on 24 January 1941 in London, an address to the Architectural Association (see *The Times*, 25 January 1940 and *The Architectural Association Journal*, **LVI** (648), February 1941); and on 28 March 1941 in Oxford, an address to the conference organized by the Town and Country Planning Association – see F.E. Towndrow (ed.), *Replanning Britain*, a summarized report of the conference (1941), pp. 100–105.

15 *MDT*, 25 February 1941.

16 *Standard*, 8 March 1941. See also other critical comments in *Truth*, 7 March 1941; meeting of the Warwickshire Law Society, 18 February 1941, appendix 3 (iii) of HLG 79/130, op. cit., note 2; and the seconding speech to adopt Gibson's plan, made by Councillor A.R. Grindlay (Progressive Party, deputy mayor and vice-chairman of the CRC) reported in *MDT*, 25 February 1941.

17 See, for example, Alderman Stringer at the city council meeting of 25 February 1941; ibid.

18 The explanation can be found in HLG 68/70, *Letter from the Town Clerk to the Ministry*, 30 January 1941.

19 As for his written statement of resignation and a written reply from Hodgkinson, see *Standard*, 15 March 1941.

20 CRC, 17 December 1940.

21 City Council, 24 December 1940. As for the debate there, see *CET*, 24 December 1940.

22 At the chamber's monthly meeting of 20 January 1941. See *CET*, 21 January 1941 and *Standard*, 25 January 1941. As for their criticisms of Gibson's plan, see, for example, 'Interview with representatives of the Coventry Chamber of Commerce, 11 February 1941', appendix 3(i) of HLG 79/130, op. cit., note 2.

23 CRC, 29 January 1941.

24 CRC, 14 May 1941, approved by the city council on 27 May 1941.

25 CRC, 4 March 1942.

26 For instance, the committee dismissed the suggestion from Gibson and Ford that as a result of further bombing, Hertford Street could be widened on its present line and retained as a main approach to the city centre: CRC, 24 August 1942. The officers' report is in CRO SEC/CF/1/9464, 'Suggested amendments to the central area replanning scheme', to CRC, dated 30 July 1942.

27 HLG 79/131, *Letter from G.L. Pepler to the Town Clerk*, 7 December 1942.

28 CRC, 17 December 1942.

29 HLG 79/131, *Letter from E.H. Doubleday to K.S. Dodd*, 15 April 1943.

30 Ibid.

31 HLG 79/132, Ministry of Town and Country Planning Advisory Panel on Redevelopment of City Centres, 'Minutes no. 3', 13 July 1943.

32 HLG 79/132, Ministry of Town and Country Planning Advisory Panel on Redevelopment of City Centres, 'Minutes no. 4', 19 July 1943.
33 Ibid.
34 Ibid.
35 HLG 79/132, *Letter from E.H. Doubleday to A.M. Jenkins*, 19 July 1943.
36 *CET*, 9 October 1943.
37 At the conference of the Lockhurst Lane Co-operative Party; *Standard*, 23 October 1943.
38 CRC, 25 October 1943.
39 CRC, 22 September 1943.
40 City council, 5 October 1943.
41 CRC, 24 November 1943.
42 CRO SEC/CF/1/10446(A), 'Report on redevelopment of Coventry's shopping facilities' by Coventry Retailers' Advisory Committee on Town Planning appointed by the Chamber of Commerce, 18 January 1944, and CRC, 18 February 1944.
43 CRC, 18 February 1944.
44 At the annual general meeting of the Council of the Chamber. See *CET*, 22 February 1944 and *Standard*, 26 February 1944.
45 CRO SEC/CF/1/10446(A), 'Alternative proposals of the Coventry retailers' Advisory Committee on Town Planning', 11 May 1944.
46 The argument is based on the report from Gibson and Ford to CRC, 26 May 1944 in CRO SEC/CF/1/10446(A).
47 CRC, 19 June 1944.
48 HLG 79/131, *Letter from E.H. Doubleday to B. Gille*, 14 February 1944.
49 HLG 79/131, 'Note of a meeting at Coventry', 24 February 1944.
50 Ibid.
51 HLG 79/132, 'Note on conference held at Coventry, 4th May, 1944', by H.W. Wells, 10 May 1944.
52 HLG 79/131, *Letter from H.W. Wells to G.L. Pepler*, 10 May 1944.
53 Ibid.
54 HLG 79/131, 'A note of the discussion between Neal, Pepler and Gille on 4 May 1944', by Gille, 8 May 1944.
55 HLG 79/131, *Letter from B. Gille to G.L. Pepler*, 18 May 1944.
56 HLG 79/131, *Letter from E.H. Doubleday to B. Gille*, 16 May 1944.
57 Ibid.
58 Ibid.
59 CRC, 19 June 1944.
60 CRC, 19 June 1944. SEC/CF/1/9462, *Letter from Clerk to the Ministry*, 5 July 1944.
61 *CET*, 29 June 1944.
62 HLG 79/131, *Letter from W.M. Fox to B. Gille*, 10 July 1944.
63 The provisional agreement from the Ministry of War Transport on the location of the inner ring road was given to Coventry by early August. CRO SEC/CF/1/9462, *Letter from A.J. Lyddon (Chief Engineer of the Ministry of War Transport) to the Town Clerk*, 9 August 1944.
64 HLG 79/132, *Letter from E.H. Doubleday to B. Gille*, 24 August 1944.
65 HLG 79/131, *Letter from F.G. Downing to G.L. Pepler*, 28 October 1944.
66 CRO SEC/CF/1/9464, 'The TCP Act, 1944: Preliminary report of the town clerk', 22 November 1944.
67 HLG 79/131, *Letter from E.H. Doubleday to F.G. Downing*, 24 November 1944.

68 CRC, 29 November 1944.

69 CRO SEC/CF/1/9464, 'Memorandum of conference between the City Redevelopment Committee and the Chamber of Commerce – 14th December, 1944'.

70 CRO SEC/CF/1/10313, 'Memorandum on Coventry redevelopment shopping facilities' by Coventry Retailers' Advisory Committee on Town Planning by Chamber of Commerce, sent to the town clerk on 8 February 1945.

71 CRC, 11 April 1945 and 13 June 1945.

72 *Standard*, 19 May 1945.

73 HLG 79/131, note of an informal meeting between Professor Holford, Doubleday and the corporation officers, 10 May 1945.

74 The idea of this road was forwarded by, first, the multiple traders at the meeting with the planning officers in May: CRO SEC/CF/1/10313, 'Short memorandum of interview between the chamber of commerce and the planning officers', 23 May 1945.

75 Reported in *CET*, 12 July 1945.

76 CRO SEC/CF/1/10446(A), report by Gibson and Ford on the interview with the Committee of the Chamber of Commerce, 20 June 1945.

77 CRC, 11 July 1945.

78 HLG 79/131, *Letter from E.H. Doubleday to F.G. Downing*, 7 March 1945.

79 HLG 79/127, 'Note of conversation between Pepler and Professor Holford', by Pepler, 3 October 1945.

80 Summarized in the minutes of CRC, 13 June 1945.

81 CRC, 13 June 1945.

82 CRC, 13 June 1945.

83 HLG 79/127, 'Note on Coventry plan' by H.E.C. Gatliff, 2 October 1945.

84 Ibid.

85 *MDT*, 22 October 1945.

86 *MDT*, 9 October 1945.

87 Ibid.

88 See, for example, *Coventry Town Crier Special Edition*, January 1945.

89 As for the detailed election results, see *CET*, 2 November 1945. As for Labour's stance during the election campaign, see *Standard*, 20 and 27 October 1945. As for the Progressive Party, see *CET*, 27 October 1945.

90 Hodgkinson, in *CET*, 3 November 1945.

Chapter 5: Replanning the city centre: Southampton 1940–45

1 SRO D/Mat/10/4, Councillor Matthews' private note titled 'Re-Planning Southampton', n.d.

2 Borough Council, 1 January 1941. Discussions reported in the *Southern Daily Echo* (hereafter *SDE*), 2 January 1945.

3 Ibid.

4 The Highways and Town Planning Sub-committee, 9 January 1941.

5 *SDE*, 21 March 1941. Pepler had already visited Southampton on 3 February. Although locally it was thought that Southampton was not to be included as one of the test cases (see *SDE*, 4 February 1941), Pepler did (see HLG 71/1570, etc., his report 'Bombed areas – redevelopment', 28 February 1941).

6 Highways and Town Planning Sub-committee, 8 April 1941.

7 Highways and Town Planning Sub-committee, 23 April 1941.

8 *SDE*, 16 May 1941.

9 SRO D/Mat/10/4, his private note, no title, n.d.

10 Borough Council, 18 June 1941. See the debates between Aldermen Woolley and Mouland, reported in *SDE*, 19 June 1941.

11 *SDE*, 12 August 1941.

12 Town Planning and Development Sub-committee (thus renamed), 5 August 1941. The recommendation was confirmed by the Council, 17 September 1941.

13 *SDE*, 9 September 1941.

14 S. Adshead, *Town planning and town development* (London, 1923), p. 75. He was not so young and, probably because of this, not so keen on the ideas of, for one thing, Le Corbusier, as Gibson and his staff in Coventry's City Architect's Department were. See S. Adshead, 'Camillo Sitte and Le Corbusier', *Town Planning Review* (1930), **14**(2), 85–94.

15 S. Adshead, *A new England* (London, 1941). On p. 25, he declares: 'Now in the year 1941, surely it is not too early to prepare plans for a New England, a New England that must be built with good, though not necessarily lasting materials, but which avoids the vacillating mistakes of the past.' This is cited in A. Ravetz, *Remaking cities* (London, 1980), p. 19.

16 As for Cook's background, see *SDE*, 18 September 1941. The creation of the new department caused the conflict between the borough engineer and the town planning and development officer regarding the latter's duties (see the files in SRO TC Box 26 and SRO SC/BA/2/38), which was settled by the planning sub-sub-committee's decision to formulate the duties in Cook's favour. Town Planning and Development Sub-committee, 2 December 1941, confirmed by the Council, 17 December 1941.

17 Borough Council, 18 February 1942. The plan and report were soon published as *The replanning of Southampton* (Southampton, 1942). The *SDE* reported the features of the report in a series of nine articles, 'The New Southampton', between 27 April and 6 May 1942, which was soon published as a pamphlet.

18 See the strong criticism from F.J. Osborn, (Hon.) Secretary to Town and Country Planning Association, of this proposal in his letter to *SDE*, 15 May 1942.

19 *The replanning of Southampton*, op. cit., note 17, pp. 31–2.

20 Ibid., pp. 12–13.

21 Ibid.

22 The council agreed to the creation of this new committee on 8 February 1942. As for Alderman Mouland's resignation, see Borough Council, 15 July 1942 in *SDE*, 16 July 1942.

23 SRO SC/EN/13/5/2/2, *Letter from H.T. Cook to S.L.G. Beaufoy* (then Ministry of Health), 21 May 1942.

24 Reported in *SDE*, 4 June 1942.

25 See H.T. Cook's report to the Town Planning and Development Committee, (hereafter TPDC), 24 February 1943.

26 TPDC, 27 January 1943.

27 SRO SC/BA 2/39, *Letter from S.D. Adshead to H.T. Cook*, 8 June 1943.

28 H.T. Cook, op. cit., note 25.

29 Borough Council, 17 March 1943, reported in *SDE*, 18 March 1943.

30 Ibid.

31 SRO BA/2/39, *Letter from S.D. Adshead to H.T. Cook*, 29 March 1943.

32 Ibid.
33 SRO SC/BA/2/39, *Letter from H.T. Cook to S.D. Adshead*, 3 April 1943.
34 SRO SC/BA/2/39, *Letter from S.D. Adshead to H.T. Cook*, 4 June 1943.
35 *SDE*, 10 June 1943.
36 SRO SC/BA/2/39, *Letter from H.T. Cook to S.D. Adshead*, 7 July 1943.
37 See, for example, SRO SC/EN/13/5/2/2, *Correspondence between H.T. Cook and S.L.G. Beaufoy*. See also SRO SC/BA/40, *Correspondence between H.T. Cook and G.L. Pepler*. After the Advisory Panel of the Ministry of Town and Country Planning visited Southampton, H.W. Wells also kept in touch with Cook. See SRO SC/EN/13/5/5/2 and SRO SC/EN/13/5/6/6.
38 Cook had conversations with traders and property firms, both local and outside the town, the Southern Railway Company, other departments of the Corporation, etc. See SRO SC/EN/13/5/2/4–5, SRO SC/EN/13/5/3/2–5, SRO SC/EN/13/5/4/103, SRO SC/EN/13/5/6/1 and 3, SRO SC/BA/36, etc.
39 There were many conferences and much correspondence, especially with the MOWT. See, for example, SRO SC/EN13/5/2/1 and 2, SRO SC/EN/13/5/6/5, SRO SC/EN/7/4/13, SRO SC/EN/9/6/5.
40 HLG 88/9, Ministry of Town and Country Planning Advisory Panel on Redevelopment of City Centres, Minutes no. 2, 25 June 1943.
41 Ibid.
42 HLG 88/9, 'Outline of a Report on Southampton's Redevelopment Plan', 24 June 1943.
43 Ibid.
44 HLG 88/9, Minutes no. 2, op. cit., note 40.
45 HLG 88/9, 'Ministry of Town and Country Planning Advisory Panel on Redevelopment of City Centres', Minutes no. 3, 13 July 1943.
46 HLG 88/9, 'Ministry of Town and Country Planning Advisory Panel on Redevelopment of City Centres', Minutes no. 4, 19 July 1943.
47 HLG 88/9, 'Outline of a Report on Southampton's Redevelopment Plan'.
48 HLG 88/9, Minutes no. 2, op. cit., note 40.
49 H.T. Cook's report to the TPDC, 23 February 1944.
50 TPDC, 9 May 1944.
51 Report of the Planning Scheme Sub-committee, 13 September 1944, submitted to the TPDC 18 September 1944.
52 Borough Council, 11 October 1944, reported in *SDE*, 12 October 1944.
53 Ibid.
54 Ibid.
55 TPDC, 30 November 1944.
56 H.T. Cook's report to the TPDC, 9 January 1945.
57 Borough architect's report to the TPDC, 13 December 1944.
58 H.T. Cook's report to the TPDC, 9 January 1945.
59 TPDC, 24 January 1945.
60 TPDC, 22 November 1944.
61 TPDC, 24 January 1945.
62 At a conference held by the Southampton Labour Party. Reported in *SDE*, 30 January 1945.
63 CAB 124/841, note by the Southampton Chamber of Commerce sent to Regional Controller of the Board of Trade, 4 May 1944. The Chamber feared that building work in the immediate post-war period was to be confined solely to housing, thus delaying the restoration of the city centre. Accordingly, they

sent a letter to Lord Woolton, Minister of Reconstruction at the end of 1944. The Chamber wanted an assurance that adequate labour and materials should be allocated to reconstruction of business and commercial buildings as well. The matter involved several government departments, but no decisive answer was given. See materials in CAB 124/841.

64 CAB 124/841, note entitled 'Southampton war damage', 9 January 1945.

65 SRO SC/EN/13/5/2/1, Ministry of Town and Country Planning's note on the meeting, sent to Southampton. See also SRO D/Mat/10/4, Councillor Matthews' private note, 'Towns and Country Planning Bill debates', n.d.

66 Borough Council, 21 February 1945, reported in *SDE*, 22 February 1945.

67 Councillor Lane speaking at the Ratepayers' Party meeting in *SDE*, 28 September 1945. Alderman Lewis, leader of Labour, later suggested to the council that 'the best way to deal with Sir Sidney was to let him make his statements, cast votes, and get on with the next business' (see *SDE*, 16 May 1946). As for Alderman Kimber, see his book, *Thirty-eight years of public life in Southampton 1910–1948* (Southampton, 1949).

68 SRO SC/EN/13/5/4/2, *Letter from H.T. Cook to H. Bennett*, 7 March 1944. As for the difficult relationship between Cook and Bennett, see SRO SC/EN/13/5/4/2 and SC/EN/13/5/6/4. The conflict between Cook and Bennett was not only confined to the city centre. For instance, regarding the layout of the Millbrook area, which the original report of 1942 thought as most suitable for a future industrial and housing site, they could not agree. As Cook wrote to Bennett:

> On a number of occasions recently you have made it clear that you consider yourself free to disregard the planning proposals for this area ... and I should be interested to know what authority you have for adopting this course of action (SRO SC/EN/13/5/6/4, *Letter from H.T. Cook to H. Bennett*, 30 December 1944.).

69 TPDC, 23 May 1945.

70 He revealed it at a special meeting of the borough council, 11 October 1945, reported in *SDE*, 12 October 1945.

71 At a meeting of the Ratepayers' Party, reported in *SDE*, 28 September 1945.

72 See *SDE*, 7 December 1944, introducing Frank Leslie Wooldridge, new borough engineer.

73 SRO D/Mat/10/4, F.L. Wooldridge's report, 'Reconstruction and redevelopment of the central area of the town', October 1945, p. 1.

74 Ibid.

75 Ibid., pp. 2–3. In June 1945, he proposed a traffic scheme to the works committee for the central area which involved the alterations of bus stops, the provision of traffic roundabouts, and the conversion of Millbrook Road, New Road and Civic Centre Road into one-way streets. He was 'convinced that Above Bar and High Street can be relieved of docks traffic by means of the existing highways system, if adequate signposting is made use of' (*SDE*, 7 June 1945).

76 F.L. Wooldridge, op. cit., note 73, pp. 4–5.

77 Ibid., p. 4.

78 Ibid., p. 7.

79 TPDC, 10 July 1945.

80 Borough Council, 18 April 1945, reported in *SDE*, 19 April 1945.

81 Revealed by Alderman Goulden, at a meeting of Labour, reported in *SDE*, 29 October 1945.
82 TPDC, 10 July 1945.
83 Borough Council, 18 July and 3 October 1945.
84 *SDE*, 13 and 18 September 1945. The *SDE* was obviously not in favour of compulsory purchase.
85 *SDE*, 20 October 1945.
86 Letters from the Chamber of Commerce and W. Dixon (President of the High Street Association) read at Borough Council, 11 October 1945.
87 HLG 71/597, 'Notes for a conference with the minister on progress with the redevelopment of blitzed towns', 30 August 1945.
88 Letter dated 29 September 1945, read at Borough Council, 11 October 1945.
89 Borough Council, 11 October 1945.
90 At a meeting of the Ratepayers' Party, reported in *SDE*, 26 October 1945.
91 Councillor Powdrill, at a meeting of the Ratepayers' Party, reported in *SDE*, 19 September 1945.
92 Councillor Hugh, reported in *SDE*, 26 October 1945.
93 Councillor Hugh, at a meeting of the party, reported in *SDE*, 9 October 1945.
94 SRO D/Mat/22/1, 'Southampton present and future', the Labour Party's election manifesto, October 1945.
95 The total number of votes cast was 75 434, made up as follows:

Labour	43 052
Ratepayers	26 598
Independent	5 566
Communist	218

The state of the party strengths in the new council was:

	Old council	New council
Labour	28	41
Ratepayers	39	26
Independent	1	1
Total	68	68

(*Source*: *SDE*, 2 November 1945).

The poll was, as Alderman Woolley pointed out at the Ratepayers' Party's after election meeting, very low, i.e. 42 per cent. Nevertheless, he admitted that it was Labour's sweeping victory. See *SDE*, 6 November 1945.
96 *SDE*, 8 November 1945.
97 See D/Mat/10/4, Matthews' note entitled 'Town and Country Planning Bill debates', n.d., prepared for the Labour Party's 1945 municipal election manifesto, 'Southampton present and future', October 1945. In this note Matthews described the joint report by the borough engineer and the borough architect:

On its merits it is a better plan. It uses existing roads more, is more practicable, less costly, can be more quickly brought into operation.

98 HLG 82/14, Councillor Matthews, 'Southampton regional report', final report for the Nuffield College Reconstruction Survey, December 1942.
99 Ibid., p. 20.
100 Ibid., p. 25.

101 HLG 88/9 (also to be found in BT 64/3407), 'Notes preliminary to a visit to Southampton', 9 June 1943. See also *SDE*, 7 September 1944, where Matthews was speaking of the possibility of developing Southampton as a tourist centre after the war.

102 Sub-committee *re* war damage repairs, 12 October 1944.

103 In his address to the 'Planning and Industry' conference organized by the Southampton Employers' Mutual Aid Group, reported in *SDE*, 4 October 1944.

104 BT64/3407, 'Note of Mr. Fairweather's interview with Mr. H.T. Cook, Town Planning Officer, Southampton, on 16th November, 1944'.

105 Ibid.

106 SRO D/Mat/22/1, 'Southampton present and future', op. cit., note 97.

107 *SDE*, 16 February 1946.

108 SRO D/Mat/10/4, H.T. Cook's report to the TPDC, 2 January 1946.

109 Ibid.

110 HLG 79/132, 'Notes on employment and labour conditions at Coventry', 9 July 1943.

111 HLG 79/132, *Letter from H.W. Wells to L. Neal*, 26 July 1943.

112 HLG 79/132, *Letter from B. Gille to G.L. Pepler*, 30 September 1943.

113 See, for example, A. Shenfield and P. Sargant Florence, 'The economics and diseconomics of industrial concentration: The wartime experience of Coventry', *The Review of Economic Studies* (1944–5) **XII** (2).

114 HLG 79/131, *Letter from Town Clerk to the MOTCP*, 22 May 1944; HLG 79/132, *Letter from Town Clerk to Board of Trade*, 10 August 1944.

115 HLG/88/9, Minutes no. 4, op. cit., note 46 and 'Note on an unofficial discussion at Coventry', 13 July 1943. It should be noted that, because of the pressure from Whitehall after the war to enhance Coventry's existing industrial base in the context of the export drive and then of Korean War rearmament, the city inevitably failed in later years to diversify its industrial structure or to control its population size (see Nick Tiratsoo, *Reconstruction, affluence and Labour politics: Coventry 1945–1960* (London, 1990), esp. chs 3 and 7.

116 HLG 88/9, Minutes no. 2, op. cit., note 40. Ironically, Southampton continued its industrial expansion after the war, especially with the growth of the oil refining industry, the telephone and cable industry, and the construction of light commercial vehicles. As a local historian argues, much of this new development in employment was attributed to the city's natural advantages as a growth centre in Southern England and its emergence as a sub-regional centre for extensive office space as well as city centre shopping. See A. Rance, *Southampton: An illustrated history* (Portsmouth, 1986), esp. ch. 13.

117 *SDE*, 13 May 1942.

118 *SDE*, 11 December 1942.

119 The annual meeting of the civic society in November 1944, reported in *SDE*, 24 November 1944. At the meeting it was reported that only 15 members had as yet paid their subscriptions for 1944.

Chapter 6: Replanning the city centre: Bristol 1940–45

1 HLG 88/9, 'Notes preliminary to a visit to Bristol', 22 September 1943. The chamber of commerce published some important ideas about town planning, which, however, did not deal with city centre replanning as such. See, for

example *Bristol Evening World* (hereafter *BEW*), 8 December 1942, reporting the interim report of the Replanning Advisory Committee set up under the auspices of the chamber, which placed particular emphasis on national and regional planning. See also the *BEW*, 17 January 1942, about the discussions on the question of satellite towns, and the *Bristol Observer* (hereafter *Observer*), 1 January 1944, about their discussions on neighbourhood units.

2 BRO 38605/A/49, 'Report of the Council of the Chamber of Commerce', for the year 1940–41, July 1941, pp. 21–2.

3 *The Times*, 9 April 1941.

4 *Bristol Evening Post* (hereafter *BEP*), 8 April 1941.

5 Planning and Public Works Committee (hereafter PPWC), 9 April 1941.

6 *BEP*, 11 April 1941.

7 *BEP*, 11 May 1941.

8 For instance, in September 1943, when the city engineer was in the very middle of his consultations with the interested bodies about his preliminary replanning proposals, the chamber of commerce and the Bristol Society of Architects proposed to the planning committee the immediate appointment of a town planning consultant responsible for a long-term replanning scheme (Planning and Reconstruction Committee (hereafter PRC), 1 September 1943, Letters from the Bristol Society of Architects, dated 11 August 1943, and from the Chamber of Commerce, dated 13 August 1943) without success (PRC, 1 September 1943). The case for a consultant was pressed again by the chamber in June 1944 following the city engineer's submission of his replanning proposals to the city council in March of that year. Colonel Whitwill, president of the chamber, stated in a letter to the planning committee that he was convinced that it would be the wish of corporation officials that Professor Abercrombie or some other specialist of equal eminence should be consulted before any further steps were taken in connection with the planning of the city centre. In reply, the committee intimated that they were satisfied that the replanning of the city would best be left to the city engineer and other corporation officers, and that they had no intention of appointing an outside consultant, requesting the chamber not to publish its statements related to a consultant (PRC, 5 July 1944). The chamber's recommendation for a consultant was made at the special meeting of the Council of the Chamber, 16 June 1944. See BRO 38605/M/38.

9 BRO 38605/A/49, 'Report of the Council of the Chamber', op. cit., note 8, p. 23.

10 *BEP*, 13 May 1941.

11 *BEP*, 14 May 1941. As for these three, see R. Whitefield, The Labour Movement in Bristol 1914–1939 (unpublished M.Litt thesis, University of Bristol, 1982), appendix III, 'Biographical notes on leading Labour Movement activists in Bristol', pp. 395–404. See also *BEP*, 27 September 1941 and PPWC, 2 October 1941 on the death of Alderman Winchester, and *Observer*, 17 April 1943 on the death of Alderman Cox. Hennessy was a sort of vocal maverick, causing some trouble around this time to Labour in connection with the question of squatters. See J. Hinton, 'Self-help and socialism: The Squatters' Movement of 1946', in *History Workshop*, Spring 1988, issue 25.

12 Report of the PPWC on 'Replanning and Reconstruction', 15 July 1941.

13 *BEP*, 16 July 1941.

14 *BEP*, 17 July 1941.

15 PPWC, 3 September 1941.

16 PPWC, 20 August 1941.
17 PPWC, 17 September 1941, a letter from the Chamber dated 8 September 1941.
18 *BEP*, 17 September 1941.
19 PPWC, 17 September 1941.
20 BRO 38605/A/50, 'Report of the Council of the Chamber for the year 1941–42', July 1942, pp. 24–5.
21 PPWC, 31 December 1941, 'Note of the meeting between the Conference of Officers and the Replanning Advisory Committee', 11 December 1941.
22 PPWC, 29 April 1942.
23 Report by Town Clerk, 11 September 1942.
24 PPWC, 21 October 1942, reported in *BEW*, 5 November 1942.
25 *BEP*, 8 December 1942.
26 PRC, 29 December 1942.
27 PRC, 3 February 1943.
28 PRC, 29 December 1942.
29 'Note of the Conference of Officers on planning in Bristol and District and the duties of the officers engaged thereon,' 7 January 1943.
30 PRC, 3 February 1943, based on the report of a special sub-committee on the question of duties, consisting of Aldermen Inskip and Cox and Councillors Rowat and Evans, 26 January 1943.
31 PRC, 17 February 1943.
32 PRC, 3 March 1943.
33 PRC, 17 March 1943.
34 Ibid.
35 PRC, 26 and 28 May 1943.
36 PRC, 23 June 1943.
37 PRC, 7 July 1943.
38 PRC, 15 September 1943.
39 HLG 88/9, 'Notes preliminary to a visit to Bristol', op. cit., note 1.
40 HLG 88/9, Ministry of Town and Country Planning Advisory Panel on Redevelopment of City Centres. Minutes no. 9, 12 October 1943.
41 HLG 88/9, Ministry of Town and Country Planning Advisory Panel on Redevelopment of City Centres. Minutes no. 11, 26 November 1943.
42 PRC, 15 September 1943.
43 PRC, 27 October 1943.
44 PRC, 10 November 1943.
45 Ibid.
46 City engineer's report on the proposals for the 'Planning and reconstruction of the central area of the city', 25 February 1944.
47 Ibid., p. 2.
48 Ibid., p. 3.
49 Ibid., pp. 3–4.
50 Ibid., pp. 5–7.
51 Ibid., p. 9.
52 PRC, 1 March 1944.
53 *BEP*, 15 March 1944.
54 PRC, 29 March 1944.
55 This point is found in W.A. James, 'Redevelopment of the central shopping area of Bristol', *Journal of Royal Institute of Chartered Surveyors* (April 1954), **XXXIII**, part X, p. 741.

56 PRC, 26 April 1944.
57 BRO 38505/M/38, Minutes of the Chamber's meetings on 26 May and 16 June 1944.
58 PRC, 16 August 1944; *BEP*, 21 September 1944; *Observer*, 23 September 1944. In April 1945, they produced a bird's eye view of the redeveloped Victoria Street. See *BEP*, 16 April 1945.
59 The city engineer's list of 'Suggestions and representations submitted by societies and from other sources' (hereafter 'City Engineer's List'), 13 September 1944, scheduled number A4 and A54. See also BRO 38505/M/38, Minutes of the Chamber's meetings of 26 May and 16 June 1944.
60 *Observer*, 24 June 1944.
61 W.A. James, op. cit., note 55, p. 742.
62 PRC, 21 September 1944.
63 *Observer*, 19 August 1944. See also City Engineer's List, op. cit., note 59, J4 and J31.
64 Ibid., J34.
65 W.A. James, op. cit., note 55, p. 742.
66 PRC, 7 June 1944.
67 PRC, 16 February 1944.
68 *BEP*, 21 June 1944.
69 *BEP*, 15 June and *Observer*, 17 June 1944.
70 *BEP*, 9 August 1944.
71 At the opening of 'When we build again' exhibition. See *Observer*, 22 July 1944.
72 BRO 38605/M/38, Meeting of the Council of the Chamber, 26 May 1944.
73 City Engineer's List, op. cit., note 59, J39.
74 PRC, 5 January 1944.
75 City Engineer's List, op. cit., note 59, J18 and J19. It was understood that the advisory committee, and the Multiple Traders' Federation in particular, were in support of a plan prepared by E.S. Rex which envisaged the Broadmead area as a shopping precinct and the Castle Street/Wine Street area as a civic centre. See PRC, 30 August 1944.
76 *BEP*, 12 October 1944.
77 PRC, 21 September 1944.
78 *Observer*, 21 July 1945.
79 *BEP*, 17 July 1945.
80 PRC, 21 September 1944.
81 PRC, 31 January 1945.
82 PRC, 23 May 1945.
83 PRC, 20 June 1945.
84 City Council, 12 June 1945.
85 PRC, 25 April 1945.
86 PRC, 6 June 1945.
87 HLG 71/597, *Letter from Prof. Holford to H.W.J. Heck*, 5 June 1945.
88 Ibid.
89 *BEP*, 17 July 1945.
90 *Observer*, 21 July 1945. The new plan also included the enlarged area for the markets, and, on the request of the Education Committee of the City Council, an educational precinct to the east of the inner circuit, including colleges of art, technology and commerce, and youth headquarters. For the new plan as such, see the report of the PRC, 12 July 1945.

91 *BEP*, 13 July 1945.
92 Ibid.
93 *Observer*, 28 July 1945. See also *BEP*, 23 July 1945.
94 *BEP*, 13 July 1945.
95 *BEP*, 17 July 1945.
96 BRO 38605/M/39, Note of the meeting of representatives of the chamber of commerce, the Bristol Replanning Association and the Rotary Club, 12 October 1945.
97 The Labour Party's municipal programme, in *BEP*, 3 September 1945.
98 The Citizen Party's statement for the election, in *BEP*, 1 October 1945.
99 Ibid.
100 'Why I ask you to vote Citizen', in *BEP*, 22 October 1945.
101 The municipal election results:

Year	Electors eligible to vote	Poll	Votes cast		Unopposed	Contested seats won	Gains
1938	129 599	50 803	(Labour)	27 412	7	4	1
			(Citizen)	37 452	4	13	3
			(Independent)	503	0	0	0
1945	229 156	43 640	(Labour)	95 312	9	22	9
			(Citizen)	87 056	0	19	0
			(Independent)	433	0	0	0

Source: BEP, 2 November 1945.

   After the election of aldermen, the Labour Party's majority on the city council stood at 24 (Labour: 17 aldermen and 51 councillors, total = 68; Citizen: 11 aldermen and 33 councillors, total = 44) (*Source: Bristol Labour Weekly*, 10 November 1945).
102 *Bristol Labour Weekly*, 17 November 1945.
103 *Observer*, 26 August 1944.
104 See City Engineer's list, op. cit., note 59.
105 There was, for instance, a strong feeling among small traders in the chamber of commerce against multiple stores, which led to the establishment of a separate retail organization rather than their being a section of the chamber. See BRO 38605/M/38 and 39, especially the meeting between the officers of the chamber and the representatives of the retail traders' section, 5 September 1945.
106 See 'A survey of the life of the architect in Bristol', *The Architects' Journal*, 1 June 1950. See also L. Wright, 'The Bristol Society of Architects, 1850–1950', *Journal of the Royal Institute of British Architects* (April 1950), **57**.

Chapter 7: City planning in the immediate aftermath of war: 1946

1 HLG 71/600, Note of meeting between the Minister and the Blitzed Towns

Advisory Committee of MPs, December 1945. See also *The Times*, 18 January 1946, *re* Silkin's press conference.

2 HLG 71/597, *Letter from A.M. Jenkins to L. Neal*, 6 December 1945.

3 See various reports in HLG 71/597, especially 'Blitzed towns' by Neal to Minister, 30 October 1945; 'Advice to local authorities on redevelopment plan' by Hill to Minister, 31 October; and 'Notes on difficulties which are preventing the early submission of declaratory orders under Section 1 of the 1944 Act for blitzed cities and possible lines of action' by Hill to Minister, 10 December 1945.

4 HLG 79/131, 'Discussion on reconstruction of Coventry between the minister and representatives of the city council held at the Ministry of Town and Country Planning', 30 January 1946.

5 HLG 71/597, 'Notes for a conference with the minister on progress with the redevelopment of blitzed towns', Neal to Whiskard, 30 August 1945.

6 HLG 71/597, Hill to Minister, 10 December 1945, op. cit., note 3.

7 See various reports in HLG 71/597, op. cit., note 3.

8 HLG 71/597, op. cit., note 2.

9 HLG 79/131, op. cit., note 4.

10 Ibid., see also HLG 71/597, 'Southampton reconstruction problems: Conference with Minister of Town and Country Planning', 23 January 1946.

11 Ibid.

12 *Observer*, 9 March 1946.

13 HLG 79/60–64 as to miscellaneous materials of Bristol inquiry.

14 PRC, 10 April 1946 and 8 May 1946. These compulsory purchase orders were sought under Section 2-(I) (a) of the 1944 Act, which states 'a local planning authority may be authorised to purchase compulsorily any land in this area as to which an order under section one of this Act is in force declaring the land to be subject to compulsory purchase for dealing with war damage'.

15 See memorandum of the Officers to PRC, 16 July 1947.

16 BRO 38605/M/39, Minutes of a meeting of the Chamber of Commerce and the Replanning Association, 29 March 1946.

17 Ibid., see also the draft form of objection, BRO 33199 (16), attached to the Minutes of a meeting of the executive committee of the Replanning Association, 3 April 1946.

18 HLG 71/597, *Letter from the RPO to F.E.L. Shearme*, 1 February 1946.

19 PRC, 5 December 1945.

20 PRC, 8 May 1946.

21 *BEP*, 14 June and *Western Daily Press and Bristol Mirror*, 15 June 1946.

22 *Western Daily Press and Bristol Mirror*, 22 June 1946.

23 Ibid., 18–29 June 1946.

24 *BEP*, 13 June 1946.

25 Ibid.

26 *BEP*, 12 June 1946.

27 *Western Daily Press and Bristol Mirror*, 27 June 1946.

28 Ibid., 22 June 1946.

29 Ibid., 27 June 1946.

30 *BEP*, 13 June 1946; said by Webb.

31 *Western Daily Press and Bristol Mirror*, 22 June 1946.

32 HLG 79/131, *Letter from E.H. Doubleday to Gatliff*, 17 January 1946. See also HLG 79/131, Note by Assistant Regional Planning Officer.

33 CRC, 7 January 1946.

34 Ibid.
35 CRC, 21 February 1946.
36 CRC, 5 March 1946.
37 CRC, 25 March 1946.
38 Interview by Tony Mason and Bill Lancaster, transcript held at the Centre for Social History, University of Warwick.
39 *CET*, 6 February 1946.
40 As for the background of Barratt, see *CET*, 27 February 1946. In June 1946, Marshall gave a paper at the Institute of Municipal Treasurers' and Account-ants' conference. Here he maintained that the ideal solution for the compre-hensive redevelopment was public ownership of land. As the government would not go that far, however, he also emphasized, as a practical initial step, the importance of the provision of temporary shops to give 'psychological stimulus to blitzed areas'. See *CET*, 21 June 1946.
41 CRO Sec/CF/1/10621, *Letter from City Guild to Town Clerk*, 21 May 1946.
42 *CET*, 27 February 1946.
43 CRC, 7 January 1946.
44 *CET*, 8 June 1946.
45 *CET*, 21 March 1946.
46 *CET*, 5 January 1946.
47 CRC, 21 February 1946.
48 *CET*, 6 March 1946. Mrs Allen was supported by Halliwell. His criticism of the CRC's redevelopment policy is found in 'Whose new city?', *Coventry Tribune*, 9 November 1946.
49 *CET*, 6 March 1946.
50 CRC, 15 April 1946.
51 *CET*, 8 June 1946.
52 *CET*, 8 June 1946. See also the *CET* editorial, 10 June 1946, again praised the ceremony as well as the plan.
53 Detailed analysis of 259 objections is found in *CET*, 25 June 1946 and in CRO Sec/CF/1/9464, 'Report of town clerk to CRC upon the public inquiry into the corporation's application for a declaratory order in respect of the area of extensive war damage (No. 1),' 4 July 1946. See also HLG 79/128–9 and 133 as to miscellaneous information on the inquiry.
54 *CET*, 25 June 1946.
55 *CET*, 28 June 1946.
56 Ibid.
57 *CET*, 12 July 1946.
58 *CET*, 27 June 1946.
59 *CET*, 29 June 1946.
60 Ibid.
61 *CET*, 13 July 1946.
62 *CET*, 25 June 1946.
63 *Standard*, 20 July 1946.
64 *CET*, 26 June 1946.
65 SRO SC/EN/13/6/5, 'Note of Conference', 19 November 1945.
66 SRO SC/EN/13/6/5, *Letter from F.E.C. Shearne (Ministry of Town and Country Plan-ning) to Town Clerk*, 27 November 1945.
67 SRO SC/EN/13/6/5, *Letter from R.B. Walker (RPO of Ministry of Town and Country Planning) to Town Clerk*, 1 December 1945.

68 SRO SC/EN/13/6/5, Town clerk's note of the conference on 29 November 1945 to the planning committee, 21 December 1945. The second conference was held between the officials of the ministries and the corporation.

69 Ibid.; as for notes 65–69, the same materials are also found in SRO D/Mat/10/4.

70 TPDC, 2 January 1946.

71 *SDE*, 17 January 1946.

72 SRO D/Mat/10/4, Cook's reports to the planning committee, 2 January 1946 and 18 March 1946.

73 TPDC, 18 March 1946.

74 Borough Council, 27 March 1946.

75 Borough Council, 17 April 1946.

76 SRO D/Z/778/1, Minutes of the first general meeting of the association, 23 May 1946.

77 SRO D/Z/778/1, 'Proposed Central Area Association of Southampton', 1 April 1946.

78 *SDE*, 24 May (at the first meeting of the central area association) and 9 August 1946 (speech at the Round Table).

79 Ibid.; see also a hint of Cook's bitterness against Wooldridge and Matthews expressed at the public inquiry in *SDE*, 26 September 1946.

80 For example, the chamber of commerce at their annual meeting; see *SDE*, 11 April 1946.

81 Regarding the chamber, see *SDE*, 29 November 1945 and 11 April 1946 (op. cit). See also *SDE* 10 April and 1 June 1946, about the Southampton Non-Party Organization (a body of property owners).

82 SRO D/Z/778/1, the first meeting of the Association, 23 May 1946, reported in *SDE*, 24 May 1946.

83 At the council meeting on 16 January 1946, reported in *SDE*, 17 January 1946, he continued that they were 'now getting down to something that could be done very quickly directly they got a right of way from the Government'.

84 The Southampton Non-Party Organization for instance complained that the Council adopted the new plan without letting the public take any part at all. See *SDE*, 10 April 1946.

85 Alderman Kimber at the council meeting on 15 May 1946, reported in *SDE*, 16 May 1946. Also see the letter from G.E.H. Prince to *SDE*, 31 May 1946.

86 TPDC, 9 May 1946, adopted by the Council, 15 May 1946.

87 *SDE*, 16 May 1946.

88 *SDE*, 7 October 1946.

89 *SDE*, 24 September 1946.

90 *SDE*, 1 October 1946.

91 *SDE*, 28 September 1946.

92 *SDE*, 27 September 1946.

93 *SDE*, 24 September 1946.

94 Regarding various objections, especially that from traders, see *SDE*, 2, 3, 7 and 10 October 1946.

95 *SDE*, 5 October 1946.

96 *SDE*, 27 September 1946.

97 *SDE*, 28 September 1946.

98 *SDE*, 25 September 1946.

99 The Winchester Diocesan Re-Organization Committee, a statutory body set up to deal with blitzed areas in the way of the reconstruction of church life,

withdrew their objection just before the inquiry opened, while the Southern Railway and the Harbour Board expressed their general agreement with the corporation scheme. See *SDE*, 24 September (for the churches), 30 September (for the Harbour Board) and 8 October 1946 (for the Southern Railway Company).

100 Scragg's closing speech, in *SDE*, 11 October 1946.

101 Scragg's opening speech, in *SDE*, 24 September 1946.

102 *SDE*, 26 September 1946.

103 As a typical example, see *SDE*, 27 September 1946, about the case of Edwin Jones. The company had been offered an alternative site in High Street from the original East Street site, but refused to move. See also D/Mat/10/4, the corporation officers' reports, 4 March 1946, and the TPDC, 27 March 1946 about the question of a new site for the company.

104 Scragg, in *SDE*, 11 October 1946.

105 Ibid.

106 Scragg, in *SDE*, 24 September 1946.

107 *SDE*, 10 October 1946. See also Cook's comment on Collier's speech and the latter's reply to Cook, in *SDE*, 28 October and 21 November 1946.

108 Scragg, in *SDE*, 11 October 1946. As for the miscellaneous materials about the Southampton inquiry, see HLG 79/648–674, which include the verbatim report of the inquiry (HLG 79/660).

109 SC/T9/100, Report of the Borough Treasurer, 7 December 1945.

110 See the presidential address of the chamber of commerce (*SDE*, 23 May 1946), and Alderman Lewis' promise for speedy reconstruction (*SDE*, 12 January 1946), both expressing the concern that trade was flowing out of Southampton to neighbouring towns (*SDE*, 21 February 1946).
     In this connection, the borough council thought very much of the provision of temporary shops (*SDE*, 17 May 1945) and decided in January 1946 to apply for the compulsory acquisition for this purpose under Section 2(2) of the Town and Country Planning Act 1944 (Planning Committee, 2 January 1946, the Council, 16 January 1946). See also the *SDE*, 20 June and 4 October 1946, as to the details of the temporary shops plan.

111 See the council debates reported in *SDE*, 17 January and 28 March 1946. The only amendment he made at the council meeting in March 1946 was to stop the inner ring road passing through the parts of the old walls – one of the few proposals in Wooldridge's scheme to affect the existing layout, for the sake of the town's historic heritage. Once the amendment was defeated by a large majority, only eight members voting for it, the planning committee's recommendation to adopt the Wooldridge plan was carried by 49 votes to 1, only Alderman Kimber voting against (*SDE*, 28 March 1946).

112 Borough Council, 15 May 1946, reported in *SDE* 16 May 1946.

113 Borough Council, 9 November 1945, reported in *SDE*, 10 November 1945.

114 Borough Council, 16 October 1946, reported in *SDE*, 17 October 1946. Alderman Kimber abstained.

115 *SDE*, 8 October 1946.

116 *SDE*, 17 October 1946.

117 Alderman Lewis, at a public meeting of the Labour Party, reported in *SDE*, 8 October 1946.

118 Councillor J. Austin, *SDE*, 2 November 1946.

119 Ibid.

120 *SDE*, 5 October 1946.

Chapter 8: The fate of planning after the war

1 See materials in HLG 71/600 and 601.
2 HLG 71/601, 'Conference on reconstruction problems', a verbatim report of the conference between L. Silkin and the blitzed authorities held on 30 October 1947. Silkin organized a series of four conferences with the 38 authorities. See other verbatim reports in HLG 71/601.
3 For instance: Declaratory orders: application and confirmation.

Authorities	Applied (acre)	Confirmed (acre)
Bristol	771	245
Coventry	452	274
Plymouth	462	207
Southampton	514	270
Swansea	281	134

Source: HLG 71/601, *Letter from D.P. Walsh to E.A. Sharp*, 9 September 1947.

4 See, for example, Town and Country Planning Association, *Planning Britain's land: A summary of the Town and Country Planning Act, 1947* (1947).
5 See, for example, A.H. Marshall (City Treasurer, Coventry), 'The financial implications of the Town and Country Planning Act, 1947', *National Housing and Town Planning Council*, November 1947.
6 The circular is found, for example, in SRO TC Box 25.
7 HLG 71/601, op. cit., note 2.
8 The editors, *The Architects' Journal*, 2 October 1952, which features 'Bristol Revised'.
9 HLG 71/601, 'Conference on reconstruction problems', a verbatim report of the conference held on 23 October 1947.
10 The figures given by Councillor P.W. Barnes, chairman of the housing committee, to the borough council on 19 March 1947, reported in *SDE*, 20 March 1947.
11 Councillor Barnes to the council on 18 June 1947, in *SDE*, 20 June 1947.
12 F.E. Dyer, deputy housing manager, at the public inquiry of the Ministry of Health into the corporation's application for a compulsory purchase order to acquire 19.6 acres of land for housing purposes, in *SDE*, 8 May 1947.
13 Borough Council, 21 May 1947, reported in *SDE*, 22 May 1947.
14 Borough Council, 20 March 1946.
15 Borough Council, 26 March 1947.
16 President of the chamber of commerce, heading a deputation to the Mayor, reported in *SDE*, 14 December 1946.
17 Chairman of the Distributive Trades Committee of the Chamber, at Chamber meeting, reported in *SDE*, 8 November 1946.
18 *SDE*, 20 March 1947. For details of the building programme and the allocation of labour force, see the General Purposes Sub-committee of the TPDC, 5 March 1947.
19 Reconstruction Sub-committee of the TPDC, 17 March 1947. The TPDC resolved to make an application for a compulsory order at their meeting on 28 May 1947.

20 Borough Council, 18 June 1947.
21 Through the Ratepayers' members at borough council meetings, reported in *SDE*, 17 April and 19 June 1947.
22 The meetings of the Central Area Association, reported in *SDE*, 26 October 1946.
23 For instance, the Mayor at the annual dinner of Southampton and District Meat Traders' Association, in *SDE*, 12 February 1947.
24 SRO D/Z/778/2, Note of the meeting between the association and the TPDC, held on 3 March 1947. It seemed that the association's letter to the Minister of Town and Country Planning made the committee's hurried decision to see them. See TPDC, 26 February 1947.
25 TPDC, 2 April 1947.
26 SRO D/Z/778/1, Minutes of the association's general meeting held on 8 July 1947.
27 TPDC, 23 April 1947. Borough Council, 21 May 1947. As for the layout of the East Park-terrace site and the model of the central area, see *SDE*, 30 January 1947 and 28 January 1947 respectively.
28 For instance, a solicitor to the Central Area Association at the general meeting on 8 July 1947, SRO D/Z/778/1, op. cit., note 26, reported in *SDE*, 4 July 1947. At the meeting he pointed out that the owners of property in The Crescent, Plymouth, who had appealed successfully against the minister's confirmation of the declaratory order (see *The Times*, 13 May 1947) had been advised to withdraw their appeal to the House of Lords, because the powers under the 1947 Planning Bill would empower the minister to authorize the designation of their land and similar property for compulsory purchase. In Southampton, those who were affected by the corporation's plan realized that no useful purpose would be served by an appeal to the High Court.
29 Meeting of the Central Area Association on 8 July 1947, SRO D/Z/778/1, op. cit., note 26.
30 *SDE*, 26 June 1947. Silkin made these remarks in his interview with *The Observer* (TPCD, 23 July 1947).
31 *SDE*, 31 July 1947. The letter was dated 25 July 1947.
32 Ibid.; the Party received the letter from the minister on the morning of 31 July 1947.
33 See the map in *SDE*, 7 August 1947, showing the areas included in and excluded from the minister's confirmation of the corporation's application.
34 HLG 79/661, Technical Department of the Ministry of Town and Country Planning, 'Reconstruction Areas Technical Examination Committee, County Borough of Southampton – Central Area Application for a declaratory order under Section 1(1) of the Town and Country Planning Act, 1944', n.d., but between 16 April 1946, when the Council formally lodged the application, and the public inquiry in September 1946.
35 *SDE*, 31 July 1947.
36 SRO TC Box 25, Note of the meeting with officials of the Ministry of Town and Country Planning, held on 26 August 1947.
37 Matthews, in *SDE*, 14 October 1947.
38 HLG 71/601, 'Ministry of Town and Country Planning: Conference on reconstruction problems', held on 30 October 1947.
39 HLG 79/661, op. cit., note 34.
40 TPDC, 22 October 1947.

41 Matthews at the conference with the Ministries of Town and Country Planning and of Transport, held on 23 March 1948; note of the conference in SRO TC Box 25.

42 Ibid.

43 Ibid.; modifications to the zoning proposals were supposedly as a result of 'the 1946 Basic Survey' of buildings in the town, which analysed the users of 1939 and 1946, general statistical data relating to war damage and the age and condition of property, etc. (see SRO SC/EN/13/5/3/1, SRO SC/EN/13/5/5/1, SRO SC/BA/2/76–78 and B.T. Rees, 'Redevelopment of Southampton's central area', *Institution of Municipal Engineers* (February 1949), **75**, p. 488).

44 TCPD, 13 April 1948.

45 TCPD, 28 April 1948.

46 B.T. Rees, op. cit., note 43, p. 491.

47 Borough Council, 19 May 1948.

48 A meeting between the association and the TCPD was arranged in September, but postponed until the committee's meeting with the ministries (TCPD, 26 November 1947). The association pressed the TCPD to receive a deputation (letters sent 28 January, 25 March, 28 April and 19 May 1948) without success. Not surprisingly, the association was very discontented with the council's adoption of the plan in May 1948. See SRO D/Z/778/1, minutes of the annual general meeting, held on 27 May 1948.

49 Southampton Corporation, *Development plan: Comprehensive Development Area 3 (Central Area), written analysis*, p. 10 (submitted to the Ministry of Housing and Local Government, September 1954). The plan added by Amendment No. 1 submitted to the ministry in July 1957, still based on the 1946 plan, was eventually approved in December 1960.

50 Wilfred Burns, *New towns for old* (London, 1963), pp. 40–41.

51 Southampton Corporation, op. cit., note 49, p. 46.

52 L. Berger, 'Aspects of the civic scene: Architecture', in F.J. Monkhouse (ed.), *A survey of Southampton and its region* (Southampton, 1964), p. 310.

53 A. Rance, *Southampton: An illustrated history* (London, 1984), p. 176.

54 D.R. Childs, 'Southampton *The Architects' Journal*, 16 April 1953, p. 486.

55 Ibid., p. 485.

56 Ibid., p. 310.

57 Alderman E. Burrow (leader of the Ratepayers' Party), speaking to the High Street Association, *SDE*, 29 November 1948.

58 *Observer*, 4 July 1946. See also *Observer* 28 September 1946, where Alderman Gill, chairman of the housing committee, expressed his dissatisfaction with the amount of labour available in the building industry.

59 Colonel Whitwill, addressing the Round Table as chairman of the South-Western Regional Board for Industry, reported in *Observer*, 31 August 1946. Quite ironically, however, the rate would remain the same until April 1947, because the labour available would fall short of that required to carry out the whole programme of work planned by the corporation (see *Observer*, 17 September 1946).

60 *Observer*, 23 November 1946. See also *Observer*, 26 April 1947, reporting the housing committee's target for 6000 houses over 2 years had to face a 20 per cent cut imposed by the Ministry of Works because of the fuel crisis and the shortage of materials, especially timber.

61 *Observer*, 4 January 1947.

62 A letter from the Ministry of Town and Country Planning to the PRC, 18 December 1946. Those zones excluded from the order included land reserved for the university and hospitals in the St Michael's area, the Newfoundland Road educational precinct, and most of the King Street historic buildings site.

63 *Observer*, 21 December 1946. See a map of the confirmed order, ibid.

64 'City engineer's memorandum of conference with representatives of the Ministry of Town and Country Planning and the Ministry of Transport at London on 10th February, 1947, to discuss matters arising out of the planning and reconstruction of the Bristol central area', submitted to the PRC, 12 February 1947.

65 Ibid.

66 Ibid.; one particular point that provoked the city engineer was the ministry's criticism of the removal of industry from the city centre. The engineer pointed out that the ministry officials had no knowledge of the corporation's trading estates policy, to part of which a compulsory order had already been given by that very minister, or about the re-zoning of the Portland Square area from warehouse to industrial use after the discussions with the manufacturers there (see PRC, 5 December 1945), which was praised by the Chamber of Commerce (see BRO 38605/A/54, Chamber's Annual Report, 19 July 1946, p. 16).

67 PRC, 23 April 1947.

68 'Central area reconstruction scheme: Report by officers', submitted to the PRC, 1 May 1947.

69 'Reconstruction proposals of the Bristol City Council. Memorandum by the officers on the present position', submitted to the PRC, 16 July 1947. The memorandum was submitted to the minister for his meeting with the council representatives led by local MPs held on 22 July 1947. See also ' "B" Appendix' to the PRC minutes, 16 July 1947.

70 PRC, 16 July 1947.

71 Note of the meeting with the minister held on 22 July 1947, as 'Appendix "B" ' to the PRC minutes, 23 July 1947.

72 PRC, 23 July 1947. The committee resolved to ask the minister to postpone the inquiry at their meeting on 1 May 1947.

73 PRC, 13 August 1947.

74 See, for example, the officers' report to the PRC, 1 May 1947, op. cit., note 68.

75 The meeting with the minister on 22 July 1947.

76 PRC, 24 September 1947.

77 The meeting with the minister on 22 July 1947. The advisory committee intimated to the PRC that the two essential conditions for success of the new shopping centre were the council's absolute control of the old centre so as to prevent the permanent re-establishment of shops there, and quick development of the new centre with both temporary and permanent shops. PRC, 27 August 1947.

78 PRC, 22 October 1947.

79 BRO 38605/M/41, the meeting of the Council of the Chamber of Commerce, 20 June 1947. There had been much discussion up to then whether the chamber should proceed with the high court appeal (see the minutes of meetings in BRO 38605/M/40 and 41). It seemed that the result of the Plymouth case and the compensation clauses under the 1947 Planning Bill eventually forced the chamber to make the decision.

80 BRO 33199(16), minutes of the annual meeting of the association held on 4

June 1947. At that time it embraced about 120 members. The names are included in a letter from Colonel Whitwill, chairman, to members in May 1947, stating that it should be incorporated in the civic society. In conclusion, he stated that 'there should be no feeling of regret in the step to be taken, but rather satisfaction that we can now join up with an older Association' [BRO 33199 (16)].

81 How many members belonged to the federation is not known, but there were 18 retail organizations affiliated to it.

82 PRC, 9 October 1946. For details of the plan, see *Western Daily Press and Bristol Mirror*, 10 October 1946, and *Observer*, 12 October 1946.

83 PRC, 1 January 1947.

84 See a letter from W.R. Tyndall, chairman of the federation, to *Observer*, 3 May 1947.

85 *Observer*, 19 April 1947.

86 PRC, 13 August 1947 and *Observer*, 16 August 1947.

87 See, for example, the comment of Councillor S. Clifford, PRC member, in *Observer*, 10 April 1948, and that of Mrs D.P. Dobson, secretary of the civic society, at its annual general meeting, in *Observer*, 24 April 1948.

88 In a written reply, Silkin stated that, while he had never sought to curtail the plan itself, the compulsory orders for approximately 100 acres of land were too large in view of the present economic difficulties and, consequently, he was 'bound to ask them [the City Council] to stage the work, and spend public money only as, and when, they need to do so' (*Observer*, 1 May 1948).

89 Addressing the South-Western Conference of the National Housing and Town Planning Conference on 28 May 1948. Indeed, Miss Sharp observed in her address that 'we cannot agree more at the Ministry that planning at the moment is a nightmare'. She said that part of her work was to hammer out with other government departments an investment programme for 1949–50. As she went on:

> It is a heart-breaking job to sit there and realise the desperate straits in which this country is and the overwhelming demands of factories, schools, housing estates and the little hope at the moment for the reconstruction of the bombed cities.... We have the same sense of disappointment, frustration and almost sometimes despair as you have....
>
> Your chairman no doubt thinks that we have not been very brilliant in getting things moving for Bristol. We, too, are very unhappy about it. (*Observer*, 29 May 1948)

90 See *Observer*, 29 May 1948, 17 July 1948.

91 *Observer*, 10 and 31 July 1948.

92 A deputation was sent to see Silkin; see *Observer*, 25 September 1948.

93 *Observer*, 7 and 31 July, 28 August 1948.

94 *Observer*, 1 January 1949.

95 *BEP*, 7 July 1949.

96 *BEP*, 12 July 1949.

97 *Observer*, 8 October 1949.

98 *BEP*, 2 December 1949.

99 See Wilfred Burns, op. cit., note 50, pp. 28–32.

100 Alderman Gill, speaking of 'The new Bristol' at NALGO's annual dinner, *Observer*, 9 April 1949.

101 As for election results, see *BEW*, 13 May 1949.

102 *BEW*, 14 May 1949.

103 His letter of resignation, *BEW*, 16 May 1949.

104 Bicker, for instance, was quite sympathetic to the traders' opposition to the widening of Park Street, but, as he intimated, had been forced to decide so because of the pressure from the Ministry of Transport (see, for example, *Observer*, 9 April 1949). The traders' opposition to the widening of it went back to early 1946, when the PRC asked the Park Street and College Green Traders' Association for their opinion upon the proposal. The association received only four replies out of its 65 members, and the matter seemed to be settled (PRC, 30 January 1946). By the summer, however, they had made it clear that they were opposed to the widening (*Observer*, 13 July 1946). With the help of the replanning association [BRO 33199(16), *Letter from the Secretary of the Replanning Association to the Town Clerk*, 16 July 1946] and the chamber of commerce [BRO 38605 M(40), minutes of the joint meeting of the chamber and the replanning association, held on 15 July 1946], the long battle started. In September 1949, the PRC – now under the chairmanship of Alderman Sir John Inskip, leader of the Citizen Party, who had opposed the widening because of the cost and of too much intervention from the Ministry of Transport (*BEW*, 22 April 1949) – decided not to widen Park Street (*BEP*, 21 September 1949). The council approved this, although the Labour members of the committee were, as Alderman Hennessy put it, 'not happy in agreeing to the resolution' (*BEP*, 11 October 1949).

105 See, for example, Labour's election programme, in *BEW*, 22 April 1949.

106 BRO 33199(6), 'A record of the redevelopment proposals for the Wine Street– Castle Street area of central Bristol', the Bristol Civic Society, 18 January 1961.

107 The annual report of the Medical Officer of Health 1947, in the Local Studies Section of Coventry City Library, p. 19.

108 See, for example, *CET*, 19, 25 and 28 June 1946.

109 CRC, 24 October 1946.

110 Especially Charles Barratt, town clerk. See, for example, 'Phoenix city arises – with garden as first great act of faith', in *The Birmingham Post Survey of Coventry*, 10 July 1962.

111 See materials in HLG 171/13, e.g. a note by R.T. Kennedy, Ministry of Town and Country Planning (MOTCP), dated 5 November 1946, and a note of the meeting between the MOTCP, the Ministry of Transport and the Ministry of Health, held on 27 November 1946. The local MPs helped the council to persuade the ministries concerned. See CRC, 7 and 28 January 1947.

112 See *CET*, 24 and 26 May 1947.

113 The order was in fact ready for issue in early 1947 but had been held up because of the effect of the Plymouth judgement (see HLG 71/600, note of the meeting between the Minister and the Ministry officials, held on 2 July 1947).

114 As for the details of the excluded areas, see a note from M.G. Kirk, Ministry of Town and Country Planning, dated 31 January 1947, in HLG 71/13. As for the boundaries of the confirmed order, see *Standard*, 7 June 1947.

115 *CET*, 3 June 1947.

116 *Standard* (editorial), 7 June 1947.

117 *CET*, 22 May 1948.

118 *CET* (editorial), 22 May 1948.

119 CRC, 26 April 1948.

120 As a convenient summary, see *Letter from C.W. Gurner (Regional Controller of the Ministry of Town and Country Planning) to L. Mann (Headquarters)*, dated 6 November 1948, HLG 79/133.

121 CRC, 11 May 1949.

122 CRC, 11 May 1949.

123 HLG 79/128, 'Technical Department Reconstruction Areas Technical Examination Committee, City and County Borough of Coventry Application Under Section 1. Town and Country Planning Act, 1944. Area No. 1', n.d. (but some time in 1946, after the public inquiry in June and July of that year).

124 See, for example, HLG 71/13, a note of a conference between the officials held on 22 September 1947.

125 HLG 71/13, a note of a conference between the officials held on 9 May 1949.

126 HLG 71/13, *Letter from J.E. Cardell (Divisional Road Engineer of the Ministry of Transport) to W.B. Vince (Assistant Secretary of Ministry of Town and Country Planning)*, dated 19 April 1948.

127 HLG 71/13, *Letter from W.B. Vince to J. Earley (Ministry of Town and Country Planning)*, dated 20 April 1948.

128 HLG 71/13, op. cit., note 125.

129 *CET*, 18 July 1949.

130 *CET*, 18 July 1949.

131 See, for example, A.H. Marshall, 'The financial implications of the Town and Country Planning Act, 1947', op. cit., note 5, p. 7. See also Hodgkinson's comment on the confirmation of the declaratory order, in *Standard*, 7 June 1947.

132 The shopping precinct was regarded by the Ministry of Town and Country Planning at least 'as reasonable in principle'. HLG 71/13, 'Points for consideration with the development of the declaratory order area', March 1948. As we have seen, the same ministry did oppose the shopping precinct proposal in the case of Bristol.

133 D.R. Childs, 'Coventry', *The Architects' Journal*, 8 October 1953. See also, for example, H.V. Morton. 'Future of Coventry', *Illustrated*, 29 October 1949; R. Jenkins, 'Coventry rises from the rubble', *The Sphere*, 10 October 1953; and 'Coventry rebuilds', *Architectural Design*, December 1958.

134 W. Burns, op. cit., note 50, p. 35. See also D.R. Childs, 'A comparison of progress in rebuilding bombed cities', *The Architects' Journal*, 8 July 1954, p. 51.

135 See, for example, D. Senior, 'Coventry plan review', *The Architects' Journal*, 11 July 1962; G. Logie, 'The lessons of Coventry', *The Architect and Building News*, 11 July 1962; Professor Sir Robert Matthews, 'An enlightened attitude ... and good men promoting it', *The Birmingham Post Survey of Coventry*, op. cit., note 110.

136 CRC, 28 September, 1955. See also 'Planning: The newer concept. Applying traffic–pedestrian segregation principle to city as a whole', *The Birmingham Post Survey of Coventry*, op. cit., note 110; A. Ling, 'Coventry's pedestrian shopping centre', *Keystone*, May–June 1956, pp. 3–4.

Bibliography

I Primary sources

A Manuscript Collections

1 Public Record Office
(a) BT (Board of Trade)
    BT 64 – Registered Files of Industries and Manufactures Department
(b) CAB (Cabinet)
    CAB 87 – War Cabinet Committees on Reconstruction
    CAB 117 – Files of the Reconstruction Secretariat
    CAB 124 – Minister of Reconstruction Secretariat files
    CAB 128 – Cabinet Conclusions, 1945–48
(c) HLG (Ministry of Housing and Local Government)
    HLG4 – Planning Schemes
    HLG7 – Special War Time Functions
    HLG51 – Local Government Services: Correspondence and papers
    HLG52 – Local Government Administration and Finance
    HLG68 – 100 000 Series
    HLG71 – Town and Country Planning: Correspondence and papers
    HLG79 – Town and Country Planning: Local authority files
    HLG81 – Expert Committee on Compensation and Betterment (Uthwatt Committee)
    HLG82 – Nuffield College Social Reconstruction Survey
    HLG83 – Regional Physical Planning Committees: Minutes and papers, 1946–49

HLG86 – Ministry of Works and Buildings: Reconstruction of Town and Country Advisory Panels and Committees, 1940–45

HLG88 – War Damaged Areas: Advisory bodies on redevelopment, 1942–45

2 Bristol City Record Office

(a) Records of various organizations

Bristol Association of Engineers 1895–1966, Acc. No. 36256

Bristol Chamber of Commerce and Shipping, Acc. No. 38605

Bristol Civic Society, Acc. Nos. 30632 and 33199

Bristol Conservative Association 1920–79, Acc. No. 38036

Bristol and District Property Owners' Association 1938–68, Acc. No. 34859

Bristol Liberal Club 1886–1971, Acc. No. 36202

Bristol Trades Council, Acc. No. 32080

Wessex Society of Architects 1928–1962, Acc. No. 17561

(b) Records of the corporation

Reports of Corporation Committees and Officers, Acc. No. 35510

Industrial Surveys in the Central Area 1945–49, Acc. No. 38129

Town Planning Records disposed by the City Engineers 1919–55, Acc. No. 34414

Rating and Valuation Records, Acc. No. 34713

3 Coventry City Record Office

The Town Clerk's files (Sec/CF/1), especially:

Sec/CF/1/7602 – Materials related to the pre-war discussion on a civic centre

Sec/CF/1/7963 – City centre redevelopment, general correspondence 1940–41

Sec/CF/1/9463 – Miscellaneous correspondence, 1944

Sec/CF/1/9464 – Materials with regard to the public inquiry in 1946 into the city council's application to the Minister of Town and Country Planning for a declaratory order in respect of an area of extensive war damage, under the Town and Country Planning Act 1944

Sec/CF/1/10313 – Coventry Redevelopment Scheme, various papers, 1945

Sec/CF/1/10446(A) – Various papers related to city centre redevelopment

Sec/CF/1/10621 – Correspondence in regard to the area of extensive war damage, 1946

Sec/CF/1/10625 – Various papers related to city centre redevelopment

4 Local Studies Section of Coventry City Library

The Corporation's pamphlets on the official openings of Corporation Street (1931) and Trinity Street (1937)

M.S. Garratt, 'The redevelopment of the central area of the City of Coventry 1924–1958', November 1959.

F. Smith, 'The Town and Country Planning Act, 1932: Report of the town clerk', 5 April 1933.

J.E. Swindlehurst, 'Town planning: A preliminary report', 26 February 1912.

5 Southampton City Record Office

(a) Various papers disposed by Sir James Matthews (D/Mat), especially:

D/Mat/9 – Overcrowding, slum clearance and housing

D/Mat/10 – Various reports to the Town Planning and Development Committee

D/Mat/11 – Itchen river
D/Mat/13 – A scheme for a sea aerodrome
D/Mat/15 – Docks and port
D/Mat/17 – Industry
D/Mat/22 – Labour Party
D/Mat/27 – Himself
D/Mat   – Uncatalogued: also includes various papers on employment, housing, industry, town planning, etc.

(b) Materials disposed by the City Engineer's Department, 1928–57 (SC/EN): including papers, reports, plans, photographs, correspondence, etc.
SC/EN/1   – Committees and associated materials
SC/EN/2   – Photographs
SC/EN/3   – Property
SC/EN/4   – Plans
SC/EN/5   – Bridges
SC/EN/6   – Internal departmental administrative materials
SC/EN/7   – External work by the department
SC/EN/8   – Public inquiries
SC/EN/9   – Planning
SC/EN/10 – Unemployment and apprenticeship
SC/EN/11 – Public health
SC/EN/12 – Contracts
SC/EN/13 – Second World War
SC/EN/14 – Professional associations
SC/EN/15 – Printed matters

(c) Materials disposed by the City Architect's Department (SC/BA): SC/BA/1 and SC/BA/2 – Town Planning Records, 1928–53

(d) City Planning Records (SC/PL): coloured sketches, drawings, maps, etc.
SC/PL/29 – Various sketches, drawings, maps, etc., regarding the central area in the 1940s

(e) City Treasurer's Records (SC/T):
SC/T9 – Materials regarding the rates and the loss of rateable value through enemy action

(f) Town Clerk's Files (TC Box):
TC Boxes 24–27 – Materials regarding town planning and redevelopment 1929–67

(g) D/Z/778: Minutes of the Central Area Association, 1946–54

(h) 'Civic Centre': A pamphlet by the City Record Office regarding the history of the civic centre

6 Other Papers

(a) Labour Party (Walworth Road, London)
Minutes of the Housing and Town Planning Sub-committee of the Central Committee on Reconstruction, 1941–44

(b) *Mass Observation* (Mass Observation Archive, University of Sussex)
Topic Collections No. 2   – Reconstruction 1941–43
Topic Collections No. 40   – Post-war hopes 1944
Topic Collections No. 66   – Town and district survey 1938–49
Topic Collections No. 84   – Local council elections 1937–51
File Reports Nos. 516 and 517 – Southampton: Effect of recent raids (1940)

File Report No. 529	– The aftermath of town blitzes: Summary of research in Bristol, Southampton and Cheltenham (1940)
File Report No. 601	– Raids and morale: Bristol (1941)
File Report No. 603	– Raids and morale: Southampton (1941)
File Report No. 669	– Plan for Britain: Analysis of letters written to *Picture Post* on 'Plan for Britain' feature (1941)
File Report No. 699	– Plan for Britain: Analysis of letters sent to *Picture Post* in response to article (1941)
File Report No. 688	– The end of the war: People's hopes and fears for the future (1941)
File Report No. 790	– Coventry's preparation for next winter's blitz (1941)
File Report No. 913	– Reconstruction problems: Consideration of government reconstruction plans, Roosevelt's Four Freedoms, political problems, and economic difficulties (1941)
File Report No. 1162	– Propaganda for town planning: Talk by Tom Harrisson given at Housing Centre (1942)
File Report No. 1647	– What people in Britain are thinking and talking about: Article in New York, *New Leader* (1943)

(c) Nuffield College Library (Oxford)

Nuffield College Social Reconstruction Survey, Box N.C.S.R.S., 'Area Reports, Southampton Reports', 1941–42

B *Official papers*

1 *Central Government*
Report of the Royal Commission on Geographical Distribution of the Industrial Population (The Barlow Report) (Cmd. 6153, London, 1940).
Interim Report of the Expert Committee on Compensation and Betterment (Cmd. 6291, London, 1941).
Report of the Committee on Land Utilization in Rural Areas (The Scott Report) (Cmd. 6378, London, 1942).
Final Report of the Expert Committee on Compensation and Betterment (The Uthwatt Report) (Cmd. 6386, London, 1942).
White Paper on Employment Policy (Cmd. 6527, London, 1944).
White Paper on the Control of Land Use (Cmd. 6537, London, 1944).

2 *Hansard – House of Commons Debates, 1940–49*

3 *National Labour Party*
Reports of the Annual Conferences, 1941–45

4 *Bristol City Council*
The minutes of the City Council and its Standing Committees, 1939–49 (BRO)

5 *Coventry City Council*
The Minutes of the City Council and its Standing Committees, 1930–49 (CRO)
Annual Reports of the Medical Officer of Health 1930–49 (Local Studies Section of Coventry City Library)

6 *Southampton Borough Council*
The Minutes of the Borough Council and its Standing Committees, 1940–49 (SRO)

C Newspapers

1 Bristol
Bristol Evening Post
Bristol Evening World
Bristol Labour Weekly
Bristol Observer
Western Daily Press

2 Coventry
Coventry Evening Telegraph
The Coventry Herald
The Coventry Searchlight
The Coventry Standard
Coventry Tribune
The Midland Daily Telegraph
Town Crier

3 Southampton
Southern Daily Echo

4 Others
Birmingham Post
The Daily Herald
Everybody's Weekly
The Listener
The News Chronicle
The Observer
Reynolds News
The Times
Truth

D Books, pamphlets, plans and reports

Abercrombie, P., *Town planning* (London, 1943).
Abercrombie, P., *County of London plan* (London, 1943).
Abercrombie, P. and Watson, J.P., *A plan for Plymouth* (Plymouth, 1943).
Adshead, S., *Civic design* (Liverpool, 1909).
Adshead, S., *Town planning and town development* (London, 1923).
Adshead, S., *A new England* (London, 1941).
Adshead, S. and Cook, H.T., *The replanning of Southampton* (London, 1942).
Architectural Press, *Your inheritance* (London, n.d.).
Architectural Press, *Towards a new Britain* (London, n.d.).
Architectural Press, *Planning for reconstruction* (London, n.d.).
Bourneville Village Trust, *When we build again* (London, 1942).
Bristol Corporation, *English city: The growth and the future of Bristol* (Bristol, 1945).

Calder, R., *Start planning Britain now* (London, 1941).

Cole, G.D.H., *A plan for Britain* (London, n.d.).

Cole, G.D.H. and Postgate, R., *The common people* (London, 1946).

Cole, G.D.H. *et al.*, *Plan for Britain: A collection of essays prepared for the Fabian Society* (London, 1943).

Cole, G.D.H. *et al.*, *Can planning be democratic? A collection of essays prepared for the Fabian Society* (London, 1944).

Le Corbusier, *Towards a new architecture* (London, 1946).

Le Corbusier, *The city of tomorrow* (London, 1947).

Le Corbusier, *Concerning town planning* (London, 1947).

Le Corbusier and de Pierrefeu, F., *The home of man* (London, 1948).

Coventry Corporation, *The future of Coventry* (Coventry, 1945).

Fabian Research Group, *Government and industry*, Fabian Research Series, No. 83 (London, 1944).

Ford, P. (ed.), *Southampton: A civic survey* (Oxford, 1931).

Fry, M., *Fine building* (London, 1945).

Howard, E., *Garden cities of tomorrow* (London, 1946).

Jevons, R. and Madge, J., *Housing estates: A study of Bristol Corporation's housing policy and practice between the wars* (Bristol, 1946).

Labour Party, *Housing and planning after the war: The Labour Party's post-war policy* (London, 1943).

Laski, H.J., *Will planning restore freedom?* (London, n.d.).

Lloyd, T.A., *Planning in town and country* (London, 1935).

McAllister, G. and McAllister, E., *Town and country planning* (London, 1941).

McCallum, I.R.M. (ed.), *Physical planning* (London, 1945).

Macmillan, H., *Reconstruction: A plea for a national policy* (London, 1933).

Mass Observation, *The journey home* (London, 1944).

Mumford, L., *The culture of cities* (London, 1938).

Newbold, H.B. (ed.), *Industry and rural life: Report of the Cambridge conference of the Town and Country Planning Association 1942* (London, 1942).

Nuffield College Social Reconstruction Survey, *Britain's town and country pattern* (London, 1943).

Osborn, F.J., *Transport, town development and territorial planning of industry* (London, 1934).

Osborn, F.J., *Overture to Planning* (London, 1941).

Osborn, F.J. (ed.), *Planning and reconstruction year books* (London, 1942–46).

Osborn, F.J. (ed.), *Making plans* (London, 1943).

Osborn, F.J., *The land and planning* (London, 1943).

Pool, P. and Stephenson, F., *A plan for town and country* (London, 1944).

Pumphrey, R., *Industry and town planning* (London, 1942).

Royal Institute of British Architects, *Rebuilding Britain* (London, 1943).

Sharp, T., *The English panorama* (London, 1938).

Sharp, T., *Town planning* (Harmondsworth, 1940).

Silkin, L., *The nation's land*. Fabian Research Series, No. 70 (London, 1943).

Simon, E.D., *Rebuilding Britain* (London, 1945).

Southern Daily Echo, The new Southampton (London, 1942).

Tout, H., *The standard of living in Bristol* (Bristol, 1937).

Towndrow, F.E. (ed.), *Replanning Britain: Report of the Oxford conference of the Town and Country Planning Association 1941* (London, 1941).

Trip, H.A., *Road traffic and its control* (London, 1938).

Trip, H.A., *Town planning and road traffic* (London, 1942).

Tyerman, D., *Ways and means of rebuilding: Report of the London conference of the Town and Country Planning Association 1943* (London, 1943).

Watkins, E.S., *How will planning affect land ownership?* (London, n.d.).

Williams-Ellis, C. (ed.), *Britain and the beast* (London, 1937).

Young, G.M., *Country and town* (Harmondsworth, 1943).

E   Articles

Adshead, S., 'Camillo Sitte and Le Corbusier', *Town Planning Review*, **14**, 2 (1930).

Cart, H.P. and de la Fontaine, 'Town planning problems in the old town, Southampton', *The Builder*, 26 June 1936.

Anon., 'Southampton: Architecture at the Royal Academy', *The Builder*, 11 June 1943.

Collins, H., 'The Reconstruction of Southampton', *The Architect and Building News*, 30 May 1943.

Florence, P.S. and Shenfield, A., 'The economics and diseconomics of industrial concentration: The wartime experience of Coventry', *The Review of Economic Studies*, **XII**, 2 (1944–45).

Gibson, D., 'Some matters concerning post-war reconstruction', *The Architectural Association Journal*, **LVI**, 648 (February 1941).

Gibson, D., 'Post-war reconstruction', *The Surveyor and Municipal and County Engineer*, 18 April 1941.

Holford, W.G., 'The planning of a great seaport, Southampton', *Journal of the Royal Institute of British Architects*, 18 July 1936.

Marshall, A.H., 'The financial implications of the Town and Country Planning Act, 1947', *National Housing and Town Planning Council* (November 1947).

Pugh, A.R. and Percy, A.L., 'Planning and reconstruction in Coventry', *Journal of the Institution of Municipal and County Engineers*, 3 September 1946.

Royal Institute of British Architects' Reconstruction Committee, 'First general statement of conclusions', *Journal of the Royal Institute of British Architects*, **49**, 10 (August 1942).

II Secondary Sources

A   Books, pamphlets, plans and reports

Addison, P., *The road to 1945* (London, 1975).

Ashworth, W., *The genesis of modern British town planning* (London, 1954).

Barnett, C., *The audit of war* (London, 1986).

Bianchini, F. *et al.*, *City centres, city cultures* (Manchester, 1988).

Bild, I. (ed.), *Bristol's other history* (Bristol, 1983).

Brace, K., *Portrait of Bristol* (London, 1971).

Buder, S., *Visionaries and planners: The Garden City Movement and the modern community* (Oxford, 1990).

Burns, W., *New towns for old* (London, 1963).

Calder, A., *The people's war* (London, 1969).

Cherry, G.E., *The evolution of British town planning: A history of town planning in the United Kingdom during the 20th century and of the Royal Town Planning Institute, 1914–74* (London, 1974).

Cherry, G.E. (ed.), *Pioneers in British town planning* (London, 1981).
Cherry, G.E., *The politics of town planning* (London, 1982).
City and County of Bristol, *Development plan* (Bristol, 1952).
City of Coventry, *The development plan* (Coventry, 1952).
County Borough of Southampton, *Development plan* (Southampton, 1952).
County Borough of Southampton, *Development plan: Central area written analysis* (Southampton, 1954).
Cullingworth, J.B., *Housing needs and planning policy* (London, 1966).
Cullingworth, J.B., *Environmental planning 1939–1969, Vol. I: Reconstruction and land use planning 1939–1947* (London, 1975).
Cullingworth, J.B., *Town and country planning in Britain* (London, 1982).
Diefendorf, J.M. (ed.), *Rebuilding Europe's bombed cities* (London, 1990).
Esher, L., *A broken wave: The rebuilding of England 1940–1980* (Harmondsworth, 1983).
Eversley, D., *The planner in society* (London, 1973).
Fogarty, M.P., *Town and country planning* (London, 1949).
Friend, J.K. and Jessop, W.N., *Local government and strategic choice* (London, 1969).
Goss, A. and Tetlow, J., *Homes, towns and traffic* (London, 1965).
Hall, P., *Urban and regional planning* (London, 1982).
Hall, P., *Cities of tomorrow* (Oxford, 1990).
Halliday, J. (ed.), *City centre redevelopment: A study of British city centre planning and case studies of five English city centres* (London, 1973).
Harrisson, T., *Living through the blitz* (Harmondsworth, 1978).
Hodgkinson, G., *Sent to Coventry* (Coventry, 1970).
Houghton-Evans, W., *Planning cities* (London, 1975).
Jackson, A., *The politics of architecture* (London, 1970).
Johnson-Marshall, P., *Rebuilding cities* (Edinburgh, 1966).
Kimber, S., *Thirty-eight years of public life in Southampton 1910–1948* (Southampton, 1949).
Kirk, G., *Urban planning in a capitalist society* (London, 1980).
Knowles, B., *Southampton – The English gateway* (London, 1951).
Kuper, L. (ed.), *Living in towns* (London, 1953).
Lancaster, W. and Mason, T. (eds), *Life and labour in a twentieth century city: The experience of Coventry* (Coventry, 1986).
Lee, J.M., *The Churchill coalition, 1940–1945* (London, 1980).
Little, B., *The City and County of Bristol* (London, 1954).
MacInnes, C.M., *Bristol at war* (London, 1962).
Marriott, O., *The property boom* (London, 1967).
Monkhouse, F.J. (ed.), *A survey of Southampton and its region* (Southampton, 1969).
Morgan, K.O., *Labour in power 1945–1951* (Oxford, 1984).
Mullan, B., *Stevenage Ltd.* (London, 1980).
Mumford, L., *The city in history* (Harmondsworth, 1966).
Pahl, R.E., *Whose city?* (Harmondsworth, 1975).
Rance, A., *Southampton: An illustrated history* (Portsmouth, 1986).
Ratcliffe, J., *An introduction to town and country planning* (London, 1981).
Ravetz, A., *Remaking cities* (London, 1980).
Ravetz, A., *The government of space: Town planning in modern society* (London, 1986).
Reade, E., *British town and country planning* (Milton Keynes, 1987).
Reith, J.C.W., *Into the wind* (London, 1949).
Richardson, K., *Twentieth century Coventry* (Coventry, 1972).
Sharp, T., *Town and townscape* (London, 1968).
Smith, H. (ed.), *War and social change* (Manchester, 1986).

Sutcliff, A. (ed.), *The rise of modern urban planning 1800–1914* (London, 1980).
Sutcliff, A. (ed.), *Towards the planned city* (Oxford, 1981).
Sutcliff, A. (ed.), *Metropolis 1890–1940* (London, 1984).
Tiratsoo, N., *Reconstruction, affluence and Labour politics: Coventry 1945–60* (London, 1990).
Walker, F., *The Bristol region* (London, 1972).
Winstone, R., *Bristol in the 1940s* (Bristol, 1961).
Yates, J.A., *Pioneers to power* (Coventry, 1950).

B Articles

'Bristol conference of the Royal Institute of British Architects', *The Architects' Journal*, 1 June 1950.
'Spotlight on Bristol', *The Municipal Journal*, 5 December 1958.
'The latest proposals for Coventry's city centre', *The Architects' Journal*, 21 November 1957.
'The redevelopment of Bristol', *Official Architecture and Planning*, September 1953.
'Coventry rebuilds', *Architectural Design*, December 1958.
Childs, D.R., 'Bristol', *The Architects' Journal*, 2 October 1952.
Childs, D.R., 'Southampton', *The Architects' Journal*, 16 April 1953.
Childs, D.R., 'Coventry', *The Architects' Journal*, 8 October 1953.
Childs, D.R., 'A comparison of progress in rebuilding bombed cities', *The Architects' Journal*, 8 July 1954.
Coventry Corporation, 'Coventry – city with a future', *Municipal Review*, October 1949.
Hinton, J., 'Self-help and socialism: The Squatters' Movement of 1946', *History Workshop*, **25**, Spring 1988.
James, W.A., 'Redevelopment of the central shopping area of Bristol', *Royal Institute of Chartered Surveyors' Journal*, April 1954.
Jenkins, R., 'Coventry', *The Sphere*, 10 October 1953.
Johnson-Marshall, P., 'Coventry: Test-case of planning', *The Listener*, 17 April 1958.
Ling, A., 'Coventry's pedestrian shopping centre', *Keystone*, May–June 1956.
Logie, G., 'The lessons of Coventry', *The Architect and Building News*, 11 July 1962.
Marwick, A., 'Middle opinion in the thirties', *English Historical Review*, April 1964.
Meggeson, R.R.H., 'The historical development of Southampton', *Journal of Town Planning Institute*, **37**, June 1951.
Morton, H.V., 'Future of Coventry', *Illustrated*, 29 October 1949.
Rees, B.T., 'Redevelopment of Southampton's central area', *Institution of Municipal Engineers*, **75**, February 1949.
Samuel, R., 'The cult of planning', *New Socialist*, **34**, January 1986.
Senior, D., 'Coventry plan review', *The Architects' Journal*, 11 July 1962.
Wright, L., 'The Bristol Society of Architects, 1850–1950', *Journal of the Royal Institute of British Architects*, 57, April 1950.

C Unpublished theses

Carr, F., *Engineering workers and the rise of Labour in Coventry 1914–1939 (University of Warwick, PhD, 1979)*.
Garside, P.L., Town planning in London 1930–1960: A study of pressures, interests and influences affecting the formation of policy (London School of Economics, PhD, 1979).
Whitfield, R., The Labour Movement in Bristol 1914–1939 (University of Bristol, M.Litt, 1982).

Index